The Palgrave Macmillan Animal Ethics Series

Series Editors
Andrew Linzey
Oxford Centre for Animal Ethics
Oxford, UK

Clair Linzey
Oxford Centre for Animal Ethics
Oxford, UK

In recent years, there has been a growing interest in the ethics of our treatment of animals. Philosophers have led the way, and now a range of other scholars have followed from historians to social scientists. From being a marginal issue, animals have become an emerging issue in ethics and in multidisciplinary inquiry. This series will explore the challenges that Animal Ethics poses, both conceptually and practically, to traditional understandings of human-animal relations. Specifically, the Series will:

- provide a range of key introductory and advanced texts that map out ethical positions on animals
- publish pioneering work written by new, as well as accomplished, scholars;
- produce texts from a variety of disciplines that are multidisciplinary in character or have multidisciplinary relevance.

More information about this series at
http://www.palgrave.com/gp/series/14421

Elizabeth Tyson

Licensing Laws and Animal Welfare

The Legal Protection of Wild Animals

palgrave
macmillan

Elizabeth Tyson
Born Free USA
Silver Springs, MD, USA

The Palgrave Macmillan Animal Ethics Series
ISBN 978-3-030-50041-2 ISBN 978-3-030-50042-9 (eBook)
https://doi.org/10.1007/978-3-030-50042-9

Cover illustration: Martin Steinthaler/ Getty Images

This Palgrave Macmillan imprint is published by the registered company Springer Nature Switzerland AG.
The registered company address is: Gewerbestrasse 11, 6330 Cham, Switzerland

Series Editors' Preface

This is a new book series for a new field of inquiry: Animal Ethics.

In recent years, there has been a growing interest in the ethics of our treatment of animals. Philosophers have led the way, and now a range of other scholars have followed from historians to social scientists. From being a marginal issue, animals have become an emerging issue in ethics and in multidisciplinary inquiry.

In addition, a rethink of the status of animals has been fuelled by a range of scientific investigations which have revealed the complexity of animal sentiency, cognition and awareness. The ethical implications of this new knowledge have yet to be properly evaluated, but it is becoming clear that the old view that animals are mere things, tools, machines or commodities cannot be sustained ethically.

But it is not only philosophy and science that are putting animals on the agenda. Increasingly, in Europe and the United States, animals are becoming a political issue as political parties vie for the "green" and "animal" vote. In turn, political scientists are beginning to look again at the history of political thought in relation to animals, and historians are beginning to revisit the political history of animal protection.

As animals grow as an issue of importance, so there have been more collaborative academic ventures leading to conference volumes, special journal issues, indeed new academic animal journals as well. Moreover, we have witnessed the growth of academic courses, as well as university posts, in Animal Ethics, Animal Welfare, Animal Rights, Animal Law, Animals and Philosophy, Human-Animal Studies, Critical Animal Studies, Animals and Society, Animals in Literature, Animals and Religion – tangible signs that a new academic discipline is emerging.

"Animal Ethics" is the new term for the academic exploration of the moral status of the non-human – an exploration that explicitly involves a focus on what we owe animals morally, and which also helps us to understand the influences – social, legal, cultural, religious and political – that legitimate animal abuse. This series explores the challenges that Animal Ethics poses, both conceptually and practically, to traditional understandings of human-animal relations.

The series is needed for three reasons: (i) to provide the texts that will service the new university courses on animals; (ii) to support the increasing number of students studying and academics researching in animal related fields, and (iii) because there is currently no book series that is a focus for multidisciplinary research in the field.

Specifically, the series will

- provide a range of key introductory and advanced texts that map out ethical positions on animals;
- publish pioneering work written by new, as well as accomplished, scholars, and
- produce texts from a variety of disciplines that are multidisciplinary in character or have multidisciplinary relevance.

The new Palgrave Macmillan Series on Animal Ethics is the result of a unique partnership between Palgrave Macmillan and the Ferrater Mora Oxford Centre for Animal Ethics. The series is an integral part of the mission of the Centre to put animals on the intellectual agenda by facilitating academic research and publication. The series is also a natural complement to one of the Centre's other major projects, the *Journal of Animal Ethics*. The Centre is an independent "think tank" for the advancement of progressive thought about animals, and is the first Centre of its kind in the world. It aims to demonstrate rigorous intellectual enquiry and the highest standards of scholarship. It strives to be a world-class centre of academic excellence in its field.

We invite academics to visit the Centre's website www.oxfordanimalethics.com and to contact us with new book proposals for the series.

Andrew Linzey and Clair Linzey
General Editors

Contents

Commonly Used Abbreviations

AHVLA	Animal Health and Veterinary Laboratories Agency
ASPA 1986	Animals in Scientific Procedures Act 1986
AWA 2006	Animal Welfare Act 2006
AWR 2018	Animal Welfare (Licensing of Activities Involving Animals) (England) Regulations 2018
BIAZA	British and Irish Association of Zoos and Aquariums
BUAV	British Union for the Abolition of Vivisection
DEFRA	Department for Environment, Food and Rural Affairs
DWA 1976	Dangerous Wild Animals Act 1976
FFA	Freedom for Animals
FOIA 2000	Freedom of Information Act 2000
PAA 1925	Performing Animals (Regulation) Act 1925
PAA 1951	Pet Animals Act 1951
RSPCA	Royal Society for the Prevention of Cruelty to Animals
SSSMZP	Secretary of State's Standards of Modern Zoo Practice
WWATC 2012	Welfare of Wild Animals in Travelling Circuses (England) Regulations 2012
ZLA 1981	Zoo Licensing Act 1981

List of Figures

List of Tables

1

Introduction

Licensing regimes which regulate the use of animals generally implement a process whereby an individual must be deemed to comply with a particular set of regulations in order to be granted, and retain, a license to keep or use animals in a particular manner. The set of regulations will differ dependent on the specific use that the licensee intends to put the animals to. This book considers the efficacy of the common regulatory model of the licensing regime as a means of regulating animal use in England, with a particular focus on wild animals and the regimes' ability to ensure animal welfare needs are met. This book aims to address the gap in available information on the practical application of a number of pieces of legislation, whose provisions create licensing regimes: the Zoo Licensing Act 1981 (ZLA 1981), the, now repealed, Welfare of Wild Animals in Travelling Circuses (England) Regulations 2012 (WWATC 2012) and the Animal Welfare (Licensing of Activities Involving Animals) (England) Regulations 2018 (AWR 2018), introduced under the Animal Welfare Act 2006 (AWA 2006).

E. Tyson, *Licensing Laws and Animal Welfare*, The Palgrave Macmillan Animal Ethics Series, https://doi.org/10.1007/978-3-030-50042-9_1

1.1 A Common Legislative Approach

Given the ever-changing landscape with regard to animal use, perceptions of animals, and scale of industries and practices which involve animals, it is perhaps not surprising that animal law takes on a number of different forms and frameworks—from Acts which prohibit particular practices[1] to measures which impose a specific duty of care on the person responsible for the animal in question to treat that animal in a humane manner and avoid the infliction of unnecessary suffering.[2]

A common framework for laws pertaining to the regulation of animal use is the licensing regime. For example, the Animals (Scientific Procedures) Act 1986 (ASPA 1986) requires that licenses must be sought and awarded in order for the licensee to be allowed to carry out painful experiments on animals[3] and, likewise, the Welfare of Animals (Slaughter or Killing) Regulations 1995 set out conditions relating to certificates of competence and licenses which must be sought and granted prior to being permitted to carry out the slaughter of animals for food.[4] Both of these statutes could reasonably be considered to be seeking to protect animals from "unnecessary suffering" (during experimentation and at the time of slaughter), rather than being designed to promote the welfare of an individual animal within the more modern and holistic context of the Five Freedoms, a concept which will be examined in detail in Sect. 5 in Chap. 2 of this book. Some licensing regimes have, as their main purpose, something other than the protection of animals but include provisions which nonetheless impact upon animal welfare. An example is the Dangerous Wild Animals Act 1976 (DWA 1976), which is predominantly concerned, as the title suggests, with protecting the general public from harm but includes some basic provisions which are intended to protect animal welfare, albeit in a fairly rudimentary manner.[5] The licensing regimes under specific consideration as part of this book are some of those concerned with the protection of animals, and wild animals kept or used in captivity in particular, namely those implemented by the ZLA 1981, the WWATC 2012 and the AWR 2018. These pieces of legislations demand (or in the case of the, now repealed, WWATC 2012 demanded) that a license be sought and granted in order to carry out the practice of operating a zoo and operating a traveling circus with wild animals, and carrying out particular activities involving animals (both wild and domesticated). Licensees are subjected to an inspection regime to allow monitoring of compliance with legal standards. If standards are not deemed to be met on inspection, the license may be refused, suspended or revoked (in the case of WWATC 2012 and AWR 2018) or the establishment, or part of it, might eventually be closed down if it is governed by the ZLA 1981.

During the passage through Parliament of the AWA 2006, it was stated by the then Secretary of State for Environment Food and Rural Affairs, Margaret Beckett, that "The powers for licensing and registration [included in the Bill] will replace a range of statutes regulating such activities as performing animals, pet shops, riding schools and dog-breeding and animal-boarding establishments".[6] The specific legislation earmarked for replacement as part of this initiative were the Performing Animals (Regulation) Act 1925 (PAA 1925), Pet Animals Act 1951 (as amended in 1983), Animal Boarding Establishments Act 1963, Riding Establishments Act 1964 and 1970 and Breeding and Sale of Dogs (Welfare) Act 1999, Breeding of Dogs Act 1991 and Breeding of Dogs Act 1973. Section 13(8) of the AWA 2006 grants explicit powers to the appropriate national authority to repeal these Acts and introduce replacement legislation under the same section of the AWA 2006. In 2013, the WWATC 2012 became the first licensing regime introduced using powers granted by the AWA 2006 and the promised repeal of the remaining legislation outlined by Beckett came into effect five years later on the introduction of the AWR 2018, which covers dog and cat boarding, horse-riding establishments, dog breeding, pet shops and the use of animals in performance and exhibits.

1.2 The Special Case for Wild Animal Welfare

While it is undeniable that domesticated animals are used by humans in far higher numbers than wild animals, this book focuses largely on if and how the law protects wild animals. The reason for this is that many animal advocates argue that a special case should be made for wild animals when kept under the control of humans. Domestication of species occurs over tens of thousands of years and changes animals genetically from their free-living or "wild" forbears. The process of domestication has resulted in animals who, when all other things are equal, can live alongside and with humans without their being "kept" by humans being detrimental to their welfare in and of itself. There are arguments surrounding, for example, the riding of horses, and whether or not this is detrimental to welfare, but the general consensus is that a pet dog, for example, will not suffer if they are well cared for. The same cannot be said of, for example, a tiger or a lion "kept" by humans. Whether the tiger or lion be in a zoo, in a circus, in private ownership or in the wider entertainment industry, animal advocates argue that animal welfare needs for wild animals, who have not been domesticated over millennia simply cannot be met when they are held captive.

These arguments are based on the fact that wild animals would inhabit countries, climates and environments very different to those that can be provided when kept under human control in England. An elephant, for example, would traverse hundreds of miles of home range and live in large matriarchal groups of up to 50 individuals in Africa and Asia. Many species of monkey live in forest environments within complex, multi-generational social hierarchies. They have a very specific diet, long childhoods and extremely high levels of cognition which make them perfectly adapted to the challenging and varied life that they would naturally live in their natural habitat.

Many advocates for wild animal welfare argue that these elements of life for wild animals are of fundamental importance, as is their ability to live in freedom. The principle of an animal's right or desire for freedom will be explored in Chap. 2, but there are very strong arguments to suggest that for some, if not many or all wild animals, the very fact of being held captive can be seriously detrimental to their welfare. As such, it could be argued that animal welfare laws which, by their very nature, require animals to be kept by humans, are somewhat irrelevant for wild animals if their welfare simply cannot be met when held in any form of captivity. Discussion in this book will include how laws might be reimagined and revised in order to meet welfare needs of wild animals, as well as domesticated animals.

1.3 The Purpose and Scope of this Research: Filling the Information Gap

The limited analysis of animal welfare law and its scope that has been carried out to date has, in general, been largely from a theoretical standpoint, with philosophers and lawyers considering the legal nuances of existing legislation and its application. Discussion on this subject is often focused around whether the law goes far enough, or too far, in its consideration of animals and whether or not it is enough to simply guard against unnecessary suffering, to provide for basic welfare needs, or whether moves should be made toward granting animals identifiable and enforceable legal rights, as individuals or members of a class or species, under the law. Much of this work has been carried out with the legal system of the United States in mind, rather than England and the wider United Kingdom, and much consideration has been given to the principle of legal standing (which, at present animals do not have, in their own right, in law)[7] or to the problems associated with the legal classification of animals in law as "property".[8] Underlying these important discussions, though, is often the implicit assumption that animal welfare law, once enacted, serves the purpose for which it was introduced and is effectively enforced. Joan E. Schaffner demonstrates this point when discussing the difference between vivisection (animal experimentation) laws in the United States compared to those in the United Kingdom:

> *In comparing the [Animals (Scientific Procedures)] Act governing research animals with the United States [Animal Welfare Act], it appears that the use of animals in research is more limited and the animals who are used **are better protected** in the United Kingdom.*[9] *[my emphasis]*

The implicit assumption in Schaffner's assertion above is that the law simply works as it was intended. On the other hand, Mike Radford, of Aberdeen University, makes the point that legislation is of little value if it is not effectively enforced, and gives some examples of areas of animal law where it would seem that enforcement might be ineffective.[10] Lack of transparency and access to information made any definitive conclusion on levels of enforcement at the time that Radford's work, which was carried out in 2001, was published difficult but the subsequent introduction of the Freedom of Information Act 2000 (FOIA 2000), which came into force on 1 January 2005, has meant that enforcement by public bodies is now, to some extent, subject to public scrutiny in a way that it never was before.

Section 1 of the FOIA 2000 states:

> (1) *Any person making a request for information to a public authority is entitled—*
>
> (a) *to be informed in writing by the public authority whether it holds information of the description specified in the request, and*
> (b) *if that is the case, to have that information communicated to him.*

Whereas there used to be no means of gaining access to documentation relating to government licensing schemes if the relevant public authority was disinclined to share that information, the FOIA 2000 opened up access to a huge amount of information, including that relating to the licensing of practices involving animals. Where speculation was previously necessary, analysis can now be carried out in order to establish a clearer picture of some (but not all) industries which use animals.

For example, as a general rule, documentation, inspection reports and correspondence relating to the operation of zoos, circuses and other current or past licensable activities are now normally available under the provisions of the FOIA 2000. This is by virtue of the fact that this information is held on file by the relevant authorities (local or national), who are charged with regulation of these businesses. On the other hand, as a result of the fact that the right of access to information under the Act is not absolute and can be subject to exemptions,[11] documentation and inspection reports relating to animal testing, a practice regulated by ASPA 1986, are far more difficult (and sometimes impossible) to access. Access to information on animal testing is particularly stifled by the application of s.44 of the FOIA 2000 which provides an absolute exemption to the public body where the release of information is prohibited by a separate legislative measure. Within ASPA 1986, this prohibition of release of information can be found in s.24 which states that

A person is guilty of an offence if otherwise than for the purpose of discharging his functions under this Act he discloses any information which has been obtained by him in the exercise of those functions and which he knows or has reasonable grounds for believing to have been given in confidence.

In short, as long as s.24 of ASPA 1986 remains in force, s.44 of the FOIA 2000 can legitimately be used to refuse the release of information. This blanket prohibition on release of information has been argued to go against the spirit and explicit intention of the FOIA 2000 and has been challenged, notably by the UK-based anti-vivisection NGO, Cruelty Free International (formerly The British Union for the Abolition of Vivisection (BUAV)). The case of *Home Office v BUAV & Anor* (2008)[12] challenged the validity of s.24 of ASPA 1986 (and the subsequent use of the exemption under s.44 of the Freedom of Information Act 2000). The Court of Appeal dismissed BUAV's case. Agreeing with, and extending, the judgment of the High Court, the Court of Appeal concluded that

Where a public official reasonably believed that information had been given under a statutory procedure in circumstances which gave rise at that time to a reasonable expectation of privacy, and the statute prohibited disclosure for purposes other than those to which the Act related, that information was exempt from disclosure under the Freedom of Information Act 2000.[13]

As such, it is for the provider of the information in question to decide whether or not that information has been provided in confidence and, thus, it was within the rights of those engaged in animal testing to simply request non-disclosure of information and that information would automatically fall under s.24. Commenting on the verdict, a solicitor for the BUAV, David Thomas, noted "it … means that, as a Home Office official candidly accepted in evidence, judicial scrutiny of regulatory decisions under ASPA is all but impossible".[14]

During initial consideration of the scope for this book, the possibility of assessing the efficacy of licensing of animal experimentation under ASPA 1986 was considered as part of the author's remit; however, the inability to access meaningful information with regard to compliance with and enforcement of ASPA 1986 due to the lack of publicly available information meant that scrutiny of this industry was not possible. This is something which can be considered a concern for effective oversight of animal welfare, in and of itself.

Despite the issues identified in attempting to access information relating to animal experimentation, ongoing monitoring and research carried out by NGOs into the practical application of legislation relating to other animal-use industries and its ability to provide effective legal protection for animals has highlighted significant concerns with regard to the enforcement and delivery of the law. A study[15] commissioned by Freedom for Animals (FFA) (formerly the Captive Animals' Protection Society (CAPS))[16] in 2011, which explored a number of aspects of the zoo licensing system in England, suggested that there is widespread, long-term and persistent failure to properly meet legal obligations on the part of the zoos themselves as well as on the part of the local authorities responsible for the Act's enforcement. The study concluded that, amongst other issues including administration, poor training and lack of expertise, the way in which the Act was being implemented and enforced was a large part of the problem.[17]

The report reinforced concerns identified by the charity over a number of years as a result of ongoing monitoring (using access to information under the FOIA 2000) which suggest that lack of enforcement action under the ZLA 1981 is a major contributing factor to some zoos persistently falling below legal standard. A subsequent study carried out by the author of this book found at least 996 instances of local authority failure to take mandatory enforcement action against between the years 2005 and 2011. During these years, there were various instances in which the authorities were arguably under an obligation to close zoos due to persistent non-compliance with standards, but in no instance was such action taken.

The 2011 study by FFA[18] (commissioned by the author in her capacity as Director of the organization at the time) went some way toward explaining the way in which the licensing of English zoos was approached by the relevant authorities. Further study was required, however, in order to draw firm conclusions as to the overall efficacy of this regime and others which employ licensing with the, ostensible, intention of protecting animal welfare. Of particular interest to the author was the debate surrounding, and subsequent introduction of, the WWATC 2012. This licensing regime—the first of its kind to be introduced using powers granted to the Secretary of State under s.13 of the AWA 2006—was introduced on the premise that it "will protect the welfare of [wild animals in circuses] while they are in use in travelling circuses".[19] The ability of the regime to protect animal welfare was strongly contested by all leading animal welfare organizations in the United Kingdom.[20] This was, in large part, due to the very specific needs of wild animals and returns to the suggestion that animal welfare laws which are, by default, designed to regulate the keeping of animals in captivity are likely to fall short when it comes to protecting wild animals. This idea will be explored in later chapters. Despite opposition, the government introduced the licensing regime and made the claim that this would "dramatically improve the welfare of animals in travelling circuses".[21] The conflict of views between the animal welfare experts and vets on the one hand[22]—who all maintained that the welfare of wild animals simply cannot be met in a traveling circus environment[23] and that the new regulations would therefore inevitably be ineffective—and the views of the government and the circus industry—who maintained that welfare needs can be met if the regulations were followed—demanded further exploration.

This book seeks to consider the role of licensing regimes as a means to regulate animal use with a particular focus on their impact on animal welfare, with a particular focus on wild animal welfare. In Chap. 2, the broad theoretical and philosophical arguments surrounding human society's moral obligations toward animals will be explored. This provides the foundations upon which Chap. 3, which considers the evolution of animal welfare law in the England, is then constructed. Chapter 4 focuses specifically on the application and mechanisms of licensing regimes as a regulatory vehicle, exploring when and how licensing might be employed and to what end.

In Chap. 5, the history of the zoo industry in England and its regulation is outlined, leading to the consideration of the first piece of legislation analyzed as part of this book: the ZLA 1981.

Chapter 6 provides an original and detailed analysis of the enforcement of the ZLA 1981 in England using data from 564 zoo inspection reports completed by government inspectors between 2008 and 2019.

The results of this analysis highlight an almost complete absence of correct enforcement action being delivered against zoos found to be non-compliant with the ZLA 1981. Of 1882 instances of non-compliance noted by inspectors during the twelve-year period under analysis, not one instance of correctly executed enforcement action was noted in response. Reasons for this lack of enforcement are then explored and conclusions drawn as to the reasons for this regulatory failure.

Chapter 7 considers the way in which regulation of zoos has been dealt with in a handful of case studies from other European countries which are of interest either because of their unusual or erroneous implementation of the EC Zoos Directive or because of their progressive approach to licensing.

Chapter 8 considers the second piece of legislation under examination as part of this book: the WWATC 2012 and their origins. Chapter 9 considers how the, now repealed, WWATC 2012 were enforced and what lessons can be learned from this, the first licensing regime introduced using powers granted under the AWA 2006, to inform upcoming legislation. The AWR 2018 is considered in Chap. 10 and is compared to the WWATC 2012 to consider whether or not lessons were learned from the shortcomings of the latter.

Chapter 11 draws together the findings of the research in order to answer the question: Is licensing an effective means to regulate the use of animals, and wild animals in particular? In exploring the way in which animal welfare is necessarily limited by the "good practice" caveat inherent in the application of the Five Freedoms (see Sect. 5 in Chap. 2 for detail), the fact that none of the licensing regimes under consideration makes any demand that legal standards are complied with consistently and the fundamental acknowledgment that licensing is a regulatory tool which allows the monitoring of processes and practices in a holistic sense but is not designed to assess individual welfare, it is concluded that, contrary to claims made by industry and government, licensing (in and of itself) cannot be considered to be a viable legal vehicle for guaranteeing animal welfare. Instead, it is concluded that licensing can be used as an important tool to scrutinize industry and provide additional protection to animals by virtue of that increased scrutiny, albeit under the proviso that the licensing regime in question is considered to fit the model for "responsive regulation" and it is drafted in a way that allows it to be correctly enforced.

Chapter 12 provides a series of recommendations for change which would allow existing and future licensing regimes governing the use of animals to be put to best effect. This includes recommendations for licensing regimes introduced in the future under s.13 of the AWA 2006 as well as those licensing regimes, such as the ZLA 1981, which are introduced as stand-alone primary legislation. Finally, Chap. 13 concludes this book with some broad, closing comments and considerations. Ultimately, it is concluded that while the licensing of the use of animals can and does provide important regulatory oversight and scrutiny, claims that animals' welfare is guaranteed by such regimes should be met with caution. If we are committed to truly guaranteeing the welfare needs of animals are met, then we must begin with restructuring our core animal protection legislation (particularly the AWA 2006) with a view to facilitating the introduction of universal minimum welfare standards, based on the individual and species-specific needs of the animals themselves, regardless of the use that they are put to by either individual people or wider industries. This may result in some animals being deemed to be unsuitable to be "kept" by man as the very keeping of them may negatively impact animal welfare. At present, no such minimum standards exist and protection for animals is limited by the constraints of the particular industry using the animal or the use to which the animal is put. Until such a time as these minimum standards realized, licensing regimes implemented to protect animals will be necessarily limited as to their ability to contribute to the delivery of high animal welfare standards in England.

Notes

1. For example, The Hunting Act 2004.
2. For example, The Animal Welfare Act 2006.
3. S.3 Animals (Scientific Procedures) Act 1986.
4. S.6 The Welfare of Animals (Slaughter and Killing) Regulations 1995.
5. S.3 Dangerous Wild Animals' Act 1976.

6. HC Deb, 10th January 2006, Official Report, column, p. 167.
7. For example, Stone, C.D., (2010). *Should Trees Have Standing?*, 3rd Edition, Oxford University Press, discusses the principle of developing models for the introduction of legal standing for natural resources and, by extension, for animals.
8. For example, Francione, G., *Animals, Property and the Law*, argues that the classification of animals as "chattels" results in legal balancing which, in the vast majority of instances, leads to the animal's interests being relegated below those of its owners.
9. Schaffner, J., (2011). *An Introduction to Animals and the Law*, Palgrave Macmillan, p. 90.
10. Radford, M., (2001). *Animal Welfare Law in Britain*, Oxford University Press, pp. 356–392.
11. Ss.21–44 Freedom of Information Act 2000.
12. Secretary of State for the Home Department v British Union for the Abolition of Vivisection and another [2008] EWCA Civ 870.
13. Ibid.
14. Thomas, D. (2009). *Freedom of Information—Putting FOI to the Test.* Freedom of Information, 6(2), pp. 11–13.
15. Casamitjana, J. (2012). Inspecting Zoos: A study of the official zoo inspection system in England from 2005 to 2011. The Captive Animal's Protection Society, Manchester.
16. The author (E. Tyson) was previously the Director of this charity and commissioned and oversaw this study.
17. Captive Animals' Protection Society, (2012). *A Licence to Suffer*. [online] Manchester: CAPS, p.17. Available at: http://www.captiveanimals.org/wp-content/uploads/2012/03/CAPS_Zoo_Insp_Rep_0112_Final.pdf [Accessed 15 Jan. 2017].
18. Casamitjana, J., (2012). *Inspecting Zoos*, APC/CAPS.
19. HC Deb, 1 March 2012, c41WS.
20. For example, Born Free Foundation. (2011). *Born Free Statement on the Regulation of Wild Animals in Circuses*. [online] Available at: http://www.bornfree.org.uk/news/news-article/?no_cache=1&tx_ttnews%5Btt_news%5D=935 [Accessed 15 Jan. 2017].
21. BBC.co.uk, (2012). *BBC News—Circuses face new rules on animal use as ban ruled out*. [online] Available at: http://www.bbc.co.uk/news/mobile/uk-13697887 [Accessed 30 Jan. 2016].

22. Born Free Foundation, Captive Animals' Protection Society, RSPCA and British Veterinary Association, (2013). The Welfare of Wild Animals in Travelling Circuses (England) Regulations 2012: unethical, ineffective and unenforceable.
23. Vet Times. (2012). Draft Legislation Plan for Ban of Wild Circus Animals Welcomed. [online] Available at: https://www.vettimes.co.uk/news/draft-legislation-plan-for-ban-of-wild-circus-animals-welcomed/ [Accessed 28 March 2020].

2

Should Animal Use Be Regulated by Law and, If So, How?

The introduction to this book explored the broad scope of its contents: an examination of the efficacy of licensing regimes as a means to regulate the use of animals, with a particular interest on their impact on animal welfare, and a specific focus on the welfare of wild animals (defined in law as "an animal not normally domesticated in the United Kingdom"[1]). This chapter will explore the foundational theories which influence and inform the regulation of animal use. Because there are already numerous laws in effect which are designed to regulate animal use, asking the question "should animal use be regulated?" may be deemed a moot point. For reasons which that will be explored in-depth in later chapters, it is necessary to offer at least a brief overview of the different theories in relation to the regulation of animal use. This overview will include discussion of whether it is necessary, or indeed desirable, to regulate the use of animals at all and, if so, for what purposes and to what extent it might be necessary or desirable, as well as ways in which the proposed purpose of the regulation is to be achieved. This will provide a foundation upon which to build arguments as to the efficacy of existing laws and their potential shortcomings.

E. Tyson, *Licensing Laws and Animal Welfare*, The Palgrave Macmillan Animal Ethics Series, https://doi.org/10.1007/978-3-030-50042-9_2

It should be noted that this book seeks to consider the regulation of animal use which is, ostensibly, implemented either in full or in part in the interests of the animals, rather than for some other external purpose. For example, the licensing of the use of wild animals in circuses was implemented with the express aim of protecting animal welfare.[2] The ZLA 1981 was implemented following long-term concern for the negative impact on the welfare of animals in zoos if the industry remained unregulated.[3] The raft of new licensing laws—the AWR 2018[4]—introduced under s.12 of the AWA 2006, similarly were introduced on animal welfare grounds, as dictated by the primary legislation.

It could easily be argued that, in today's society, there is recognition that animals should not be abused or mistreated. Most reasonable people would be horrified if they saw a dog being beaten, for example, and there was national uproar when footage was released in early 2011 of an elephant in a circus being beaten with a pitchfork,[5] an act which led to the prosecution and conviction of the elephant's owner.[6] A clear indication of public concern over the mistreatment of animals is the fact that the Royal Society for the Prevention of Cruelty to Animals (RSPCA) received 1,175,193 calls during 2018 from concerned members of the public on issues relating to the treatment of animals, investigated 130,700 cruelty cases and secured 1678 convictions as a result of private prosecutions brought by the charity.[7]

Today, there is a near universal view that animals should be spared abuse, but this view has not always been prevalent. Despite the fact most would agree that family pets should not be kicked and elephants in circuses should not be beaten with pitchforks, views on the extent to which animals should be protected from the actions of people are still the cause of much debate.

The academic debate about the extent to which our treatment of animals should be restricted centers around three major areas: sentience (largely agreed to be synonymous with the ability of animals to suffer), whether (sentient) animals can be considered to possess "interests" and, though it is rarely raised as a significant factor in this debate in recent years, whether or not the kind and humane treatment of animals is necessary in order to avoid eroding our sense of humanity. The last position, which was notably championed by philosophers such as Thomas Aquinas during the thirteenth century[8] and Immanuel Kant in the eighteenth century,[9] is largely considered outdated in modern times (as the majority view is that animals possess at least some inherent worth which is worthy of protection in its own right) although mention of it can be found in Trust law for the reasons that charitable trusts under English law can only be established for "the benefit of the public", not for the benefit of animals. As such, any charitable trust with the aim of promoting the welfare of animals must do so for the public benefit, thus perpetuating the standpoint that kindness to animals is intrinsically morally good and beneficial to those who practice it, rather than desirable for the animals themselves in a more direct sense. A historical example of case law where this point was explicitly dealt with was *Re: Wedgwood Trust* [1915][10] which considered the estate of a woman who had established a charitable trust for the express purpose of benefitting animals. It was ruled that helping to "stimulate humane and generous sentiments in man towards lower animals" could be considered a charitable purpose.

The core discussion within this chapter will focus on the issue of sentience as a logical starting point followed by consideration of whether or not a sentient animal can be deemed to be a possessor of interests and, if so, what those interests may be and to what extent sentiency combined with the possession of interests may give rise to moral consideration and thus consideration for protection under law.

2.1 Can Animals Suffer at All and, If So, How Does This Affect Our Treatment of Them?

The word "suffer" is defined as to "experience something bad or unpleasant",[11] and for people, the concept of "suffering" comprehends a great number of mental states of emotions. These might include *inter alia,* pain, stress, fear, anxiety, shame, apprehension, uncertainty and depression. Aaltola provides a working definition of suffering as follows: "Suffering is substantial physical discomfort and/or mental distress which affects our whole being and sidelines most (if not all) other considerations normally important to us".[12] This section will explore how the concept of suffering applies to animals and, by extension, what the ability (or lack thereof) to suffer could mean with regard to their moral standing.

Suffering has formed the cornerstone of the debate on animal protection since the time of eighteenth-century philosopher Jeremy Bentham, who wrote the following, now famous, passage in 1789:

> *It may one day come to be recognized that the number of the legs, the villosity of the skin, or the termination of the os sacrum are reasons equally insufficient for abandoning a sensitive being to the same fate [as slaves]. What else is it that should trace the insuperable line? Is it the faculty of reason or perhaps the faculty of discourse? But a full-grown horse or dog, is beyond comparison a more rational, as well as a more conversable animal, than an infant of a day or a week or even a month, old. But suppose the case were otherwise, what would it avail? The question is not, Can they reason? nor, Can they talk? but, Can they suffer?*[13]

It is largely agreed that answering Bentham's question "can they suffer?" in relation to a being or object gives us the baseline for differentiating between those beings or objects which might require moral consideration, and those that do not. For example, if we ask ourselves the question "can it suffer?" about a rock on a beach, our knowledge of the composition of rocks and their inanimate state allows us to conclude that "no, it does not suffer". As such, it is logical that we have no reason to be concerned (for the rock) if we throw it into the sea, kick it with our shoe or bury it in the ground. It is therefore universally agreed that rocks, in and of themselves, do not require moral consideration and we do not need to consider or amend our behavior toward them to avoid causing suffering. On the other hand, most people would accept without question that, as a result of our knowledge of mammalian physiology and behavior, to kick, throw or bury alive a kitten we see on the street would *inevitably* cause suffering. As such, if it can be agreed that a kitten can suffer, it stands to reason that kittens should be granted some level of moral consideration with a view to avoid causing the kitten suffering. The extent to which the kitten (and other non-human animals) should be granted moral consideration remains subject to debate.

Few people now share the view of the seventeenth-century philosopher Rene Descartes that "animals are without feeling or awareness of any kind",[14] and, instead, it is widely agreed that at least some animals can be considered sentient or, in other words, *with* feeling and awareness. Sentience, in turn, is considered to be a prerequisite for an individual to be able to experience suffering (in that an individual with no feeling or awareness could not be considered to have the capacity to suffer). There remains debate surrounding how sentience should be defined, particularly when it is considered that those individuals deemed to be sentient might, as a result, be considered to warrant the grant of moral (and subsequently legal) consideration and those who fall outside of the definition might be deemed to warrant no such moral or legal consideration. Regan, for example, suggests that the test for sentience should be the ability to feel pain, something which is largely deemed to be an attribute of many species of animal. Regan similarly connects the ability to feel pain with the ability to suffer, on the broad basis that pain in animals should be "considered intrinsically, just as much of an evil as a comparable experience of a human being".[15] The ability to suffer, he argues, is an important criterion in classifying individuals as "subjects-of-a-life" who warrant moral consideration.[16]

Frey, on the other hand, while recognizing that many animals feel pain or, due to the fact that he believes that animals do not have the rational capacity to conceptualize pain, believes they, instead, experience "unpleasant sensations",[17] argues both that sentiency is poorly defined and open to interpretation and that pain, as a stand-alone criterion, is inadequate to establish moral significance. As such, he rejects the argument that sentience should be a deciding factor in who or what might be granted moral consideration and equally rejects the argument that the capacity to feel pain provides a sound basis from which to draw the same conclusion.

On the first point, he argues that sentience could be defined in many different ways, with not all of them necessarily indicating that the "sentient" being or object experiences pain and thus has the potential to suffer. For example, he argues that "if 'sentiency' is taken to mean 'reaction to stimuli', ... perhaps even litmus paper... [is a] candidate for having rights".[18] On the second point, he argues that pain is a "naturalistic-cum-evolutionary" experience which has "no moral status whatsoever" and makes the point that the way in which a chameleon changes color in reaction to his surroundings is a similarly naturalistic-cum-evolutionary experience which is not given any moral significance within human society.[19] He also suggests that equating pain with suffering is erroneous in that the assumption that "pain is an intrinsic evil" has not been substantiated.[20] Indeed, Frey argues that he can conceive of "someone liking a pain to which he has nevertheless given his full attention".[21] Finally, Frey points out that the ability to experience pain as the *only* criterion to establish who or what should be granted moral consideration would exclude "marginal cases" such as those people with nerve damage who could not feel pain at all in either all or part of their bodies.[22]

To consider these arguments—for and against the view that the ability to experience pain should constitute the sole criterion for establishing sentience and, in turn, that sentience is synonymous with an ability to suffer—in detail would divert from the main question under consideration which is "can animals suffer at all?", but a conclusion sufficient to allow the continued exploration of this question can be reached at this point. For the purposes of this book, it can be concluded that the nuances of Frey's argument surrounding pain not necessarily being an "intrinsic evil"[23] have merit, as do his arguments that some individuals who cannot feel pain (such as those with nerve damage) might be excluded if pain is the only criterion used to gauge sentience. However, to dismiss the ability to experience pain as a reliable indicator of the ability to suffer on the basis of the exceptions, rather than the rule, appears somewhat ill-conceived.

Pain is, as Frey suggests, an evolutionary tool and, as a general rule, experiencing pain is unpleasant. It is this very fact that will cause a young child to withdraw their hand quickly if coming into contact with an open flame despite that child not necessarily having the pre-conceived understanding and foresight that putting one's hand in a flame might cause pain and, subsequently, suffering if the hand is burned and it is this that allows us, and many other species, to avoid constant injury or accident. As such, the very ability to experience pain suggests that the individual in question *may* have a capacity to suffer in that the experience of pain is the biological warning system which helps that individual to avoid such instances of suffering. It is recognized, as Frey points out, reflexive rather than conscious reactions to painful stimuli can be found in life forms such as amoebas, which are generally agreed to lack the biological complexity (i.e., a central nervous system) to experience pain and thus lack the ability to suffer despite being "sentient" when judged against other criteria, and it is generally accepted that experiencing pain requires more than simply reflexive response and requires some feeling of negative experience which extends beyond the initial reflexive reaction. However, work carried out by Braithwaite et al. on fish concluded that fish have the capacity to both feel pain and experience "the emotional part of pain, the part that generates the negative feeling of suffering" and therefore further concluded that they see "no logical reason why we should not extend to fish the same welfare considerations that we currently extend to birds and mammals".[24]

If it can be accepted that fish have the capacity to suffer, then it seems nonsensical to suggest that mammals and birds, whose physiology is closer to our own, should lack the capacity to suffer. Indeed, writing in the 1700s, David Hume warned against denying that animals possess similar levels of consciousness to humans when evidence suggests otherwise. He opens his chapter on the existence of animal consciousness with the forthright statement: "[n]ext to the ridicule of denying an evident truth, is that of taking much pains to defend it; and no truth appears to me more evident, than that beasts are endow'd with thought and reason as well as men".[25] To conclude this part of the discussion, while Frey and those who concur with his view may dispute the rights and wrongs of affording animals moral consideration as a result of their ability to suffer, there seems to be little evidence to support the view that the suffering itself (though perhaps experienced differently between one species and, indeed one individual, and another) does not exist in many, if not most, animals.

With the above discussion in mind, it is fair to say that it is now generally accepted at least some animals have the capacity to suffer. In recent years, the debate has focused far more upon the *extent* of suffering that animals are capable of and, with this in mind, the extent to which the infliction of suffering upon animals is deemed acceptable when balanced against other factors. An outline of the main areas of discussion on suffering is provided below.

Until now, the instances of suffering mentioned have largely involved the infliction of physical pain. However, suffering is not just concerned with pain. It might be that, on reading the earlier passage about the kitten being kicked and buried alive, the scenario might invoke mental images of other forms of suffering different to mere physical pain. Dependent on your views as to the extent of animal sentience and cognition, you might imagine the kitten also feeling frightened, anxious or stressed. You might imagine that a kitten buried alive will struggle to free herself so that she does not die from suffocation. If the kitten survived her ordeal, it is reasonable to imagine her being ever fearful of people and of a nervous disposition henceforth. Any one of these reactions to the passage might be considered a reasonable response. The necessity of recognizing that suffering is not limited to experiences of pain in animals was noted in the 1965 Brambell Report,[26] published by the UK government (and considered in detail in Sect. 5 of Chap. 2 in this book), which highlighted the need to consider the cumulative effect of factors other than pain in evaluating suffering. The report noted:

> *We, for our part, must pay special attention to the possible cumulative effect on the animal of the long continuance of conditions which might be tolerable or even acceptable, in the short term. Factors producing prolonged stress, discomfort or deprivation must weigh heavily with us and may, on occasion, be of much more significance for the total welfare of the animal than more acute, but transitory, suffering.*[27]

While Cartesian theorists denied that animals were capable of suffering at all, it is perhaps fair to say that up until the 1960s, which saw the development of what became known as the Five Freedoms (introduced following the publication of the aforementioned Brambell Report, mentioned above, and discussed in detail in Sect. 5 in Chap. 2 of this book), many of those who agreed that animals could suffer physical pain were skeptical as to the ability of animals to experience emotions or mental states in the way that humans do. With the exception of the previously mentioned view of scholars such as David Hume, whose viewpoint on this issue was something of an anomaly at the time he was writing, there was a time when to attribute what were considered to be wholly human emotions, such as happiness, sadness, depression and others, to animals—and thus to anthropomorphize them—was considered to be wholly unscientific. For example, the now celebrated primatologist, Dr. Jane Goodall, was heavily criticized when she began her behavioral studies of chimpanzees in the 1960s for committing the "cardinal sin in ethology"[28] of attributing human emotions to animals (anthropomorphism). Since then, her work and that of other leading ethologists, such as Marc Bekoff,[29] have added to the growing body of clear evidence that the emotional lives of animals are far more expansive than we previously believed them to be.

Indeed, there has been a raft of experiments carried out on animals over the last six or seven decades which have established significant data to suggest that animals can feel a range of emotions including depression, grief, fear and anxiety. Some of these experiments have included giving dogs no means of escaping electric shocks in order to induce "learned helplessness", leading to the demonstration of emotions such as fear, grief and depression.[30] Beginning in the 1950s, Harlow's now infamous work on the emotional effect of social deprivation and isolation involved removing rhesus macaque monkeys from their mothers at one day old and replacing their mothers with a cloth doll. The cloth doll would, at intervals, shoot sharp brass spikes out of its "body" as the infant clung to it. Harlow's other experiments put individual monkeys in bare wire cages and monitored their development. It was found that both the monkeys with the doll "mothers" and the wire cage monkeys developed "severe persistent psychopathological behaviors similar to those seen in autistic children".[31]

On the other hand, those such as Frey continue to deny non-human animals emotions and feelings, and consider anthropomorphism misguided. In fact, he suggests that those people who, for example, anthropomorphize their pets with statements such as "he loves me" are usually "lonely people" who want to believe that their pets are "lesser human beings".[32] However, despite Frey's view, it would seem that there is reasonable evidence to suggest that animal suffering, like human suffering, is not limited to the experiencing of pain but can extend to a range of mental and emotional states as well.

So far, we have accepted that at least some sentient animals can experience physical, emotional and psychological suffering. The ability to experience suffering is largely agreed to indicate that those individuals should be granted some form of moral consideration in order for them to avoid experiencing suffering. What will now be considered is the principle of the ability to suffer alongside discussion surrounding the possession of interests.

2.2 What Are Interests?

Interests can be defined in a number of different ways. An interest might be considered to simply mean a curiosity in a particular thing or subject. One might, for example, have an interest in world history or sport. The term interest can also be found in legal terminology whereby having a legal interest in property means that one has a tangible legal claim on that particular property. Finally, there are interests which relate to individuals' needs or desires which might be considered more fundamental than those outlined above. Fundamental interests often attributed to humans might include an interest in avoiding suffering pain or an interest in continued life. What all of these uses of the term have in common is that the individual in possession of an interest is likely to suffer a disadvantage (or avoid a benefit) if a situation or turn of events compromises their interests or is likely to receive a benefit (or avoid a disadvantage) if a situation or turn of events works out, or is maintained, in favor of their interests.

For example, a world history enthusiast may take great pleasure in reading or watching documentaries on their subject of choice. The pleasure experienced is the benefit which results from pursuing their interest in world history. A person who stands to inherit a property receives the benefit of the interest when the property title is transferred to them. A person who has an interest in avoiding pain but falls from their bike and suffers a painful fractured arm is disadvantaged as their interest in avoiding pain has been compromised by the accident. A person who is free of pain avoids the disadvantage (of suffering pain) as long as the freedom from pain is maintained and thus, the interest is met.

The examples given above suggest that humans are possessors of interests and, indeed, it is universally accepted that this is the case. It should be noted though that there is significant discussion as to whether *all* humans can be considered to possess interests[33] but, for the purposes of this section, we can assume that most humans are considered to be in possession of at least some interests.

Before moving on to consider whether or not animals possess interests, the final point to make is that while the most fundamental interests, such as an interest in continued life and an interest in avoiding suffering, might reasonably be considered to be shared by most individuals, it should be noted that interests more generally are likely to differ from one individual to the next. This is particularly the case when considering those interests which might not be considered fundamental, such as an interest in watching football or an interest in taking a holiday. Some interests which might be deemed fundamental within a particular section of society or part of the world, such as an interest in receiving a university education, might be deemed less important in another section of society or part of the world. As the type of interests in question (i.e., those which have an impact upon the wellbeing of any one individual) are, by their very nature, focused on the individual, these differences are arguably inevitable.

Defining and identifying interests is important because it is interests that the law generally seeks to protect. As such, and having considered briefly what interests *are*, notwithstanding the fact that animals can suffer, it is essential to understand whether or not animals, like (most, if not all) humans, are also possessors of interests. If it can be concluded that animals are possessors of interests, then it is equally important to identify what those interests might include in order to decide how our actions toward them should be controlled and to what extent animals might require legal protection via formal regulation.

2.3 Do Animals Have Interests?

The importance of sentience (which will be used henceforth in this book as interchangeable with "the ability to suffer") in the debate on interests is based around the widely accepted principle that the ability to suffer implies that the individual in question has a life which can go well or badly for them or, put differently, sentient beings can all be considered to have a "welfare", a term defined by Fraser and Broom as follows: "Welfare defines the state of an animal as regards its attempts to cope with its environment".[34] In practice, an animal who is coping well with their environment could be considered to have good welfare and an animal who is not coping with their environment could be considered to have poor welfare. Coping might be assessed by measuring physiological reactions to the environment, or considering behavioral or emotional reactions, *inter alia*.

The connection between having a welfare and having interests is often taken for granted and is summed up by Cochrane, who suggests that "the capacity for wellbeing is synonymous with the possession of a welfare, a good of one's own, and interests".[35] However, just as Frey argues that experiencing pain is not synonymous with suffering, others argue that sentience does not necessarily indicate the possession of interests.

While it is largely agreed that sentience is one important criterion in deciding who or what possesses interests, inasmuch as anything that is not sentient tends to fall outside of the debate altogether, there is ongoing dispute over whether or not sentience alone can be considered a sufficient indicator. Some theorists, such as Francione, argue that sentience *is* the only relevant consideration[36] and, despite their differing views in other areas, Garner tends to agree with him that sentience (and thus, in his view, the possession of a welfare) is the indicator that a being is the possessor of interests.[37] As outlined above, Cochrane is in agreement that sentience, or the possession of a welfare, is important.[38] All three of these theorists agree that sentient animals all have some interests, although they do not necessarily agree on the specific nature of those interests.

Some theorists, such as Frey, believe that animals have no interests at all.[39] In line with his view that animals do not experience feelings, he argues that nor can they have interests as, I his view, interests require the possession of desires, beliefs and self-awareness (something which Frey argues animals cannot possess). Since Frey published his work on this issue, however, psychologists such as Gallup[40] and Pepperberg[41] and primatologists such as De Waal,[42] among a host of others, appear to prove that at least some non-human animals almost certainly do have beliefs, desires and self-awareness. For example, Pepperberg's work with Alex, an African Grey Parrot, appeared to demonstrate that Alex was capable of experiencing complex emotions such as jealousy[43] as well as the demonstration of complex cognitive function. As such, it would appear that even by Frey's standards, it is logical to conclude that these animals, at least, have interests.

Indeed, it is now largely accepted that most animals have at least some interest in not suffering (in both a physical and psychological capacity). However, even those that believe it to be undeniable that animals have interests find it difficult to agree on the specific detail of those interests. One of the main disputes in this regard centers around whether or not an animal needs to be consciously aware of an interest in order to possess it.

An example can be found in the discussion on whether animals have an interest in continued life, with some arguing that while animals have an interest in not suffering pain or mental distress, they cannot possibly have an interest in continued life as they lack the cognitive ability to conceptualize the meaning of their continued existence.[44] Those who hold this view might argue that animals can be killed for human use as long as the death does not cause unnecessary suffering. Others argue that animals have as much of an interest in continued life as humans do, regardless of their ability to conceptualize their existence[45] and make the point that to deny this interest to animals would also deny an interest in continued life to infant humans who are too young to have yet developed any concept of death and those with cognitive limitations who are also unable to conceptualize their existence.[46]

For the purposes of this section, it is important to acknowledge the main thrust of this dispute, which is that cognitive ability may or may not be important when ascribing interests. If sentience is deemed a sufficient stand-alone criterion for ascribing interests, then it follows that most animals are in possession of some interests. If cognitive ability, such as the ability to conceptualize an interest, is required in order to ascribe interests, then accepting animals as interest holders becomes far more problematic and might limit interest holders to a very small number of species for whom the criteria can be deemed to be met. Wise's work on this exact issue has suggested that, dependent on criteria used to assess the possession of interests, there are compelling arguments to conclude that not only great apes—largely recognized as cognitively advanced animals—and other more cognitively developed animals may be in possession of interests which require protection in law, but that animals such as bees—largely considered to be cognitively limited—may also fulfill criteria to allow us to attribute interests to them.[47]

Our purpose in this section was to establish whether or not animals have interests at all and it would appear that employing even the narrowest criteria for assessment, such a Frey's, which demand that only those with (or with potential for) sufficient cognitive ability and self-awareness can be considered to be in possession of some interests would result in at least some non-human animals being considered interest holders. Furthermore, the wider criteria employed by those such as Francione, who ascribe interests to *all* sentient individuals, allow that *most* animals have interests. Finally, even if we conclude that animals have no interests at all, there remain (admittedly outdated) aforementioned arguments such as those advanced by Kant that it is in our own interests to treat animals well and thus we should do so in order to safeguard our own humanity. For the purposes of this work, it is enough at this point to conclude that either animals do have at least some interests that might require protection by law or (though a rather less compelling and arguably outdated viewpoint) that the protection of animals by law may have the effect of upholding public morality and humanity and therefore is in our own (human) interests to do so. All of this taken together allows us to conclude that animals *should* be protected by law. The means by which this protection is achieved will be considered next.

2.4 Balancing Our Interests with Those of Animals

So far, we have progressed under the widely accepted principles that sentient animals can suffer both physically and psychologically and that animals can have an interest in not suffering. We have accepted that there may be limitations and objections to these principles, but that an exploration of those limitations and objections falls outside of the scope of this book. Now we move on to how suffering, interests and the balancing of those interests interact with each other to decide if, and to what extent, the use of animals should be regulated by law.

Most acts or omissions do not exist in isolation but have consequences which may affect a number of different things in a number of different ways. In fact, it is the recognition of this fact that drives the development of the law in the first place—we cannot act on our interests without taking into consideration the interests of others and this is, for the most part, the theory which underpins the law.

The balancing of interests is something which is accepted in day-to-day life, even without many of us realizing that we do it. If I see a bank note drop from someone's pocket, I might have an interest in picking it up and keeping it for myself. However, the person that dropped that note also has an interest in retaining it. Most reasonable people would agree that even if I gain a benefit from keeping the money myself, I have a moral obligation to catch up with the person that dropped it and hand it back. Indeed, the law recognizes the interest of the rightful owner of the note as the Theft Act 1968[48] protects against this sort of action. As such, I do not just have a moral obligation not to keep the money for myself, but I have a legal obligation not to keep the money for myself too. In this way, the interest of the rightful owner of the money is legally protected. The moral obligation that a reasonable person feels to return the money can be set within a number of moral frameworks, perhaps most effectively that of Kant's "Moral Absolutism".[49] This school of thought is based on the ancient premise of "do unto others as you would have them do unto you" and believes that certain things are, by definition, morally right or morally wrong. Stealing would be one such act and therefore, the morally correct thing to do would be to return the money, irrespective of the consequences.

We can use a similar interest-based approach to apply to the aforementioned situation of burying the kitten alive. I may have an interest in burying the kitten alive in order to amuse myself. I could argue that it would make me happy to bury the kitten alive and therefore I have a right to do what I want to the kitten in pursuit of my happiness. Most reasonable people would argue that my interest in amusing myself was of lesser importance than the pain (in both a physical and moral sense) I would create if I were to bury the kitten alive. Indeed, the law would agree; the burying of a kitten alive would almost certainly be construed as a breach of s.4(1) of the AWA 2006 which prohibits the infliction of unnecessary suffering. In this way, the interest of the kitten in not suffering unnecessarily is legally protected. However, as will become clear as the discussion progresses, this protection is not absolute.

Debate quickly arises when the interests in question are not quite so easy to weigh against one another as the examples given above. For example, what if the kitten in question was in a laboratory and I considered that the suffering I planned to inflict was necessary in order to conduct an experiment which might help medical science better understand the development of cancer cells in human children? Would a reasonable person argue that the kitten's interest in not suffering outweighs my interest, or indeed (if the belief that animal testing was useful and necessary were correct) the interests of all humanity, to further work in finding a cure for cancer in humans? What if there were a 100% guarantee that the research would provide important results? What if there was no guarantee that the research would provide any useful results at all?

What if, instead of a kitten, the animal in question was a pig in a factory farm and I was a parent who had a low income and a number of children to feed? Are my interests in feeding my family cheap and easily available meat more important than the interests of the pig not to live and die in a factory farm in order to feed my family? Would the situation be different if the pig were kept on a "free range" farm? What if we accept that a person can live healthily on a vegan diet which renders the "need" to eat meat, or other animal products, obsolete? Can we suggest that our interest in eating meat, while not necessary for our survival, is sufficient to warrant the death of the animal, a conundrum likely to be contingent on one's individual view on whether or not animals have an interest in continued life.

If Bentham's aforementioned question "can they suffer?" forms the starting point for the debate surrounding the extent to which animals should be afforded legal protection, and the attribution of interests to animals develops the debate, it is the balancing of interests in situations such as those outlined above that form the substance of it. From this discussion come the two principal schools of thought surrounding our treatment of animals: the rights theory and the welfare theory. These two schools are, in and of themselves, multi-faceted and different theorists present different approaches but it is fair to say that differences between the two theories in very general terms can be clearly identified.

2.5 Animal Welfare Theory Versus Animal Rights Theory

Animal rights theory and animal welfare theory are often confused in mainstream public discourse but, from an ideological and legal perspective, there are fundamental differences between them. The difference can be broadly summed up in the following well-used phrase:

> *Animal rights theorists advocate for no cages, animal welfare theorists advocate for bigger cages.*[50]

Some proponents of animal rights theory argue that use (and ownership) of animals by humans *inevitably* results in exploitation and/or suffering and is therefore unacceptable,[51] and this is perhaps particularly true for wild animals. Proponents of animal welfare theory might argue that animal use by humans is acceptable as long as the animal's needs are provided for and they are treated humanely or not made to suffer unnecessarily.[52]

In between the purist rights and welfare theory camps, a number of other scholars have developed their own position on the matter, taking parts from both theories. An example is Cochrane, who believes that animals can be considered to be rights holders without necessitating total liberation (i.e., he does not agree that animals have an inherent interest in liberty, as many rights advocates do who subscribe to the "no cages" approach[53]). Notwithstanding the recognition that different versions of the rights and welfare theories exist, for the purposes of this book, and for simplicity, the two "purist" positions will be used in order to further the current discussion. The animal rights stance holds that, contrary to Kantian theory, animals can never be "means to be arbitrarily used by this or that will".[54] It is argued that animals are ends in themselves[55] and, thus, their lives are not given value by the importance that humans ascribe to them (as individuals or species) but that they have inherent value of and for their own distinct purposes. Animal rights advocates who subscribe to the stance described above therefore oppose the use of animals for their flesh, milk and eggs, as well as their use in medical research. They also oppose the use of animals in entertainment and the principle of animals as chattel under the law.[56] The rights theory argues that the law should recognize that animals, like people, have fundamental rights which cannot simply be ignored or overridden arbitrarily for human (or any other) benefit.

In the lab kitten situation, the rights theory would reject the purported benefit to humanity as a valid interest as the kitten's interest in not being experimented upon should be considered fundamental and protected, in the same way that (in modern society) a human being's right not to be experimented on is (theoretically) protected. The same would apply to the pig who, from a rights perspective, should not be raised in a farm and killed for her flesh, regardless of how many children I have to feed and regardless of whether she can conceptualize her own death or if she has an interest in continued life.

From a legal perspective, animal rights advocates tend to seek to prohibit (abolish) practices which use animals and move toward fundamental legal rights for animals similar to those fundamental rights generally recognized (if not always enforced) for human beings. These rights might include the right to life, the right to liberty, the right to freedom from torture, the right to bodily integrity, amongst others. While it is recognized that these rights are not absolute, in the case of humans (those in the armed forces, for example, are killed in the line of duty and it is not considered to be a human rights breach *per se* and human rights are compromised in societies worldwide on a daily basis), however for people, these rights are ostensibly, if not practically, recognized and (should be) upheld when all other things are equal. For animals, no such benchmark exists.

For humans, the United Nations Declaration on Human Rights was adopted in 1948 as setting out "fundamental human rights to be universally protected".[57] The main driving force behind the establishment of the United Nations and the Declaration itself was the desire to ensure that the human rights atrocities carried out during the Second World War could never be allowed to happen again. The overall principle underpinning the declaration was that the "recognition of the inherent dignity and of the equal and inalienable rights of all members of the human family is the foundation of freedom, justice and peace in the world".[58]

While it is recognized that human rights, even those fundamental ones outlined in the declaration, are rarely, if ever, absolute, the principle of seeking to establish, and have universally recognized, similar (if not identical) rights for animals is a major focus for some animal rights advocates. Of course, some rights deemed fundamental for human beings, such as the right to marry or the right to freedom of religion, will be irrelevant for animals and therefore animal rights advocates do not seek to implement, arbitrarily, the *same* rights as those granted to humans but rather focus upon those in which animals can be considered, like humans, to have an *interest*. For example, freedom from torture is likely to be as important to an individual cat, dog or elephant as it is to an individual human, regardless of whether or not the individual could conceptualize the treatment in advance.

The welfare theory, as opposed to the rights theory, is the predominant basis for English legislation which regulates animal use (with some notable exceptions). The welfare theory accepts that animals are used by humans for their own benefit, such as for food, for experimentation or for entertainment. Suffering is used as a key indicator in animal welfare assessment and, as a general rule, animal welfare advocates seek change which mitigates or prevents all *unnecessary* suffering. One of the main challenges to this approach is that the term "unnecessary suffering" is subjective; there is no firm agreement on what level of suffering might be deemed "necessary" and thus legislating to ensure that only "necessary" suffering is permitted becomes inherently problematic. For example, the case of *Stuart Bandeira and Darren Brannigan v. Royal Society for the Prevention of Cruelty to Animals 2000*[59] turned on this exact point. The argument put forward by the RSPCA was that a dog who had been injured as a result of being sent into the earth of a fox or the sett of a badger by his owners when he was attacked by a fox or a badger, had been made to experience unnecessary suffering. The main thrust of the appellant's argument was that causation was very difficult to prove as animals tend to get themselves into "scraps" without being forced to do so by people. It was argued that the act of the appellants was simply "no more than putting a dog's nose and feet at the beginning of a hole in the countryside"[60] and this, in and of itself, could not be regarded as causing unnecessary suffering. The appellant's lawyer argued that "it is wrong for the law to leave a wide spectrum of uncertainty as to what amounts to ill-treatment and what can be described as causing unnecessary suffering and suchlike, because this leaves the citizen with no idea of where he stands".[61] Indeed, while RSPCA did win the case, the Court of Appeal judge cautioned that the judgment should not be used as "as a flag to wave at those who hunt with dogs or any other animals".[62] While the facts of this case suggested that unnecessary suffering had been caused in this particular instance, the judge suggested that the magistrate in future cases should be mindful of the risk posed to the animal as a deciding factor, saying "[a]s it seems to me, if the risk of injury is very high, then a finding of causation by the Magistrates is very likely. If the risk of injury is very low, then a finding of no causation by the Magistrates is very likely".[63]

In his paper, "Unnecessary Suffering",[64] Mike Radford charts the development of the concept from its first inclusion in the Prevention of Cruelty to Animals Act in 1849 and its application in case law. He quotes Hawkins J. in *Ford v Wiley*,[65] highlighting that "the amount of pain caused, the intensity and duration of the suffering, and the object to be attained, must, however always be essential elements for consideration" in cases which require a conclusion on the matter. In effect, proportionality plays a key role in reaching judgment—a position which was echoed in the later RSPCA case cited above. A wider discussion of the intricacies of decision-making with regard to what may or may not constitute unnecessary suffering is not required in the context of this book, and it is enough, therefore, for our present purposes to accept that there continue to be no clear-cut rules with regard to the application of the expression, "unnecessary suffering", despite its having been a foundational principle in animal law since its inception. In practice, the expression is interpreted on a case-by-case basis, informed by precedent.

The animal welfare theory would seek to improve conditions for animals used by humans by implementing standards of care (via both legally binding rules and non-binding guidance) and laws which seek to regulate the use of animals. An animal welfarist might deem it acceptable to use a kitten in a lab to test for a cure for cancer, as long as the kitten was cared for according to particular standards, but may not agree for the same kitten to be used to test a brand of cosmetics (which may be seen as a more frivolous or unnecessary use of the animal). An animal welfarist might accept that a pig can be raised and killed in order to provide food for my family as long as she was kept in particular conditions and killed in a way which did not cause her excessive (or unnecessary) pain or suffering. The welfare approach is often criticized by advocates for animal rights on the basis that it, on the one hand, legitimizes the ongoing use of animals for human gain and, on the other, achieves reforms too slowly and ineffectively to make any meaningful positive impact upon animals. Garner has challenged this view, notably in the book *The Animal Rights Debate*,[66] in which he and Francione go "head-to-head" on the issue. Garner bases his argument in large part on pragmatism, separating out what might be ultimately desirable in the long term from what is realistic and achievable within current political and legislative parameters. He notes that, while he largely agrees with much of the arguments put forward by animal rights theorists (and particularly those such as Francione who argues for the abolition of animal use for human benefit), the approach is fundamentally flawed as it is not taking into account the very real and prevalent interests (of people, businesses or wider societies) which act to maintain animal use. The major difference between Garner's and Francione's approach in practice is that Garner's position does not see the right to life for animals as of fundamental importance.[67] Arguing that death (so long as it does not include suffering) is of less moral importance for animals (and "marginal humans"[68]) than it is for humans generally, Garner subscribes to the view highlighted previously that, due to human's perceived greater cognitive capacity and ability to both conceptualize death and maintain hopes and aspirations for the future during life, in a way that most other animals (to our knowledge) cannot, the death of a person will inevitably count for more (morally) than the death of an animal. He notes that death will prevent future opportunities from being realized in both people and animals but that the range of opportunities available to people is richer and more complex than those available to animals.[69] That said, he recognizes that death also takes away opportunities for animals and so advises caution in accepting the argument that animal deaths have no moral significance. Garner goes on to suggest that a similar argument could be made with regard to animal liberty—another fundamental call of animal rights theorists.[70] Garner argues that animals' lack of autonomy means that liberty *per se* is not "the same denial of autonomy [as in the case of humans] through depriving animals of their liberty".[71] In other words, Garner is suggesting that denying an animal his or her freedom and autonomy is of lesser consequence to denying a human being his or her liberty. This view on liberty is also held by Cochrane and outlined in his book *Animal Rights Without Liberation*.[72] Ultimately, Garner argues that the welfarist approach is predominantly focused not upon abolishing human use of animals, but in abolishing—or at least mitigating—animal suffering to the extent possible. He argues that while animals can be considered to have an interest in avoiding suffering, they do not generally have as strong (if any) interest in continued life or liberty.[73]

As mentioned previously, it is the animal welfare theory model, not the animal rights theory model, which forms the basis of animal welfare legislation. This legislation is increasingly based around the aforementioned concept of Brambell's Five Freedoms, which are a set of needs animals are deemed to possess, as follows:

1. Freedom from Hunger and Thirst
2. Freedom from Discomfort
3. Freedom from Pain, Injury or Disease
4. Freedom to Express Normal Behavior
5. Freedom from Fear and Distress[74]

To use the terminology under consideration in this chapter, these five needs could be construed as the "interests" of the animals in question. According to the model, when these interests are met, the animal's "welfare" is considered to be provided for. It is perhaps noteworthy that in keeping with welfarist theory, animal needs within this framework are not deemed to include either the right to life or liberty. Since the development of the Five Freedoms in the mid-1960s, the needs have been incorporated into many pieces of modern animal welfare legislation worldwide, including s.9 of the overarching AWA 2006 in England and Wales, where the five needs are included, with very little amendment from their original form, as follows:

Section 9

(1) *A person commits an offence if he does not take such steps as are reasonable in all the circumstances to ensure that the needs of an animal for which he is responsible are met to the extent required by good practice.*
(2) *For the purposes of this Act, an animal's needs shall be taken to include—*

(a) *its need for a suitable environment,*
(b) *its need for a suitable diet,*
(c) *its need to be able to exhibit normal behavior patterns,*
(d) *any need it has to be housed with, or apart from, other animals, and*
(e) *its need to be protected from pain, suffering, injury and disease.*

This chapter has explored the commonalities and differences between animal rights theory and animal welfare theory. Despite differing views with regard to approach and desired end-goals, it is safe to say that one point which proponents of an animal rights theory, those supporting an animal welfare approach and those who perhaps do not fall clearly into either camp appear to agree upon is that, given the sheer magnitude of animal use currently being employed in this country, the regulation of their use under the law is not just desirable, but absolutely necessary. The way in which this regulation plays out and the impact it may have on the animals themselves is considered in the next chapter.

Notes

1. S.21 Zoo Licensing Act 1981.
2. HC Deb, 1 March 2012, c41WS.
3. For example, HC Deb 25 October 1967 vol 751 cc512-3W 512W, HL Deb 20 May 1970 vol 310 cc1049-52 1049, HL Deb 29 October 1970 vol 312 cc218-36 218 and *HL Deb 28 January 1974 vol 349 cc55-77*.

4. The Animal Welfare (Licensing of Activities Involving Animals) (England) Regulations 2018.
5. *Daily Mail,* 28th March 2011, "Anne's agony: Battered, kicked and stabbed, the desperate plight of Britain's last circus elephant".
6. *R v Bobby and Moira Roberts* (2012). Northamptonshire Magistrates' Court sitting at Northamptonshire Crown Court, 23 November 2012.
7. RSPCA.org.uk. (2019). *RSPCA Facts and Figures.* [online] Available at: https://www.rspca.org.uk/whatwedo/latest/facts.
8. Honderich, Ted, ed. (1995). "*Animals: Peter Singer*". The Oxford Companion to Philosophy. Oxford, pp. 35–36.
9. Ed. P. Heath and J.B. Schneewind. (1997). *Lectures on Ethics.* Cambridge: Cambridge University Press, p. 212.
10. Re: Wedgwood Trust [1915] 1 Ch. 113.
11. Oxford English Dictionary.
12. Aaltola, E., (2012). *Animal Suffering: Philosophy and Culture,* Palgrave Macmillan, p. 16.
13. Bentham, J., (1907). *An Introduction to the Principles of Morals and Legislation,* 1907.
14. Kemp Smith, N., (1952). *New Studies in the Philosophy of Descartes,* Macmillan, London, pp. 136 and 140.
15. Regan, T. (2010). *The case for animal rights.* 2nd ed. Berkeley: University of California Press, p.26.
16. Ibid., p. 263.
17. Frey, R. (1980). *Interests and rights: The Case Against Animals.* Oxford: Clarendon Press, p. 163.
18. Ibid., p. 34.
19. Ibid., p. 50.
20. Ibid., p. 48.
21. Ibid.
22. Ibid.
23. Regan, T. (2010). *The case for animal rights.* 2nd ed. Berkeley: University of California Press, p. 26.
24. Braithwaite, V. (2010). *Do fish feel pain?.* Oxford: Oxford University Press, p. 113.
25. Hume, D., (1739). *A Treatise on Human Nature.* p. 93.
26. Brambell, F. W. R. (1965). *Report of the Technical Committee to Enquire into the Welfare of Animals kept under Intensive Livestock Husbandry Systems.* London, Her Majesty's Stationery Office.

27. Brambell, F. W. R. (1965). *Report of the Technical Committee to Enquire into the Welfare of Animals kept under Intensive Livestock Husbandry Systems*. London, Her Majesty's Stationery Office., p. 10.
28. Goodall, J., (1990) *Through a Window: 30 years observing the Gombe chimpanzees*, London: Weidenfeld & Nicolson, p. 13.
29. For example, Bekoff, M., (2007). *The Emotional Lives of Animals*, New World Library, Novato, California.
30. Seligman, Martin E.P., (1975). *Helplessness: On depression, Development and Death*.
31. Text accompanying photographs taken of test subjects circa 1970, University of Wisconsin, United States.
32. Frey, R. (1980). *Interests and rights: The Case Against Animals*. Oxford: Clarendon Press.
33. See Singer, P. (1995). *Animal liberation*. 2nd ed. London: Pimlico, p. 18, for exploration of this concept.
34. Broom D.M., (1991). *Animal welfare: concepts and measurements*. J Animal Science. 1991; 69: 4167–4175.
35. Cochrane, A., (2012). *Animal Rights Without Liberation*, Columbia University Press, p. 25.
36. Francione, G. (2012). Sentience—Animal Rights The Abolitionist Approach. [online] Abolitionistapproach.com. Available at: http://www.abolitionistapproach.com/sentience/ [Accessed 24 Dec. 2017].
37. Francione, G. and Garner, R. (2010). The animal rights debate. New York: Columbia University Press, pp. 106.
38. Cochrane, A., (2012). Animal Rights Without Liberation, Columbia University Press, pp. 36–38.
39. Frey, R. (1980). *Interests and rights: The Case Against Animals*. Oxford: Clarendon Press, p. 2.
40. Gallup, G. (1970). *Chimpanzees: Self-Recognition*. Science, 167(3914), pp. 86–87.
41. Pepperberg, I., (2000). *The Alex Studies: Cognitive and Communicative Abilities of Grey Parrots*. Harvard University Press.
42. De Waal, F., (1982). *Chimpanzee Politics: Power and Sex among Apes*, John Hopkins University Press.
43. Pepperberg, I. (2008). *Alex and me*. New York: HarperCollins Publishers, FAQs.
44. Regan, T., (2001). *Defending Animal Rights*, University of Illinois Press.

45. Francione, G., (2008). *Animals as Persons: Essays on the Abolition of Animal Exploitation*, Columbia University Press.
46. See Singer, P. (1995). *Animal liberation*. 2nd ed. London: Pimlico, p. 18, for exploration of this concept.
47. Wise, S. (2013). *Drawing the line*. Cambridge, Mass: Perseus Books.
48. S.3(1) of the Theft Act 1968 defines "appropriation" as including "where he has come by the property (innocently or not) without stealing it". The test in the Theft Act is that the property must be appropriated "dishonestly", which would include knowingly keeping the money mentioned above while knowing that it belonged to someone else.
49. Plato.stanford.edu. (2016). Kant's Moral Philosophy. [online] Available at: https://plato.stanford.edu/entries/kant-moral/ [Accessed 24 Dec. 2017].
50. Origin Unknown. Example of use: Bbc.co.uk. (n.d.). BBC—Ethics—Animal ethics: Introduction to animal rights. [online] Available at: http://www.bbc.co.uk/ethics/animals/rights/introduction.shtml [Accessed 24 Dec. 2017].
51. For example, Francione in Francione, G. and Garner, R. (2010). The animal rights debate. New York: Columbia University Press, p. 15.
52. For example, Garner in Francione, G. and Garner, R. (2010). The animal rights debate. New York: Columbia University Press, p. 122.
53. Cochrane, A. (2012). Animal rights without liberation. New York: Columbia University Press, p. 210.
54. Immanuel K., (1785). *Groundwork for the Metaphysics of Morals*.
55. Regan, T. (2010). The case for animal rights. 2nd ed. Berkeley: University of California Press.
56. Francione, G.L., (1995). *Animals, Property and the Law*, Philadelphia: Temple University Press.
57. Description used by the United Nations of the Declaration's purpose. See Un.org. (n.d.). Universal Declaration of Human Rights. [online] Available at: http://www.un.org/en/universal-declaration-human-rights/ [Accessed 24 Dec. 2017].
58. Preamble, Universal Declaration of Human Rights (1948).
59. Stuart Bandeira and Darren Brannigan v. Royal Society for the Prevention of Cruelty to Animals (2000) LTL 28 February 2000.
60. Ibid.
61. Ibid.
62. Ibid.

63. Ibid.
64. Radford, M. (1999). *"Unnecessary suffering": the cornerstone of animal protection legislation considered.* Criminal Law Review, 702–13.
65. Hawkins J in Ford v Wiley (1889) 23 QBD 205 at [219].
66. Francione, G. and Garner, R. (2010). *The animal rights debate.* New York: Columbia University Press, pp. 103–170.
67. Francione, G. and Garner, R. (2010). The animal rights debate. New York: Columbia University Press, p. 125.
68. See Singer, P. (1995). *Animal liberation.* 2nd ed. London: Pimlico, p. 18 for exploration of this concept.
69. Francione, G. and Garner, R. (2010). The animal rights debate. New York: Columbia University Press, p. 117.
70. Francione, G. and Garner, R. (2010). The animal rights debate. New York: Columbia University Press, p. 129.
71. Francione, G. and Garner, R. (2010). *The animal rights debate.* New York: Columbia University Press, p. 118.
72. Cochrane, A. (2012). *Animal rights without liberation.* New York: Columbia University Press.
73. Francione, G. and Garner, R. (2010). The animal rights debate. New York: Columbia University Press, pp. 117 and 129.
74. The Farm Animal Welfare Council (Foundation, Internet. "[ARCHIVED CONTENT] UK Government Web Archive—The National Archives". National Archives (UK). Web. 6 June 2016).

3

How Is Animal Use Regulated and How Does This Protect Them?

The previous chapter concluded that, while there remains debate surrounding the extent to which animals should be protected by law and the best approach to achieve protection, it has long been a majority-held belief that animals should be afforded some protection under the law. In practice, animals are protected by law in a variety of ways. Some legislation has the protection of animals as its main purpose and other legislation might offer some level of protection to animals as a consequence (whether intended or otherwise) of some other goal or aim. This chapter seeks to lay out the history of animal law in England and then consider the various mechanisms and frameworks by which the use of animals is regulated by legislation.

3.1 Changing Approaches to the Regulation of Animal Use in England

Since the introduction of the Driving of Cattle, Metropolis Act of 1781[1] and the later, but more comprehensive, "Martin's Act" to prevent the "wanton … and cruel … beating, abuse, or ill-treatment [of] any Horse,

E. Tyson, *Licensing Laws and Animal Welfare*, The Palgrave Macmillan Animal Ethics Series, https://doi.org/10.1007/978-3-030-50042-9_3

Mare, Gelding, Mule, Ass, Ox, Cow, Heifer, Steer, Sheep, or other Cattle" in 1822,[2] legislation specifically concerned with, or including provision for, the protection of animal welfare in the England has increased to become a significant body of law in its own right. In 2001, there were over 3500 individual pieces of legislation relating to animal welfare in force in the United Kingdom[3] and that number is on the increase, with at least 917 legislative measures that include the term "animal welfare" having been introduced in the United Kingdom since that time.

Animal law in England has been shaped by a great number of factors, including political influences (domestic, European and global), public opinion, industry stakeholders and pressure groups. The first legislation concerned with the protection of animals was ostensibly focused upon preventing overt cruelty toward animals, rather than assuming the more modern approach of protecting welfare more generally. It should be noted that some scholars have questioned whether or not this early anti-cruelty legislation was, in fact, introduced with the aim of protecting the animal as an individual possessing of, at least some, intrinsic worth or if the rationale was rooted in other concerns. For example, it has been suggested that in cases such as bull baiting, which was outlawed in 1835 following the introduction of the Cruelty to Animals Act 1835 (later repealed by the Protection of Animals Act 1911), the reasoning had *something* to do with concern for the animals themselves but that societal factors also had significant influence. For example, in the initial attempts to see bull baiting banned, discussion in Parliament centered not exclusively around cruelty to animals. Sir William Pulteney, who sponsored the Bill gave his reasoning for its proposal as follows:

> *The practice was cruel and inhuman; it drew together idle and disorderly persons; it drew also from their occupations many who ought to be earning subsistence for themselves and families; it created many disorderly and mischievous proceedings, and furnished examples of profligacy and cruelty. In short, it was a practice which ought to be put a stop to.*[4]

It is clear from Pulteney's description of bull baiting that his concern was not limited to the cruelty inflicted on the bulls themselves. He was also concerned that the practice increased nuisance and public disorder, and he implied that it encouraged people to become idle and shun work. The extent to which his view was founded is irrelevant for the purposes of this research, but it could certainly be concluded that at least some stakeholders in this early piece of animal welfare law had motives other than, or in additional to, the protection of animals in mind when supporting its implementation.

Whether motivated in part or full by the desire to bring an end to overt cruelty to animals, early statutes made no attempt to impose duties upon those responsible for animals to promote and protect their welfare in a more holistic way, beyond refraining from specific cruel acts, and the development of the concept of "animal welfare" in law, as it is now understood, came much later. Over time, the justification for legislation designed to protect animals, both from cruelty and, increasingly, to promote or protect their welfare, has been given significant weight by an ever-expanding understanding of the sentiency of animals and their myriad needs—needs which go far beyond simply avoiding being beaten as well as going beyond simply needing to be fed, watered and provided with veterinary care. Work in the fields of animal welfare science and ethology has explored the behavioral, social, psychological and environmental needs of animals which, in turn, have served to inform policymakers on the development of the law.

As society's view of animals changes and, importantly, as its use of animals changes, law has been developed to reflect this. The first laws were concerned largely with cattle and horses, but today, while our general concern for animals might be heightened, our use of them has grown immensely. Industries using animals in enormous numbers, such as farming (every year in the United Kingdom approximately 2.6 million cattle, 10 million pigs, 14.5 million sheep and lambs, 80 million fish and 950 million birds are slaughtered for human consumption[5]) which expanded rapidly following the end of the Second World War[6] and vivisection (3.94 million scientific procedures with live animals were employed in 2016[7]). This, in turn, led to growing concerns surrounding the treatment of animals used by such industries. For example, the boom in the intensive farming industry in the 1950s and 1960s led to the publication of the book *Animal Machines* by Ruth Harrison in the mid-1960s.[8] Harrison's book highlighted the major welfare concerns for animals used in the factory farming industry, which grew as a response to food shortages and what was deemed to be an overreliance on import of foreign meat following the Second World War. Subsidies were given to farmers who increased production using new technology and this led to animals increasingly being raised and killed in "production line" style farms with higher stocking densities than traditional farms.[9] While these farms increased production significantly, they also severely jeopardized animal welfare. In part as a result of Harrison's publication, the government commissioned a study that whose outcome would contribute toward the development of a framework within which animal welfare standards could be assessed, initially with a specific focus upon farming. This study resulted in the formulation of the aforementioned "Brambell's Five Freedoms". The Five Freedoms outlined the five fundamental welfare needs that animals were deemed to possess. By assessing the extent to which these needs were provided for, an assessment of welfare standards could be carried out using the new framework. The freedoms were defined as follows:

1. Freedom from Hunger and Thirst
2. Freedom from Discomfort
3. Freedom from Pain, Injury or Disease
4. Freedom to Express Normal Behavior
5. Freedom from Fear and Distress[10]

While it would take some time for the Five Freedoms to become fully entrenched in law, this framework provided a foundation upon which welfare assessment could be based and, soon afterwards, the first piece of legislation which explicitly empowered the relevant minister to introduce regulations with a view to protecting animal welfare—The Agriculture (Miscellaneous Provisions) Act 1968—was introduced. Section 2(1) of the Act gave powers to the relevant minister(s) to introduce regulations which may in particular include provision:

(a) *with respect to the dimensions and layout of accommodation for livestock, the materials to be used in constructing any such accommodation and the facilities by way of lighting, heating, cooling, ventilation, drainage, water supply and otherwise to be provided in connection with any accommodation;*

(b) *for ensuring the provision of balanced diets for livestock and for prohibiting or regulating the use of any substance as food for livestock and the importation and supply of any substance intended for use as food for livestock;*

(c) *for prohibiting the bleeding of livestock and the mutilation of livestock in any manner specified in the regulations, and for prohibiting or regulating the use of any method of marking or restraining livestock or interfering with the capacity of livestock to smell, see, hear, emit sound or exercise any other faculty.*

In 1876, the Cruelty to Animals Act was introduced to regulate by license the use of animals in vivisection. It was repealed by the Animals in Scientific Procedures Act 1986 (ASPA 1986). The law is not strictly a piece of animal welfare legislation (although it is often touted as such by the vivisection industry itself). Instead, and as the name of the original iteration of the law suggests, these laws are designed to control the administering of explicitly cruel practices on animals or, in other words, to license activities which would otherwise be outlawed as cruelty to animals in other circumstances. This principle comes back to the earlier discussion of "necessary suffering" and the balancing of interests.

Around the same time that ASPA was introduced, the growing concern for animals in general led to other establishments, such as zoos and aquaria, having industry-specific regulations imposed upon them.[11] While the ZLA 1981, as it was originally enacted, contained no explicit reference to "animal welfare", Hansard records show that the rationale behind its introduction was deeply rooted in a concern for animal welfare.[12] Even more recently (2002), the ZLA 1981 was updated to include the provisions of the EC Zoos Directive[13] which imposed further regulation on zoos and extended protection of animals to include an obligation to provide an environment suited to the species' specific biological and behavioral needs as well as a further obligation for the zoo to make a contribution to conservation or education.[14] This appeared to be a move toward recognition in law that animals should not be kept in zoos for purely entertainment purposes, but that that their captivity is justifiable only on the basis that the zoo makes a contribution to conservation of biodiversity. The British government's 2012 announcement that it intends to pursue a ban on the use of wild animals in traveling circuses on ethical grounds, with the law finally introduced in January 2020, despite a purported lack of scientific evidence to categorically prove suffering occurs,[15] is an interesting development which suggests that more consideration than ever is being given to an animal's implicit "right" not to be used without justifiable cause.

In 2007, the AWA 2006 was introduced as the core animal welfare law for England. This new legislation was the first to entrench the Five Freedoms into rule of law and shifted the regulatory focus from mere prevention of cruelty toward animals to a more holistic promotion of welfare approach.

While the law has developed to recognize that animals should be protected from certain types of suffering and some, albeit limited, policy decisions are made based on ethical reasoning rather than on purely evidence-based, animal welfare science considerations, animals are still classed as property in law and do not have enforceable legal rights of their own. Instead, the way in which animal welfare law operates is by regulating the actions of the people that engage in practices encompassed by the legislation. Following is more detailed consideration of how these various approaches to animal law play out in practice.

3.2 Animals as Property

"There is no question that animals are regarded as property under the law and have held the status of property for as long as anyone can remember".[16] This property status is something which advocates of animal rights theory have sought to change—with animal rights theorists such as Francione arguing that the property status of animals results in the outcome that "the regulation of animal use does not, as a general rule, transcend that level of protection that facilitates the most economically efficient exploitation of the animal".[17] However, the ownership of property confers on the owner certain rights which, in turn, provide some limited protection to the animal when that property happens to be an animal. Statutes which impact upon animals as property include the Theft Act 1978 which provides in s.1 that "A person is guilty of theft if he dishonestly appropriates property belonging to another with the intention of permanently depriving the other of it". An offense under this Act carries a maximum sentence on conviction of seven years imprisonment.[18] The Criminal Damage Act 1971 provides in s.1(1) that "A person who without lawful excuse destroys or damages any property belonging to another intending to destroy or damage any such property or being reckless as to whether any such property would be destroyed or damaged shall be guilty of an offence" with an offense under this section carrying a maximum prison sentence of ten years on conviction.[19]

On the surface, it would appear unlikely that these Acts offer any meaningful protection to animals, but may offer a remedy to the owner of the animal in the event of theft, injury or death caused to the animal. However, they may also have the practical impact of acting as a deterrent to those thinking of injuring an animal or stealing an animal from his or her owner and, in this way, may provide a modicum of protection to the individual animal in question as a result. Perhaps, a good example of this can be found in *Hamps v Darby* 1948,[20] where a pigeon fancier's birds flew onto the neighbor's land and fed on his crop of peas. The neighbor shot and killed four of the birds and injured another. While any court verdict could do nothing to protect the birds from harm or death after the event, in finding for the plaintiff, it is perhaps reasonable to assume that the neighbor would be unlikely to kill or injure birds again if they were to stray onto his land in future.[21]

Of course, the limited protection that may be provided to an animal by virtue of his or her property status is arguably negated by the fact that the owner is not bound by the same standards. As such, while an owner would be regulated by the Animal Welfare Act 2006 to not treat their animal cruelly or fail to promote their animal's welfare, if the owner chose, for example, to (humanely) kill their pet dog because they were bored of them, then there is nothing to prevent them doing so. As such, the property status of animals puts them in a very vulnerable position in relation to their owner.

3.3 Prevention of Cruelty

As highlighted in the introduction to this chapter, the original laws dealing with the protection of animals in England sought to protect animals from cruelty by prohibiting specific practices. Bear baiting, cock fighting and beating of cattle were all outlawed. These laws created a negative duty for people to abide by: they must not carry out certain prohibited acts and generally these involved the infliction of deliberate or wanton cruelty to an animal.

The very first piece of legislation focused specifically on the protection of animals was the aforementioned "Martin's Act" of 1822. The statute was concerned with the prohibition of "wantonly and cruelly beat[ing], abus[ing], or ill-treat[ing]" the animals most used in that day (cows, horses, mules, etc.). The underlying principle of the Act was that animal use is permitted unless the practice was deemed cruel and thus explicitly prohibited or it was deemed to cause "unnecessary suffering" (howsoever defined—the concept of unnecessary suffering is considered in Sect. 5 in Chap. 2 of this book).

The Protection of Animals Act 1911 was repealed and replaced by the AWA 2006 in 2007, and the older statute's main provisions in relation to cruelty were carried over to the AWA 2006, with some practices (using animals in fighting, poisoning animals, etc.) remaining explicitly prohibited in the new law. In addition to these clauses, the principle of "unnecessary suffering" was maintained in s.4 of the AWA 2006.

3.4 Ensuring the Welfare of the Individual Animal

A more modern approach to animal protection law has been to move away from the simple responsibility to not inflict unacceptable harm on animals (via the principle of unnecessary suffering) toward a demand for people responsible for animals to take active responsibility to attempt to ensure the *welfare* needs of the individual animal are met. As previously noted, a working definition of the term "welfare" can be found in the work of Fraser and Broom as follows: "Welfare defines the state of an animal as regards its attempts to cope with its environment".[22]

Good welfare might, therefore, be considered to represent not just an animal who is free from suffering (whether unnecessary or otherwise) but an animal who is coping well with their environment. In layman's terms, the promotion of welfare might be considered to seek to provide an animal with a "good life" or a "life worth living". The way in which animal welfare has been measured in modern legislation in England is via assessment against the Five Freedoms, which are incorporated into s.9 of the AWA 2006.

3.4.1 The Animal Welfare Act 2006

Since 2007, the main statute concerned with the protection of the welfare of individual animals in England is the AWA 2006. The term "protected animal" is defined by s.2 of the Act as follows: "If (a) it is of a kind which is commonly domesticated in the British Islands, (b) it is under the control of man whether on a permanent or temporary basis [see discussion above], or (c) it is not living in a wild state". This definition effectively captures a huge number of animals within its remit including pets, farm animals, animals in zoos, animals in circuses and, with some exceptions,[23] animals used in other industries.

As already discussed, the Act also includes the more traditional protection against deliberate cruelty, as outlined in s.4, which deals with the prevention of unnecessary suffering. Section 9 ensures that people responsible for a protected animal promote his or her welfare, to the extent required by good practice, in line with the Five Freedoms, which are outlined in S.9(2) of the Act. Having said this, animals used in scientific procedures under ASPA 1986 are expressly excluded from protection under some sections of the Act[24] and nothing which occurs during the normal course of fishing falls under the Act.[25] Furthermore, there are specific exemptions found in the Mutilations (Permitted Procedures) (England) Regulations 2007 (made under the AWA 2006) which outline which mutilations can be carried out on animals as exemptions to the broad prohibition of mutilation found in s.5 of the AWA 2006. These exemptions speak to the prior discussion of balancing of interests in Sect. 4 in Chap. 2 of this book. Returning to the case of the kitten and his or her interest in not being used in painful experiments, as a matter of law the interests of scientific research may take precedence over those interests should the experiments in question meet the criteria demanded within ASPA 1986[26] and therefore the protection of the kitten from suffering is not absolute—*some* suffering might always be deemed necessary or acceptable. Indeed, under ASPA 1986, extreme suffering can be inflicted with the correct permission in place. A similar observation can be made with regard to the mutilations of animals that are allowed due to exemptions included in the AWA 2006. Many of these exemptions relate to practices involved in farming—for example, the "de-beaking" of chickens (a process whereby part of the beak of a young bird sliced off, without the use of anesthetic). The purpose of this mutilation, despite "induc[ing] pain and physiologic stress in birds",[27] allows the birds to be kept in high-density farming conditions, where they would likely resort to attacks on one another and/or cannibalism if they had their beaks intact. The mutilation is therefore permitted in the interests of the birds only to the extent that it does not impact the proper functioning of the farming industry in that it is designed to prevent the (unnatural) cannibalism behavior which occurs as a direct result of keeping birds in these conditions. As with the case of the kitten, protection of otherwise "protected animals" is far from absolute.

Theoretically then, the AWA 2006, if effective, should ensure that the welfare of all animals which fall within the definition of "protected animal" and are not subject to exceptions, should have their needs met to the extent required by good practice.[28] However, given the huge variation in species, environments and uses of animals that the Act covers, combined with the fact that each individual animal will potentially have her own specific individual needs, it seems reasonable to conclude that one piece of legislation could not possibly encompass all of the relevant needs. Indeed, returning to the argument that some, if not all, wild animals may suffer poor welfare by virtue of being kept "under the control of man", then encompassing welfare needs within the law for those animals may simply be impossible.

In recognition of this, it is largely accepted that the AWA 2006 forms the foundation for protection of animal welfare, but additional legislation or guidance which puts the Act into context with regard to a particular use or type of animal is often necessary.[29] With this in mind, the Act includes powers for the relevant national authorities to introduce secondary legislation which serves to place specific obligations upon those using animals for particular purposes or on those keeping particular species of animals.[30] Since its implementation, regulations of this type have been introduced under s.12 or s.13 of the Act to provide specific protection to farmed animals and wild animals in circuses.

Furthermore, non-binding Codes of Practice have also been introduced under s.14 of the Act to further clarify the law. While these have no legal force in and of themselves, their purpose is to give meaning to the provisions of s.9 of the Act with regard to the needs of the individual animal or use of the animal in question. Non-compliance with the codes cannot lead to prosecution,[31] but they can be used to support a prosecution in order to show that needs have not been met with a view to establishing liability.[32] The codes contain information relating to the welfare needs of the animals in question and outline actions an owner might take in order to meet the obligations laid out in s.9 of the AWA 2006. For example, in the case of dogs, the relevant code demands that, in order to meet your dog's need for a "suitable environment" (S.9(2)(a) of the Act), one must carry out, *inter alia*, the following actions[33]:

- *Provide your dog with a safe, clean environment. Make sure that you provide adequate protection from hazards.*
- *Provide your dog with a comfortable, clean, dry, quiet, draught-free rest area.*
- *Provide your dog with somewhere it can go to avoid things that frighten it.*

The animals for which codes have been established to date are horses and other equidae, cats, dogs and privately kept non-human primates (the Primate Code), and their efficacy remains a subject of debate. For example, the Codes of Practice for dogs, cats and equidae have not been formally reviewed, but an inquiry carried out by the Environment, Food and Rural Affairs Committee in 2014 asked stakeholders to submit feedback on the efficacy of the Primate Code. The author of this book, along with a number of NGO and academic representatives, raised concerns at this time with regard to the efficacy of the Primate Code, highlighting, among other concerns, that the code lacked specificity and was not easily interpreted in line with legal obligations outlined in the AWA 2006 (despite being implemented specifically to interpret the Act).[34] Regardless of the detail of the code, it was also argued by all leading animal protection organizations involved in the consultation that the principle of a code of practice was flawed because it was not possible to meet the welfare needs of non-human primates in captivity.

Notwithstanding the exemptions already noted, whereby it is clear that the protection of the welfare of otherwise "protected animals" is not absolute, vital to understanding the extent to which the AWA 2006 protects animal welfare is the interpretation of what is considered "good practice" in the context of s.9. As no demand is ever made of responsible persons to meet *all* of the animals' welfare needs in full, and instead the Act demands only that needs are met "to the extent required by good practice",[35] the definition of "good practice" is a vital point for consideration.

3.4.2 "Good Practice" Considered

Good practice can be considered in a number of different ways. Recognizing that individual animals belonging to the same species share generally the same welfare needs, the concept of good practice with regard to provision of animal welfare would lend itself to establishment of some kind of universal minimum welfare standards for a species of animals. These universal standards could then be used to assess whether or not welfare needs are met for the animals in practice, regardless of the particular use to which the animal is put.

For example, if it could be agreed that a capuchin monkey (*Cebus spp.*) requires a social group, a specific amount of space, a particular diet and particular climate, *inter alia*, in order to have their welfare needs met, it stands to reason that anyone keeping a capuchin monkey should have to provide for those needs, regardless of what use the animal might be put to. It makes little sense that demands in relation to welfare provision for individuals belonging to the same species should differ in accordance with the situation which they happen to be kept in: a capuchin monkey kept in a zoo, a capuchin monkey kept in a circus and a capuchin monkey kept as a pet will share the same physical, behavioral and psychological needs as those of his or her free-living counterparts. However, in practice, it would appear that policymakers responsible for the introduction of animal welfare legislation in the United Kingdom do not use any kind of universal minimum standards based on the needs of the species as their benchmark for good practice and, instead, use the parameters of the specific industry as the measure of good practice. For example, best practice in zoos will be used to devise welfare standards for zoos; best practice in circuses will be used to devise welfare standards for circuses. The result of this is what O'Sullivan refers to as the "internal inconsistency",[36] whereby the same animals are given different levels of protection according to the use they have been put to.

A good example of how this "internal inconsistency" plays out can be found in two pieces of government guidance, published just a few months apart and by the same government department (Department for Environment, Food and Rural Affairs (DEFRA)) in 2012. The guidance in question pertained to the welfare of animals in zoos (the Secretary of State's Standards of Modern Zoo Practice (SSSMZP)) and the welfare of animals in circuses (Guidance on the, now repealed, WWATC 2012). The zoo standards seek to provide guidance to how to apply the provisions of the ZLA 1981 and "also provide practical guidance in respect of provisions made by or under the Animal Welfare Act".[37] The circus guidance specifically seeks to interpret the WWATC, which were introduced under s.13 of the AWA 2006. As such, each guidance document seeks to interpret the same piece of legislation.

Despite seeking to interpret the same legislation, the welfare standards set out in the two guidance documents differ from one another. For example, the welfare guidance for zoos demands that elephants not be chained by the leg unless in exceptional circumstances.[38] In circuses elephants can be chained by the leg every single night of their lives.[39] This discrepancy in standards suggests, therefore, that policymakers do not consider good practice to be universal and based on the animals' needs, but to be defined by the parameters of the particular use. From a practical perspective, if elephants are to be kept in circuses, they must be kept in such a way which prevents them from escaping. The temporary nature of accommodation in a traveling circus (often a tent) requires that chaining is used to hold the animals for much of the time. In zoos, which have permanent structures in which elephants would live, there should be no need to chain the elephants unless in exceptional circumstances.

This outcome of these varying standards which are arguably based upon the limitations of the industry in question, rather than the needs of the animals themselves, is that animals kept in conditions which might be deemed illegal under the AWA 2006 in one place can be kept in the same conditions elsewhere and the person responsible for them be deemed compliant with the same law. What should be emphasized at this point is that, unlike the exceptions in relation to mutilation and animal experimentation described above, the different welfare standards mandated for elephants in zoos and elephants in circuses are not the result of explicit exemptions included in the Act. The situation occurs in the interpretation of the same clause for the same animals who share the same welfare needs.

So, while many people may assume "good practice" within the context of the AWA 2006 references the implementation of universal minimum/best practice standards for the treatment of animals (based on species or kind), but the foregoing discussion makes it clear that this is not the case. For the purposes of this section, it is important to recognize that the AWA 2006 makes no demand upon persons responsible for animals that they ensure that the animals' welfare needs are met in full, or even in part. They are simply required to meet them to the extent required by "good practice", where the term "good practice" refers to good practice within the specific industry in question which is using the animals, rather than using as a starting point the needs of the animals themselves. This is in keeping with the spirit of the original Five Freedoms upon which the "needs" referred to in s.9(2) of the 2006 Act are based. The Farm Animal Welfare Council noted explicitly in its introduction of the Five Freedoms that

> *They form a logical and comprehensive framework for analysis of welfare within any system together with the steps and compromises necessary to safeguard and improve welfare* ***within the proper constraints of an effective livestock industry***.[40] *[My emphasis]*

Fundamental to the interpretation of the Five Freedoms, therefore, is that they were intended to "safeguard" and "improve" welfare within the "proper constraints of an effective livestock industry". In other words, the Five Freedoms seek to provide a framework within which animal welfare can be improved, but not to the extent that it interferes with industry productivity. As such, in introducing the term "to the extent required by good practice" clause into s.9 of the AWA 2006 and understanding that policymakers interpret "good practice" as having its basis on standards of good practice within the particular industry being regulated, it becomes apparent that there is unlikely to be any demand placed upon any person responsible for an animal to meet his or her welfare needs in full. Instead, the extent to which needs are required to be met is relative to the extent to which it is possible to meet needs without impacting upon the effective (one assumes that this can be interpreted as profitable) operation of that particular business or industry. If it were possible to fully meet animal welfare needs without the proper functioning of industry being constrained, which is very unlikely, it is theoretically possible that an animal could have his or her welfare effectively protected in full. The extent to which this happens in practice will be explored as part of this research.

In Chaps. 12 and 13 we will explore how legislation might be better constructed to recognize universal standards of animal welfare, even if this means accepting that some animals cannot have their needs met when kept "under the control of man" and therefore cannot be kept at all and, thus, do away with the "internal inconsistency".

3.5 Abolition of Practices

Abolition of practices may come about as a result of the fact that certain practices cannot be carried out without seriously compromising the welfare of animals. In other words, acts which inevitably cause unnecessary suffering are so cruel as to be unacceptable or which are considered to be wholly incompatible with the ability to make provision for welfare needs may be banned outright, rather than allowed to continue under regulated conditions. As has already been recognized, the approach of outlawing cruel practices was one of the earliest approaches to animal welfare law and examples include the historic (and ongoing) prohibition of bear baiting and dog fighting, fox hunting and fur farming.

Proponents of the animal rights stance outlined in Chap. 2 argue that abolition of animal use in its entirety, not the outlawing of specific cruel practices, is the only way to truly confer rights on animals.[41] Only one piece of legislation relating to animals in the UK statute book currently prohibits practices relating to animals not on welfare grounds, but on grounds of ethical opposition, namely the ban on fur farming (Fur Farming Prohibition Act 2000). While this law arguably could have been introduced on welfare grounds, due to research demonstrating the negative welfare impact of fur farming on at least some species (e.g., mink),[42] it was instead introduced in response to public opposition to the practice. In other words, its introduction was based on an explicitly moral judgment of what was believed by the government at the time to be right and wrong. The decision was taken that it is wrong to farm animals for their fur, regardless of the absence or presence of welfare issues.

Speaking in the House of Commons on the subject, the Minister at the time, Baroness Hayan said:

> *The Government are, of course, conscious of the concern that many have for the welfare of farmed mink. We share that concern and so we have sought to ensure that the highest possible standards are applied as long as fur farming continues. But this Bill is introduced on wider grounds and on the basic philosophy that animals should not be killed simply for the business of stripping their skins off their backs. That is, we believe, quite simply inappropriate in the 21st century.*[43]

Since that time, the ban on the use of wild animals in traveling circuses has been introduced in England on explicitly ethical grounds in January 2020. In 2012, the government committed to introducing this law despite the perceived lack of evidence to show that the welfare of wild animals in traveling circuses is any more compromised than in other captive environments.[44] This legislation is distinctly rights-based in nature given that it has responded on ethical and not welfare concerns. In fact, the ethical basis for the ban is described succinctly by government in the draft Bill's accompanying explanatory note:

We should feel duty-bound to recognize that wild animals have intrinsic value, and respect their inherent wildness and its implications for their treatment.[45]

3.5.1 Ethical and Welfare Approaches to Legislation

The above discussion of welfare or ethical grounds may appear arbitrary and, indeed, law introduced on welfare grounds and ethical grounds have little to tell them apart once enacted and one may only be aware of the ethical basis of a piece of legislation after its implementation by researching Hansard records and government archives. The very fact that animal welfare is deemed important is *because* we make ethical assessments of our treatment of animals, and so the two concepts are logically and inextricably linked. Indeed, the entire foregoing discussion on interests and how they may (or may not) give rise to moral consideration hinges on this specific point. However, the UK government has been insistent that the two approaches (the welfare approach and the ethical approach) to legislation are mutually exclusive with the strong implication that animal welfare law introduced on the basis of empirical scientific evidence is preferable to legislation based on ethical decision-making. A major part of this reason is that the government believes that irrefutable empirical evidence that animal welfare suffers in a particular situation (e.g., in a traveling circus environment) forms a stronger basis for legislation which will be less open to legal challenge than legislation based on ethical or moral grounds alone.

The government's clear distinction between legislation introduced on the grounds of welfare and that introduced on grounds of ethics was made clear during the long period of debate and lobbying surrounding the issue of wild animals in traveling circuses. The then Animal Welfare Minister, James Paice MP, expressed concern that a ban implemented ostensibly on welfare grounds but without empirical scientific evidence that animal welfare is irrevocably compromised by their use in traveling circuses "might well be seen as disproportionate action under the European Union services directive and under our own Human Rights Act 1998" and thus open the UK government up for legal challenge.[46] Having clearly and explicitly rejected the possibility of introducing a ban on welfare grounds under the Animal Welfare Act 2006 due to this perceived lack of evidence of welfare compromise, the same government promised to begin work on a ban on ethical grounds early the following year.[47] Their preference for legislation based on welfare grounds is evident from the fact that the potential for a ban on welfare grounds was examined and exhausted before a ban on ethical grounds was considered.

In addition to the belief that legislation based upon sound scientific evidence is more watertight than legislation based on, potentially moveable, ethical principles—the wider context of animal welfare legislation must be understood to be able to properly understand the apparent aversion to legislation based on ethical grounds. It comes back to the principle of the "good practice" approach (outlined in detail in Sect. 4.2 in Chap. 2 of this book) which applies different levels of protection to the same animals when kept in different situations. While empirical scientific evidence is used as the basis to decide how animals are treated, it is possible to consider their treatment and welfare provision in any specific industry or practice independently of any other. The result of this is that one industry might be subject to stricter controls than others. If these controls are based upon an ethical premise that, for example, "the use of animals in circuses is immoral", then lawmakers are forced to make a distinction between the morality of using wild animals in circuses and why, for example, it is unacceptable in comparison to animals kept in zoos, which is deemed morally acceptable. In reality, there might be little difference between the lived experience (and thus the welfare) of the animals in a circus or a zoo and so the ethical stance tends to appear somewhat shaky, and thus, open to challenge. This is exactly the situation that the government seeks to avoid.

Indeed, this specific point was raised during the passage of the, now implemented, ban on wild animals in circuses. During the debates on the issue in the House of Lords, multiple peers raised the concern that the ethical position of one person may differ significantly from the ethical position of another and to legislate on the basis of an ethical position is contentious. For example, Lord Trees stated:

> *Her Majesty's Government have not introduced the Bill as a result of welfare concerns. It is introduced on the basis of ethics; it is an ethical decision. In that*

context, I submit that this leads us on to very contentious ground. I have been impressed by one of the briefings many of us may have received from Professor Ron Beadle, a professor of organisation and business ethics at Northumbria University. He argues that it is difficult on ethical grounds to single out animals in travelling circuses from animals involved in almost any other relationship with humans—such as, among others, zoos, displays of birds of prey and horseracing, through to eating meat and even keeping pets.[48]

While many proponents of animal welfare and animal rights would agree with Lord Trees, his point speaks to the difficulty that the government faces in the absence of empirical scientific evidence of welfare compromise as a direct result of a particular activity or use (i.e., the use of wild animals in traveling circuses). Laws introduced on ethical grounds run the risk of opening up a veritable Pandora's Box of scrutiny of other similar activities which could be considered equally immoral when examined through a similar ethical lens.

If, however, there is evidence of welfare provision being consistently less in circuses than in zoos based on an animal welfare science approach, then this evidence can be used to rebut challenges that zoos and circuses provide the same level of welfare provision as one another. Examples which would support the contention that animal welfare is inevitably compromised in circuses might include testing stress levels (via cortisol testing), documenting what are known as stereotypic behaviors, which are repetitive behaviors such as pacing or self-harming and are recognized as a sign of mental distress in animals. High instances of illnesses or high mortality rates in circuses might provide further concrete evidence as to the way in which animal welfare might be compromised in circuses in comparison to zoos.

3.6 The Extent to Which Regulation of Animal Use Protects Animals

If we consider the extent to which regulating the use of animals protects them, it would appear that, in the context of protecting welfare, current legislation demands this is met "to the extent required by good practice",[49] with good practice being defined by the limitations of the industry or practice itself rather than by the fundamental needs of the animals. Other statutes, such as those dealing with curbing trade in endangered species or wildlife protection, may grant more fundamental protection (e.g., non-interference) to animals according to their species or their status as free-living, as opposed to captive. This concept will be explored as part of this research due to the fact that one of the two pieces of legislation under consideration as part of this research, the ZLA 1981, was initially conceived with a view to protect animal welfare but has since been updated to incorporate the demands of the EC Zoo Directive (Directive 1999/22-EC) whose major concern is the conservation of biodiversity. As such, the overarching aim of the ZLA 1981 is not animal welfare, but conservation of biodiversity. This allows for comparison between the efficacy of this, and WWATC 2012 and the AWR 2018, which have no conservation element to it, but is introduced directly under the AWA 2006.

This chapter has provided a broad overview of the various ways in which animals are protected by the law, as well as considering historical development of the different types of legal protection. The next chapter will provide a more detailed exploration of the specific legal mechanism under examination in this book: the regulatory licensing regime.

Notes

1. The Driving of Cattle, Metropolis Act 1781 (21 Geo. III, c.67).
2. The Cruel Treatment of Cattle Act 1822 (*3 Geo. IV c. 71*).
3. Radford, M., *Animal Welfare Law in Britain*. Oxford University Press, 2001.
4. Cobbett, W. (1806). *Cobbett's parliamentary history of England*. London: Published by R. Bagshaw, p. 103.
5. Hsa.org.uk. (n.d.). Frequently Asked Questions. [online] Available at: https://www.hsa.org.uk/faqs/general#n1 [Accessed 16 November 2019].
6. See Environmental Challenges in Farm Management. (n.d.). Post War Agriculture. [online] Available at: http://www.ecifm.rdg.ac.uk/postwarag.htm [Accessed 28 Dec. 2017].

7. Statistics of Scientific Procedures on Living Animals Great Britain 2016, Home Office, 2017 [Available: https://www.gov.uk/government/statistics/statistics-of-scientific-procedures-on-living-animals-great-britain-2016].
8. Harrison, R. (1966). Animal machines. New York: Ballantine Books.
9. See Environmental Challenges in Farm Management. (n.d.). Post War Agriculture. [online] Available at: http://www.ecifm.rdg.ac.uk/postwarag.htm [Accessed 28 Dec. 2017].
10. The Farm Animal Welfare Council (Foundation, Internet. "[ARCHIVED CONTENT] UK Government Web Archive—The National Archives". National Archives (UK). Web. 6 June 2016).
11. The Zoo Licensing Act 1981.
12. See Sect. 2 in Chap. 5 of this book for further information.
13. COUNCIL *DIRECTIVE* 1999/22/EC.
14. ZLA 1981 (as amended by SI 2002/3080) s.1A.
15. See Sect. 2 in Chap. 8 for further information.
16. Francione, G. (1995). *Animals, property, and the law.* Philadelphia: Temple University Press, p. 34.
17. Ibid., p. 5.
18. S.7 Theft Act 1978.
19. S.4(2) Criminal Damage Act 1971.
20. Hamps v. Darby [1948] 2 K.B. 311 (C.A.).
21. S. A. C., (1949). Tort—Homing Pigeons—Right of Farmer to Kill in Defence of Crops—Property in Pigeons. Cam. Law. J., 10(02), p. 270.
22. Broom, D.M., (1991). *Animal welfare: concepts and measurements.* J Anim Sci 1991; 69: 4167–4175.
23. For example, S.59 of the AWA 2006 expressly states that "Nothing in this Act applies in relation to anything which occurs in the normal course of fishing".
24. S.58 Animal Welfare Act 2006.
25. S.59 Animal Welfare Act 2006.
26. The criteria for what kind of project will be permitted a license are outlined in S.5(3) of ASPA 1986.
27. AVMA (2010). *Welfare Implications of Beak Trimming.* Literature Reviews—American Veterinary Medical Association (Animal Welfare Division). [online] American Veterinary Medical Association, p. 4. Available at: https://www.avma.org/KB/Resources/LiteratureReviews/Documents/beak_trimming_bgnd.pdf [Accessed 22 Oct. 2017].

28. S.9(1) Animal Welfare Act 2006.
29. For example, Gov.uk. (2013). Animal welfare—GOV.UK. [online] Available at: https://www.gov.uk/guidance/animal-welfare [Accessed 22 Oct. 2017].
30. Ss.12 and 13 Animal Welfare Act 2006.
31. S.14(3) Animal Welfare Act 2006.
32. S.14(4) Animal Welfare Act 2006.
33. S.1 Code of Practice for the Welfare of Dogs.
34. Tyson, E., (2014). Written Evidence: Primates as Pets. [Available at: http://data.parliament.uk/writtenevidence/committeeevidence.svc/evidencedocument/environment-food-and-rural-affairs-committee/primates-as-pets/written/4982.html].
35. S.9(1) Animal Welfare Act 2006.
36. O'Sullivan, S. (2011). *Animals, equality and democracy*. Houndmills, Basingstoke, Hampshire: Palgrave Macmillan, p. 31.
37. *The Zoo Expert Committee Handbook*, DEFRA, 2012, p. 3.
38. The SSSMZP, DEFRA, p. 58.
39. Guidance on the WWATC 2012, DEFRA, p. 50.
40. Webarchive.nationalarchives.gov.uk, (2009). [ARCHIVED CONTENT] Farm Animal Welfare Council—5 Freedoms. [online] Available at: http://webarchive.nationalarchives.gov.uk/20121007104210/http:/www.fawc.org.uk/freedoms.htm [Accessed 30 Jan. 2016].
41. For example, Francione in Francione, G. and Garner, R. (2010). The animal rights debate. New York: Columbia University Press.
42. For example, Mason, G., Cooper, J. and Clarebrough, C. (2001). *Frustrations of Fur-Farmed Mink*. Nature, 410(6824), pp. 35–36.
43. HL Deb 19 July 2000 vol 615 cc1130-56.
44. Radford, M., (2007). The Report of the Chairman of the Circus Working Group (The Radford Report).
45. DEFRA. (2013). *Wild animals in circuses*. London: HM Stationery Office. [Available at: http://www.official-documents.gov.uk/document/cm85/8538/8538.pdf].
46. HC Deb, 19 May 2011, c497.
47. HC Deb, 1 March 2012, c41WS.
48. HL Deb 19 June 2019 vol 798 c796.
49. S.9(1) Animal Welfare Act 2006.

4

Regulatory Licensing Regimes as a Legislative Framework

4.1 The Circumstances in Which Regulatory Licensing Regimes Are Employed

Regulatory licensing regimes are employed in various circumstances. They may be implemented in cases whereby a widespread activity is considered to present the potential for risk if allowed to continue without any control, but for which it is believed that risk can be mitigated by the imposition of regulation. For example, s.4(2) of the Licensing Act 2003, dealing with, *inter alia*, the regulation of sale of alcohol, outlines the licensing objectives as follows:

- the prevention of crime and disorder;
- public safety;
- the prevention of public nuisance;
- the protection of children from harm.

If the licensing regime were not in place, the implication is that the unrestricted sale of alcohol may result in crime and disorder, a threat to public safety, public nuisance and a risk to children. By subjecting the

E. Tyson, *Licensing Laws and Animal Welfare*, The Palgrave Macmillan Animal Ethics Series, https://doi.org/10.1007/978-3-030-50042-9_4

business selling alcohol to scrutiny and licensing, it both identifies those businesses carrying out the sale of alcohol and imposes duties upon the licensee which, if complied with, should have the practical effect of mitigating or avoiding the risks identified. Importantly, when balanced against the option of prohibiting the sale of alcohol altogether, it has clearly been deemed that the sale of alcohol in and of itself is not so inherently dangerous so as to warrant such action. The mechanism by which control is (theoretically) achieved is by creating offenses under the Act which, if not complied with, will result in sanctions. For example, under s.145 of the Act, the sale of alcohol to children is punishable on summary conviction to a fine not exceeding level 3 on the standard scale.[1] In addition, s.129 mandates that a license can be suspended or forfeit on demand in the case of conviction for a relevant offense, of which any offense under the Act is categorized as a relevant offense.[2]

Other licensing regimes, such as that implemented under the Motor Vehicles (Driving Licences) Regulations 1996 (as amended), seek to ensure that a level of competency is achieved prior to an individual being able to carry out a particular activity (in this case, driving a vehicle) which could pose a risk if carried out by incompetent individuals. In addition, the regime provides a mechanism for revoking licenses and disqualifying those individuals who do not comply with the law from driving in the future. In this way, incompetent, dangerous or reckless drivers can be prevented from driving, while competent and safe drivers can continue without unnecessary or burdensome interference. Like the Licensing Act 2003, the mechanism by which license conditions are enforced is by making it an offense to drive particular classes of vehicles without a license[3] or to drive in a particular way which could be considered reckless or dangerous (e.g., driving under the influence of drugs or alcohol[4]). Offenses, depending on severity and circumstance, can lead to "points" being added to a license (for offenses requiring "obligatory endorsement" such as exceeding the speed limit) which have a cumulative effect and, if 12 points are received, the license is revoked for the minimum period,[5] which can be six months, one year or two years, depending on whether previous disqualifications apply and are to be taken into account. Alternatively, more serious offenses, such as causing death by dangerous driving,[6] can result in a maximum prison term of 14 years[7] on indictment. As with the sale of alcohol, legislators have clearly decided that driving, if carried out within the constraints of the regulations, is not so inherently dangerous so as to warrant outright prohibition.

The Dangerous Wild Animals Act 1976 implements a licensing regime for those people who keep animals classed as "dangerous" in the schedule of the same. The purpose of the Act is to mitigate safety risks inherent in keeping dangerous animals. Section 3 of the Act outlines the conditions under which a license should be granted, including ensuring the secure nature of the animal's enclosure, ensuring that provisions are put in place in the event of accidental release or escape and that the person responsible for the animal is a suitable person. Section 3(c) includes some provision for basic welfare needs for the animal and demands that a license cannot be granted if the accommodation is unsuitable or if adequate bedding, food and water are not provided.

As highlighted in the three examples above, while licensing regimes are introduced across a broad range of activities, including sale of alcohol, driving and the keeping of animals, they generally share a number of common elements. These include the following:

- The licensable activity presents some risk. This may be a risk to public safety generally (in the case of alcohol licensing or driving licensing), a risk to a specific group or class of individuals (children, the owners of dangerous animals, etc.) and a risk to non-human animals (in the case of licensing introduced to protect animal welfare—to be explored in detail later in this book).
- It is believed that it is possible to mitigate the risks to such an extent that prohibition is unnecessary or disproportionate. In effect, the risk exists if the practice is carried out badly/recklessly, but the risks are mitigated (or even removed altogether) if the practice is carried out to a defined standard. For example, the most obvious way to remove any risk related to the keeping of dangerous wild animals would be to prohibit the keeping of wild animals. It is clearly believed by legislators that the risk posed is high enough to warrant oversight and regulation to ensure standards are met, but not so high that the practice should be outlawed altogether.

- The actions required in order to mitigate the risk are measurable and relatively uniform across an activity and may be carried out on a widespread basis. For example, in order to gain a driving license, every person must demonstrate the same minimum level of competency in both driving and theory. This level of competency must be measurable in order for the regime to be effective.
- The grant and retention of a license is subject to certain conditions and, where necessary, periodic assessment against conditions is carried out to ensure ongoing compliance. If compliance is unsatisfactory, the license can be amended, suspended or revoked. This has the effect of ensuring that those people who do not (or cannot) carry out the actions required to mitigate the risks identified as arising from the activity are prohibited from taking part in that activity, while those who meet the requirements can continue without undue interference.
- Carrying out a licensable activity without a license is deemed an offense and carries sanctions under the relevant regime. While (as with any law) this will not guarantee that nobody carries out the activity without a license, it gives an automatic means of redress in law if an individual or business is found to be operating without a license and acts as a deterrent for those considering operating outside of the law.
- Potential benefits of licensing regimes might include the following:

  - Systems of licensing allow for a standard benchmark to be understood and adhered to. It allows for a central core of inspectors to compare standards "like-for-like" across an industry or activity rather than subjective decisions being made on each and every establishment by a number of different people based on their own opinion as might be the case if industries were assessed on an ad hoc basis as a result of complaints or concerns and which may, in turn, lead to private prosecution. With a licensing regime with defined standards and assessment criteria, it means that there can be increased certainty and consistency, with everyone knowing where they stand and what is required of them.
  - Licensing, accompanied by inspection, theoretically allows for issues to be noted and action to be taken to remedy problems, or potential problems, before they become too serious and without

potentially lengthy, costly and protracted court proceedings which might be required if the licensing regime and accompanying standards were not in place.

4.2 Licensing Regimes and Animals

Licensing regimes which relate to activities involving animals may be implemented, as noted in relation to the Dangerous Wild Animals Act 1976, in the interests of public safety. Others might be implemented with a view to safeguard the public and provide for the welfare of the animals. An example of this is, now repealed, WWATC 2012. Other systems of licensing may have additional aims such as monitoring and assessing contribution to conservation of biodiversity and education, as in the case of the ZLA 1981. Whether or not the possession of a license in relation to activities involving animals provides guarantees that animal welfare needs are being met, is a point which will be explored in detail in this book. It is worth noting at this stage, however, that the possession of a license is often seen as an indicator that animal welfare needs are being met in full.

With regard to the types of licensing regime under consideration—those which seek to mitigate recognized risks inherent in particular activities—it should be noted that the absence of a license does not necessarily imply that the business or individual in question is carrying out the activity in a way which would be automatically be deemed unacceptable if a license were to be sought for the first time. Indeed, it may well be that an unlicensed zoo provides the exact same standards of care, the exact same contribution to conservation or education that a licensed zoo does, for example. Notwithstanding this fact, it would seem that the purpose of regulation is not only to ensure standards are met but to ensure that those carrying out the activities are identified and monitored for compliance. In effect, the activity has been deemed unsuitable for self-regulation and, for this reason, regardless of the standards being delivered by the business, to operate without a license is considered an offense. Conversely, as we will see later in this book, the possession of a valid license does not necessarily indicate that standards *are* being met.

4.3 Secondary Legislation and the Animal Welfare Act 2006

In the presentation of the draft Animal Welfare Bill (now the AWA 2006), the rationale behind incorporating the ability to introduce secondary legislation under the mantel of the Act was outlined as follows:

> The Bill will also provide powers to introduce secondary legislation and codes of practice to protect the welfare of non-farmed animals kept by man. This enabling power is already available for farmed animals and our aim is to ensure that in future all domestic and captive animals will be protected by legislation that can be easily revised to take account of changing welfare needs and increased scientific knowledge.[8]

It is recognized that the AWA 2006 effectively seeks to protect the welfare of each every individual animal of any species in each and every situation where they could be considered to be "under the control of man", as long as they fit the description of "protected animal" and they are not subject to exemptions (such as those animals used in scientific research, as previously discussed). This means that the Act covers billions of individual animals in a diverse range of situations, from farming to pet ownership to use of animals in sports and entertainment. To attempt to create a piece of primary legislation which encompassed all eventualities would have been a gargantuan task and any future amendments would have been cumbersome. By allowing the relevant Secretary of State (usually the DEFRA Minister) wide powers to introduce secondary legislation under the parent Act, this allows (via consultation) for expert input into specific animal species or uses and it allows for secondary legislation to be amended and improved relatively easily as knowledge relating to animal welfare increases and expands. From a purely practical perspective, if it were necessary to find parliamentary time to introduce new primary legislation each time it was found a specific practice was not adequately covered by the AWA 2006, this would be likely to hinder the progress of animal welfare law due to the likely lower priority animal welfare legislation is given when compared to laws relating to people, the economy and national security, for example. A prime example of this point is the English ban on the use of wild animals in traveling circuses. The initiative was deemed inappropriate for introduction as secondary legislation under the AWA 2006 and thus was drafted as new piece of primary legislation. That law remained in draft form from 2013 to 2019 and the government argued during that period that there was no time to introduce it. After concerted campaigning from the public and animal welfare organizations, the government finally introduced the Bill, which was passed and implemented in January 2020. In comparison, a whole raft of new licensing legislation was passed as secondary regulations under the AWA 2006 during the same period.

Secondary legislation under the AWA can be introduced under a number of sections including s.1, s.5 and s.6 for reasons including extending the definition of "animal" under the Act, exempting certain procedures from the blanket prohibition on mutilations and defining inspectors' functions.

Section 12 grants a broad power to the appropriate national authority (currently DEFRA) to introduce regulations for the purposes of promoting the welfare of animals and their progeny. This might include, but is not limited to, the implementation of specific requirements to ensure welfare is met, the facilitation or improvement of coordination between people carrying out different functions in relation to animal welfare or the creation of bodies which advise on animal welfare. Regulations can create offenses, confer post-conviction powers (such as deprivation or disqualification orders), provide for payment of fees, make provision for different cases, provide exemptions and make incidental provision or savings. The authority may provide that an offense may be a relevant offense for the purposes of s.23 (search of premises under warrant).

To date, the only regulations that have been introduced under s.12 are the Welfare of Farmed Animals (England) Regulations 2007. These regulations outline welfare standards that are required to be met. Failure to comply with the provisions of the regulations is an offense and renders the offender liable for prosecution. Possible penalties under the regulations include imprisonment of not more than 51 weeks and/or a fine not exceeding level 4 on the standard scale (currently set at £2500).

Regulations introduced under s.12 are not a focus of this research as, instead, we are concerned with the introduction of regulations under s.13

of the Act. These are regulations which facilitate the introduction of schemes of licensing or registration. Anyone carrying out an activity governed by s.13 automatically commits an offense if they are not in possession of a valid license or have not registered (whichever is relevant).

4.3.1 The Introduction of Licensing Regimes Under s.13 of the Animal Welfare Act 2006

As previously noted, licensing regimes can be introduced under both primary and secondary legislation. The ZLA 1981 is an example of a piece of primary legislation which creates a system of licensing and inspection. The purpose of this type of licensing regime is to govern a particular activity—in this case, the operation of a zoo—and licensing conditions include conservation obligations, public safety and animal welfare demands. Licensing regimes introduced under the AWA 2006 as secondary legislation, on the other hand, can only be introduced for the purposes permitted by the parent Act—that is, to promote animal welfare. As such, a licensing regime introduced under s.13 of the AWA 2006 must focus exclusively on animal welfare and cannot include conditions or obligations relating to other concerns (such as public safety or conservation). The way in which licensing regimes can be implemented under s.13 is described below.

As outlined previously, s.13 of the Act provides that the relevant national authority may introduce licensing regimes, or systems of registration, in order to regulate or better monitor certain activities involving animals. According to government guidance, "The registration procedure would be used in cases where it is necessary for the enforcement authority to know of the existence and location of organizations or individuals who are keeping specific animals or carrying on particular activities, but where the additional controls and costs of a licensing regime are either unnecessary or would be unduly burdensome".[9]

While registration will not be considered in any detail, the reason for its mention at this point is to recognize that, from its description in relation to registration, licensing is apparently deemed a more stringent measure by virtue of its "additional controls and costs". It is unclear whether "costs" in this instance refer to costs imposed on the industry or on the government/authority costs in administrating a scheme. As no schemes of registration have yet been implemented under the Act, it is unclear where the line may be drawn with regard to which practices require licensing and which may be subject to the, ostensibly less stringent, measure of registration.

4.3.2 The Scope of Regulations Introduced Under S.13 of the Animal Welfare Act 2006

The purpose of s.13 is to allow for the relevant national authority to introduce systems of licensing or registration for activities involving animals. As a general rule, these regulations can only be introduced for the purposes of promoting animal welfare. The promotion of animal welfare is one of two major principles embodied in the Act, with the other being the prevention of unnecessary suffering. These two principles and their development have been discussed in some detail in Sect. 5 in Chap. 2 of this book.

The infliction of unnecessary suffering, outlined in s.4 of the Act, is deemed a more serious offense than failure to promote welfare (outlined in s.9). As such, the sanctions for the offense of infliction of unnecessary suffering are more stringent under the Act than those for failure to promote welfare. This is demonstrated by the fact that breach of s.4 can result in a maximum of 51 weeks imprisonment or a fine of £20,000. Breach of s.9, on the other hand, can result in a maximum of 51 weeks imprisonment and a fine of no more than 5 on the standard scale (currently £5000).[10]

Furthermore, failure to meet the provisions of s.9 can result in the issuing of an improvement order in place of immediate prosecution. This allows the owner of the animal to come into compliance with the Act prior to the instigation of formal legal proceedings against them. If they comply within the timescale, which is decided at the discretion of the inspector, then it will be deemed that no offense has been committed. There is no equivalent of an improvement order for an offense under s.4. It is clear that the legislators deem the infliction of unnecessary suffering a more serious offense than failure to promote welfare, and this is clearly reflected in the available sanctions and enforcement mechanisms under the Act.

When devising regulations under s.13 of the AWA, the appropriate authority is limited to the sanctions that may be applied to any offense committed to a fine not exceeding level 5 on the standard scale (currently £5000) or a term of imprisonment not exceeding 51 weeks. These are the same limits set for offenses committed under s.9 of the Act (failure to promote welfare) rather than the more stringent sanctions available for contravention of s.4 (the infliction of unnecessary suffering) which allows for a fine of up to £20,000. It seems clear that regulations introduced under s.13 of the Act can be introduced for the purposes of promoting welfare but, due to the lesser sanctions available to legislators when drafting regulations under s.13, it can be inferred that offenses related to the infliction of unnecessary suffering fall outside of the scope of regulations introduced under s.13.

The first regime introduced under s.13 of the Act was the, now repealed, WWATC 2012. It was stated at the time of their introduction that the regulations would "fulfil undertakings given by the Government to Parliament to introduce secondary legislation under the Animal Welfare Act 2006 to protect further the welfare of wild animals in travelling circuses".[11] What is clear is that, while animals are generally protected by the Act, the introduction of the licensing regime was explicitly intended to "protect further" (than the basic provision of the Act) the welfare of animals. Arguably, this "further protection" does not mean that those circuses governed by licensing are expected to exceed the provisions of the Act, but are given specific obligations, usually in the form of binding license conditions, which aim to ensure that the provisions of the Act are effectively delivered. Failure to meet license standards may lead to the suspension or revocation of a license. In this way, and via the enforcement of license conditions, licensing can be argued to help clarify and uphold the law.

The WWATC 2012 was the first licensing regime to be introduced using powers granted to the appropriate national authority (DEFRA) under s.13(7) of the Act then, in 2018, licensing of riding schools, dog breeders, boarding kennels and pet shops was brought under new regulations introduced using the same legal mechanism.

In addition to the option of licensing regulations, Codes of Practice are one of the other tools available under the AWA 2006 to aid interpretation, and thus clarify and uphold the law. Codes of Practice are introduced under s.14 of the Act and have already been described in Sect. 4.1 in Chap. 3 of this book. If it is deemed that a particular activity requires further scrutiny or specific regulation, secondary legislation requiring registration or licensing might be introduced as well as or instead of a Code of Practice, which have been referred to as a "light touch" by DEFRA officials in the past. In the Impact Assessment published following consultation on the way in which the trade in primates as pets in England might be managed, DEFRA stated, "The code is light touch as it is advisory and, coupled with targeted publicity when it is launched, will have a better chance of reaching the intended audience. There is not enough evidence to justify formal regulations".[12] In addition to putting demands to meet welfare on a more formal footing, regulation via licensing and registration may also serve to clarify the specific steps which the owner of an animal or the proprietor of a business might need to take in order to ensure that welfare needs are met. This potentially serves the important purpose of seeking to ensure that legal standards are met consistently and to reduce the potential of offenses being committed as a result of ignorance or lack of understanding of the law.

If all animal owners and business proprietors were required to follow their own interpretation of the needs outlined in s.9 of the Act, it is likely that interpretation, and thus delivery of welfare standards for animals, would differ drastically from place to place as any one individual's understanding of which is required will invariably differ to a greater or lesser extent from another's. This could lead to some animals being afforded extremely high standards of welfare provision but also to other animals being afforded extremely low standards. In addition, open interpretation of the demands of s.9 would mean that decisions relating to whether legal obligations have been breached would be left to the courts. It has already been suggested that secondary legislation is beneficial as it allows the involvement of experts in technical areas on which MPs might not be qualified to make decisions, as well as expediting the implementation process. The clarity provided by secondary legislation also holds benefits if and when cases come to court. Given that judges, like MPs, are unlikely to have the requisite knowledge to draw conclusions on the point at which an offense is committed in any and all situations relating to animals, delivering judgments on the basis of provisions contained in detailed secondary legislation in place of the broad principles of the AWA 2006 theoretically helps to avoid inconsistencies in enforcement and sanctions across different cases.

The introduction of licensing regimes as secondary legislation under s.13 of the AWA 2006 can therefore be considered not only to provide oversight, monitoring and assessment, but also to offer clarity to allow individuals to understand how to meet the requirements of the Act in the first instance. This should, in turn, result in fewer offenses being committed as those responsible for animals understand the parameters within which they must operate. One of the main questions which this book seeks to answer is whether or not it necessarily follows that the implementation of a licensing regime will improve animal welfare provision or even, as has been suggested by those under regulation, that the possession of a license under such a regime demonstrates that animal welfare needs *are* being met.[13]

4.4 License Conditions

Licenses are usually issued with a series of conditions which must be complied with in order for the license to be retained. If the licensing regime employs a system of inspection, it is against these conditions that compliance is assessed on inspection. License conditions may be generalized, individual, statutory or imposed under powers granted to particular authorities. One license might be subject to one type of condition or a variety of different types of condition. For example, a license held under the ZLA 1981 must be issued subject to the statutory provisions of s.1A of the Act,[14] therefore guaranteeing that certain mandatory conditions are imposed on each and every licensee. In addition, the license can also be subject to such additional conditions specific to that establishment "as the local authority think necessary or desirable for ensuring the proper conduct of the zoo during the period of the license".[15] These are examples of individual conditions.

Failure to comply with license conditions may constitute a breach of the law or may give rise to discretionary or mandatory action on behalf of the relevant authority in order to encourage or enforce compliance. A thorough examination of license conditions pertaining to the statutes under consideration and their enforcement will be carried out in Chaps. 7 and 8 of this book.

4.5 Systems of Inspection

In addition to license conditions, most licensing regimes involve a system of inspection. The increased scrutiny which results from inspection regimes which monitor the conditions in which animals are kept or used arguably places the animals held under licensing regimes in a position of better oversight and protection than those animals whose keeping is not governed by such a system. This is because failure to meet welfare needs is more likely to be recognized when industries are subject to scrutiny via inspection than when animals are kept or used in activities which have not been deemed to present a risk requiring monitoring and assessment. It should be recognized, however, that simple identification of failure to meet animal welfare does not automatically lead to an improvement in animal welfare standards or to the meeting of required standards in the future. Indeed, enforcement of sanctions when and if failure to meet welfare needs has been identified during inspection or monitoring is vital to ensure that standards are raised and maintained at the level required by the licensing regime. Simply recognizing failure will not solve animal welfare problems.

Licensing regimes vary with regard to the regularity of inspection. For example, the inspection under the ZLA 1981 are carried out annually (albeit formal inspections by government officials are only required once every three years), the Dangerous Wild Animals Act 1976 mandates an inspection once every two years, and the Welfare of Wild Animals in Travelling Circuses (England) Regulations imposed three inspections each year on licensed businesses during the time it was in force.

Theoretically, it is via a combination of licensees having clear conditions to meet, regular inspections being carried out and effective enforcement of license conditions being carried out in the event that they are not met that the licensing regimes might be able to achieve their objective of ensuring that animals used in licensable activities are better protected than if licensing were not in place. This should not be conflated with the assumption that welfare needs are met in full (or in part) simply because the practice in question is subject to licensing and inspection as that depends whether or not the implementation of the standards in question has the practical effect of protecting animal welfare. As we have already seen, there is never a demand that welfare needs are met in full under the AWA 2006 as the Act merely demands that animal welfare needs are met "to the extent required by good practice",[16] so while we can be certain that inspection regimes increase scrutiny (on the proviso that inspections are properly utilized and executed), as will be shown, it does not automatically follow that welfare provision is increased to the standard required (or even if it is, that animal welfare needs are met in practice) as a result of a system of licensing and inspection being in place. This point has been remarked upon with regard to the special case of wild animals will be explored in detail in later parts of this book.

Having provided a broad overview of the circumstances in which licensing regimes might be implemented to regulate the use of animals, when implemented as both primary and secondary legislation, we will now continue to consider the statutes in question, beginning with the ZLA 1981.

Notes

1. S.145(9).
2. Schedule 4, Clause 1.
3. S.87 of the Road Traffic Act 1988.
4. S.4 of the Road Traffic Act 1988.
5. S.35 of the Road Traffic Offenders Act 1988.
6. S.1 of the Road Traffic Act 1988.

7. Schedule 2, Part One of the Road Traffic Offenders Act 1988, amended by s.235 of the Criminal Justice Act 2003.
8. HL Deb, 14th July 2004, cWS61.
9. Animal Welfare Act 2006, Explanatory Notes, Chapter 45, s.69.
10. In October 2017, it was reported that the government intends to consult on increasing protentional prison terms relating to certain animal welfare offenses from the current maximums to five years but, at the time of writing, these measures had not yet been published.
11. HC Deb, 1 March 2012, c41WS.
12. DEFRA (2009). Impact Assessment of the Code of Practice on the Welfare of Privately Kept Non-Human Primates. [online] London: DEFRA, p. 1. Available at: http://webarchive.nationalarchives.gov.uk/20100713195239/http://www.defra.gov.uk/corporate/consult/welfare-cop-primates/ia-primates.pdf [Accessed 24 Nov. 2017].
13. For example, Penarth Times. (2016). Animal charity raises concerns over wild animals as circus comes to the Vale. [online] Available at: http://www.penarthtimes.co.uk/news/14424591.Animal_charity_raises_concerns_over_wild_animals_as_circus_comes_to_the_Vale/ [Accessed 17 Jun. 2016].
14. S.5(2A) Zoo Licensing Act 1981.
15. S.5(3) Zoo Licensing Act 1981.
16. S.9(1) Animal Welfare Act 2006.

5

Primary Licensing Legislation: The Regulation of Zoos

The preceding chapter considered regulatory licensing regimes in both broad terms and in the context of their application in the interests of animal welfare. This chapter will examine the way in which one of the industries under consideration as part of this research (the zoo industry) is comprised and the history of its regulation in England.

5.1 The Size and Shape of the Zoo Industry in England

There are estimated to be 465 establishments which can be considered to meet the definition of "zoo"[1] in the United Kingdom, with 299 currently listed in England alone,[2] including those businesses which have been granted a dispensation under s.14(1)(a) of ZLA 1981 which exempts certain zoos which hold either very few animals or are of a very small size from the provisions of the Act. According to government records, there are 233 zoos which are currently operating with licenses granted under the Act in England.[3] Zoos range from small farm parks with a handful of

E. Tyson, *Licensing Laws and Animal Welfare*, The Palgrave Macmillan Animal Ethics Series, https://doi.org/10.1007/978-3-030-50042-9_5

wild animals to safari parks covering multiple acres and traditional city center zoos with a huge variety of species and individuals.

Most recent figures suggest that there are more than 200,000 individual animals in zoos in England with an average of 700 animals per establishment. Fully licensed zoos (those which have been granted no dispensation under s.14) hold an average of 2145 animals. The largest zoo in terms of numbers of animals in England is Regent's Park Zoo (London Zoo) in London. The zoo houses over 18,500 individuals.[4]

Exact numbers of establishments and animals held therein are difficult to ascertain due to a variety of factors, including the fact that licensing of zoos is governed by individual local authorities and there is no central register held of all zoos in the United Kingdom. The animal health section of the government's Department of Environment, Food and Rural Affairs (DEFRA), the Animal Health and Veterinary Laboratories Agency (AHVLA), theoretically holds a list of zoos in England, but monitoring has shown that this is not always accurate with evidence of licensed zoos not being included on the list and zoos that are no longer operating remaining on the list. According to the AHVLA, "the list will be reviewed annually"[5] but, in practice, is usually updated sporadically (and sometimes only at the request of researchers). Furthermore, a disclaimer published as part of the list confirms that "AHVLA cannot guarantee that the information will be absolutely complete or up to date". Indeed, the list has not been updated by DEFRA since November 2012.

Finally, there is some evidence that not all establishments which fall under the legal definition of a zoo as outlined in s.1(2) of the Act are correctly licensed, or indeed licensed at all. Most recent estimates based on research carried out by NGO researchers suggest that there are up to 465 establishments which meet the definition of "zoo" operating in the United Kingdom (either licensed or unlicensed).[6] Of the 26 newest zoos listed in the most recent AHVLA list, published in November 2012, at least four of those zoos were operating without a license for some time prior to being brought to the relevant local authority's attention.[7] Only upon the local authority becoming aware of the zoo's existence was the licensing process carried out. It is thus possible that there are a number of zoos operating without a license at any one time. This could be due to ignorance of the law on the part of the zoo operators or the relevant local authority or a result of a deliberate attempt to avoid the rigors (and related costs) of licensing on the part of the business.

An example of apparent ignorance of the law can be found in the case of "The Tortoise Sanctuary", a rescue center which operated for a number of years under the mistaken belief that as it considered itself to be a "sanctuary", rather than a zoo, it did not require a license under the ZLA 1981. Following an enquiry made by an anonymous person, the local authority investigated the establishment and concluded that a license was in fact required as it met the legal definition of a zoo outlined in the Act. The sanctuary started a publicity campaign, which was supported by the local MP, against the local authority's decision. The sanctuary argued that it should be granted a complete exemption under the Act on the basis that it was a "sanctuary" and not a "zoo". While there might be considered to be differences between legitimate, well-run sanctuaries and zoos—largely in that sanctuaries are places of rehabilitation, offer animals a home for life and will rarely breed animals, and zoos are largely places which exhibit animals as their primary purpose—there exists no legal differentiation between the terms "sanctuary" and "zoo". The particular business in question fell firmly within the definition of zoo within the Act. The council maintained its position and insisted a license was required. The sanctuary did not apply for the license, subsequently closed and the animals were rehomed.[8]

A further example of a business which sought to avoid zoo licensing can be found in the case of Tropical Inc., which had run for a number of years as a "mobile zoo". This type of business is not currently deemed to fall within the jurisdiction of the ZLA 1981 due to the fact that its premises are not open to the public in the same way that traditional zoo premises are. In 2012, the business applied for planning permission to establish a permanent center which would be open to the public. Permission was granted. The author, in her then capacity as Director of Freedom for Animals (FFA), contacted the council to request information on the progress of the zoo license which would be required for the business to operate as a zoo and was told that it was understood that a license was not required. This was queried with the council as it was not clear why the decision had been taken that a license would not be required given that the proposed site and business operation appeared to meet all of the criteria necessary for a zoo. CAPS was told that the business owner had informed the council planning committee that a license was not required and they had simply taken his word for it. Following a complaint, the council reconsidered the position and agreed that a license would be required in order for the permanent site to operate and thus began to pursue licensing with the owner.[9] No evidence of a zoo opening on the site is available so it can be assumed that the proposed zoo never opened and/or the application was never pursued.

In light of these two case studies, it is possible that there are more businesses such as the Tortoise Sanctuary and Tropical Inc. which are currently operating (whether deliberately or ignorantly) in contravention of the ZLA 1981.

5.2 The Development of Zoo Regulation in Great Britain

Prior to 1981, there was no specific legislation which governed the operation of zoos in England. When the move toward zoo regulation, and the subsequent implementation of the ZLA 1981, is considered in its historical context, the desire that any statute should have animal welfare at its heart was clearly indicated during the debate and discussion in Parliament which led to its introduction. Indeed, Hansard records show that the purpose of its enactment was largely in response to concern for animal welfare.

In 1970, the first suggestion of a specific Act to protect animals in zoos was mooted by the Earl of Mansfield who asked the House of Lords to consider a licensing regime for zoos in order to protect animal welfare. He suggested that inaction was not an option, saying

> Do not Her Majesty's Government realize that if they persist in this attitude of cynical indifference many hundreds, and probably thousands, of interesting wild animals will eke out a miserable existence and come to a premature death.[10]

At the time, the government was satisfied that the Federation of Zoological Gardens of Great Britain and Ireland (now known as the British and Irish Association of Zoos and Aquariums—BIAZA), which had been established in 1967, was sufficient to monitor and control the conduct of zoos in conjunction with the Protection of Animals Act 1911. The Earl of Mansfield pointed out that the Federation was a voluntary organization and so zoos that did not want to be regulated by it could simply choose to refrain from joining.[11] In addition, BIAZA is also an industry trade body, whose membership is made up predominantly of zoos and their committees staffed predominantly by management-level zoo staff. As such, it could be argued that any level of regulation imposed by BIAZA is not only just effective on those zoos which choose to join, but would also quite clearly be a form of self-regulation.

It took another decade to see the introduction of the ZLA 1981, but the ongoing assertion by those who supported legislative measures in both Houses of Parliament was that the welfare of animals in zoos must be protected by regulation.[12] It should also be noted that, at this stage, there was no legal basis for the promotion of animal welfare in law as we understand it today as the duty to promote welfare was introduced on the implementation of the AWA 2006. This is certainly not to suggest that the ZLA 1981 (or other animal-related legislation prior to 2006) contained no provisions which might benefit animal welfare in practice, but that the introduction of the 2006 Act "created a new offence of failing to take reasonable steps to ensure an animal's welfare (the so-called 'duty of care' clause)".[13] In effect, this new offense raised the demands placed upon those caring for animals and gave those demands legal basis.

5.3 The Original Zoo Licensing Act 1981

The legislation's stated purpose is "to regulate by license the conduct of zoos"[14] and, interestingly, in spite of the strong focus on the need to protect animal welfare in zoos during the debates which led to the implementation of the Act, the original statute contained no specific welfare provisions. There was opportunity to introduce standards (presumably, including those relating to animal welfare) by virtue of powers granted to the Secretary of State under s.9 to devise standards for the management of the zoo or the animals as s/he saw fit. Indeed, the detailed Secretary of State's Standards of Modern Zoo Practice are updated at intervals, most recently in 2012, and contain comprehensive guidance relating to animal welfare. Importantly, these Standards are not, and never have been, directly enforceable. The original text also made reference to the grant of a license being subject to the local authority being satisfied that the well-being of the animals would be met at the zoo, but no further clarification on what standards might ensure that wellbeing was met were included.

As a result, the welfare of animals in zoos at the time that the Act was introduced was dependent on a number of factors. The first was the good judgment of the team of inspectors, who were required, under ss.10–12 of the original Act, to inspect the zoo at intervals and in special circumstances. A report was required after each periodical inspection which

> may include advice on the keeping of records and recommendations for any practicable improvements designed to bring any features of the zoo up to the normal standards of modern zoo practice; and for this purpose the inspectors shall have regard to any standards known to them which have been specified by the Secretary of State under section 9.[15]

If standards were found, during inspection, to fall below those required of the zoo, the inspectors could outline the problems, and the action required to remedy them, in the relevant report. The local authority could then obligate the zoo to meet welfare (and other) standards by attaching a condition outlining the relevant requirements, and the timescale in which they must be met, to the zoo's license by virtue of powers granted by s.16 of the Act. It was by this mechanism of transposition into license conditions that it was possible for the Secretary of State's Standards of Modern Zoo Practice to be enforced. Failure to comply with a condition without good reason was an offense under s.19 of the Act and could lead to a license being revoked under s.17, among other sanctions.

The arguable weaknesses of the original system were that a zoo could not commit an offense under s.19 of the ZLA 1981 until a condition had been attached to the license and the business had subsequently failed to comply (without good reason) within the agreed timescale. This suggests that problems might persist for a number of years before the zoo could be sanctioned. The inspection regime only required formal inspection once every two to three years, which might have the effect of exacerbating potential delay in rectifying issues. Furthermore, as there were no mandatory license conditions outlined in the Act, there was a wide degree of discretion on the part of the local authority as to which of the Secretary of State's Standards to enforce, and to what extent. This suggests a degree of uncertainty for the zoos in question with license conditions (and thus their obligations under the law) varying between zoos depending on who inspected the premises (which differs between zoos and from year-to-year within the same zoo) and which local authority's jurisdiction the zoo fell within.

A license could be revoked under s.17 of the Act for reasons other than breach of license conditions, namely as a result of the zoo being conducted in a "disorderly manner" or in such a way as to cause a nuisance or following the conviction of the owner or one of the keepers under other relevant legislation listed in s.4(4). All of the legislation listed in s.4(4) relates in some way to animal welfare and a conviction under any of the statutes listed also gives rise to grounds to refuse a license application in the first instance. In this way, it could be argued that the original Act protected animals from being exposed to people that might cause them harm or fail to provide for their welfare by preventing these people from running, or working for, zoos.

A benefit of the flexible nature of the enforcement mechanisms within the Act was that it was possible to accommodate businesses of varying size and make-up, from small collections to city center zoos to safari parks within the regime by virtue of the wide discretion discussed above. Indeed, the necessity for a level of flexibility and discretion is still recognized today within the current SSSMZP which states: "due to the widely differing nature of zoo collections, not every Standard will apply equally to all zoos".[16]

5.4 The EC Zoo Directive

It was only with the transposition of European Council Directive (EC Directive) 1999/22/EC into the amended Zoo Licensing Act in 2003 that duties on zoos directly related to welfare were included in the body of the statute. As it was the EC Directive that prompted the inclusion of what can be interpreted as welfare provisions into the Act, it is important to consider the purpose of the Directive itself.

The aim of the Directive is outlined in Article 1 of the same, as follows:

> The objectives of this Directive are to protect wild fauna and to conserve biodiversity by providing for the adoption of measures by Member States for the licensing and inspection of zoos in the Community, thereby strengthening the role of zoos in the conservation of biodiversity.

It is clear that the Directive is concerned, as its primary purpose, not with the promotion or protection of animal welfare, but with zoos' role in the conservation of biodiversity. In fact, the term "welfare" appears nowhere in the EC Directive. Despite this, the wording from Article 3 of the Directive concerned with housing of animals and provision of veterinary care, which is reproduced with only minor textual amendments in s.1A(c) of the ZLA 1981, can be recognized as dealing directly with factors which impact on animal welfare. Section 1A(c) reads as follows:

> The following are conservation measures to be implemented in zoos in accordance with this Act—
>
> S. 1A (c) accommodating their animals under conditions which aim to satisfy the biological and conservation requirements of the species to which they belong, including—
>
> (i) providing each animal with an environment well adapted to meet the physical, psychological and social needs of the species to which it belongs; and
> (ii) providing a high standard of animal husbandry with a developed program of preventative and curative veterinary care and nutrition

It would appear from the wording used that the effective delivery of the provisions outlined in s.1A(c) should have the practical effect of ensuring that the animal welfare needs are met in zoos.

Not only did the Directive introduce welfare provisions into the Act but, importantly, made compliance with the provisions of s.1A mandatory. Failure to comply was subject to new sanctions introduced under the new ss.16A–16G of the Act. Zoos which persistently failed to comply with license conditions relating to the delivery of s.1A provisions would be subject to closure, or partial closure.

Finally, provisions were included for the welfare and disposal of the animals following zoo closure for the first time.[17] Prior to this amendment, while a zoo license could be revoked, thus preventing the ongoing operation of the zoo, no provisions were in place to protect the welfare of the animals in the event of the revocation of a license.

The transposition of the Directive into the amended Act in 2003 thus had the effect of incorporating animal welfare standards, albeit without explicitly labeling those standards as being concerned with animal welfare, into the main body of the Act for the first time. What had not, and still has not, been formally questioned was whether or not welfare needs for wild animals in zoos can be met at all.

5.5 The Zoo Licensing Act (as Amended)

The ZLA 1981 (as amended) has been described by the government department currently charged with its oversight, the Department of Environment, Food and Rural Affairs (DEFRA), as follows:

> The Zoo Licensing Act 1981 sets out how zoos in Great Britain are inspected and licensed. This ensures that zoos are safe for the public to visit, that high standards of welfare are maintained and that zoos make a contribution to conservation of wildlife. It also implements European Council Directive 1999/22/EC in the UK.[18]

It would thus appear that the purpose of the Zoo Licensing Act 1981, in the view of the government, is now threefold:

1. It ensures that zoos are safe to for the public to visit;
2. It ensures that high standards of animal welfare are maintained; and
3. It ensures that zoos make a contribution to the conservation of wildlife.

The areas of consideration for this research will focus predominantly on the ability of the legislation to "ensure high standards of animal welfare" but will also consider the contribution to conservation of wildlife as a related matter. The public safety element of the Act is not relevant to the topics explored in this book and so will not be considered in any great detail.

5.6 The Secretary of State's Standards of Modern Zoo Practice

The stated purpose of the SSSMZP is to specify "standards with respect to the management of zoos and the animals in them".[19] No more is said in the Act as to what the standards might contain and so the Secretary of State is granted wide discretion as to their contents. Indeed, given that s.9 states that the Secretary of State "may" (as opposed to "must") specify standards, included in that wide discretion is the option to deem standards altogether unnecessary.

Notwithstanding this discretion, and as mentioned previously, a version of the standards has been in place for a number of years and is updated periodically. The earliest version of the SSSMZP held by DEFRA at present dates to 2004 and no information is held by the government department on when the first standards were published or what their contents may have entailed. Notwithstanding this, it is understood that a version of the SSSMZP has been in existence since at least 1984, when their publication was referred to during a debate in the House of Commons.[20] In practice, the current standards offer detailed guidance to zoos with regard to a number of areas of management. A strong weighting toward animal welfare is apparent, with ss.1–5 dealing specifically with the "five freedoms[21]" and s.6 dealing with the transport of animals, with a specific focus on welfare during transport and related legislation.

Conservation and education is dealt with in s.7, public safety in s.8, stock records in s.9, staff and training in s.10, public facilities in s.11 and rules on display of the zoo's license in s.12. There are a series of appendices dealing in more detail with some of the provisions already outlined and with the demands of the EC Zoos Directive specifically. The document as a whole runs to 94 pages.

In addition to specific guidance with regard to the ZLA 1981, the standards "also provide practical guidance in respect of provisions made by or under the Animal Welfare Act".[22] Section 14 of the AWA 2006 allows for the Secretary of State to devise and implement Codes of Practice to fulfill the exact aim outlined above. Section 14(3) confirms that "A person's failure to comply with a provision of a code of practice issued under this section shall not of itself render him liable to proceedings of any kind", but s.14(4) concedes that failure to comply with any code "may be relied upon as tending to establish liability" in the event of legal proceedings. Given that the SSSMZP have been devised and implemented under powers granted by s.9 of the ZLA 1981, rather than under s.14 of the Animal Welfare Act, it is unclear whether or not the standards could be treated in the same manner as part of legal proceedings as those codes that have been introduced under s.14 (i.e., to be used to establish liability). Consequently, while the SSSMZP may be used to inform zoo operators on how to meet the provisions of the AWA 2006, there does not appear to be a way of directly enforcing those standards that relate to the provisions of the AWA 2006. As such, any failure to meet welfare standards would be dealt with separately under the AWA 2006.

There have been very few prosecutions brought against zoos under the ZLA 1981 since its implementation, and those that have been brought have been conducted in the magistrate's court. As a result, there are no detailed judgments available on record to understand judicial opinion on the interplay between the SSSMZP and the Act itself. One of the few cases for which information on the court's handling of breaches of the ZLA 1981 is available involved the 2013 prosecution of the proprietors of Pets Corner Petting Zoo by Waveney District Council for breach of existing zoo license conditions. The defendants were found guilty on six counts and issued with a fine. It was reported that "Waveney District Council inspectors found Pets Corner in Oulton Broad lacked proper veterinary care, had poor record keeping and contaminated water",[23] but no further detail is available on the specific breaches committed.

Notwithstanding the SSSMZP's dual purpose of providing guidance on both the ZLA 1981 and, since 2007, the AWA 2006, a number of practices outlined in the standards appear to conflict with the provisions of one or the other of these pieces of legislation.

An apparent conflict between the ZLA 1981 and the AWA 2006 can be found in s.5 of the standards and deals with the feeding of live vertebrates to animals in a zoo, a practice which is accepted as part of the SSSMZP. The standards state that "Although the Animal Welfare Act 2006 does not prohibit the feeding of animals with live prey, the live feeding of vertebrate prey should be avoided save under exceptional circumstances, and only under veterinary advice".[24] It is the case that very few practices are explicitly outlawed in the Animal Welfare Act[25] and, instead, practices are generally considered under the lens of s.4 and or s.9 on a case-by-case basis. As such, the implicit suggestion that because a practice is not explicitly outlawed, it is legal, makes little sense. By the same logic, one could argue that the act of putting a dog in an oven and switching it on is not explicitly outlawed either and is thus legal. It was argued by the author during the most recent revision of the SSSMZP in 2012 that the feeding of live vertebrate prey should be considered to constitute a breach of s.4 or, at the very least, s.9, but the standards were not amended in line with this view. It remains unclear how this practice can be legally justified given that causing a protected animal[26] to be eaten alive would certainly be detrimental to the animal's welfare and could easily be conceived as "unnecessary suffering". Of course, this would need to be tested in the courts but the government's pre-emptive statement advising zoos that the practice is not illegal appears to be ill-advised.

An apparent conflict with the provisions of the ZLA 1981 can also be found within the standards in that the "pinioning" of birds is explicitly allowed in zoos.[27] The practice of pinioning involves the amputation of the end of a bird's wing at the carpal joint a few days after birth in order to prevent the bird from ever experiencing flight. While the practice is legal by virtue of the fact it is included within the permitted procedures listed in the Mutilations (Permitted Procedures) Regulations 2007, it is unclear how permanently removing a bird's ability to fly can be considered to meets the requirement of s.1A (c)(i) of the Act which demands that animals should be provided with "an environment well adapted to meet the physical, psychological and social needs of the species to which is belongs".

Notwithstanding the conflicts noted above, the standards offer comprehensive guidance on animal welfare and specific information for animals that are either considered to have very specialized welfare needs (such as elephants[28]) or animals that belong to a particular taxonomic class that share some similar characteristics (such as reptiles[29]).

No explanation as to the legal status of the SSSMZP is offered in the Act itself, the standards, the Zoo Expert Committee Handbook (see below) or the Guidance to the provisions of the Zoo Licensing Act (see below). Reference is made in s.5 of the Act that local authorities should "have regard" for any standards specified by the Secretary of State under s.9 and s.10 demands that inspectors "have regard" for them in considering their recommendations for improvements during and following inspections. What is clear from the Act is that the standards are not directly enforceable against zoos and so non-compliance does not constitute an offense under the ZLA 1981 per se. Indeed, until a condition detailing what is required of the zoo is attached to the zoo's license, standards contained within the Act cannot be directly enforced against a zoo at all.

5.7 The Zoo Expert Committee Handbook

The SSSMZP are "supplemented by the Zoo Expert Committee Handbook which provides further detail and guidance",[30] but the Zoo Expert Committee Handbook does not form part of the standards. It is explicitly stated that the handbook is a "non-statutory and simply contains guidance with recommendations that all zoo stakeholders … should find helpful".[31] Inspectors need not "have regard" to the handbook and neither do local authorities in the same way that they need to "have regard" for the standards. The handbook has no independent legal force and derives none from the Act. It therefore acts as guidance which may be followed voluntarily. As a result of its non-statutory nature, the handbook will not be considered in any detail as part of this book.

5.8 Guidance to the Provisions of the Zoo Licensing Act 1981

In addition to the SSSMZP, the ZLA 1981 is supplemented by legal guidance to the Act's provisions produced by DEFRA and targeted toward local authorities, which are the bodies responsible for the enforcement of the legislation.[32] As with the SSSMZP and the Zoo Expert Committee Handbook, the guidance is explicitly recognized as a non-statutory document. It is noted within the introduction that "this guidance should not be taken as an authoritative statement of the legal effect of the Act".[33] This is interesting when considering the explicit statements relating to feeding of live vertebrate prey and pinioning, already discussed. In these instances, DEFRA appears confident in making explicit statements over the application of the law, despite interpretation falling outside of the department's jurisdiction.

Most recently updated in late 2012, the guidance explains the Act, provision-by-provision, and seeks to clarify any ambiguous areas with regard to, for example, how to distinguish whether or not a collection falls within the definition of a zoo or how to distinguish whether or not a species of animal can be classed as "wild" for the purposes of the Act.

The guidance also includes flowcharts for local authorities to use to understand the licensing process and model documents which can be used as templates.

Relevant sections of the guidance will be considered in the chapter(s) examining the practical enforcement of the legislation.

5.9 The Extent of the Welfare Provisions Under the Zoo Licensing Act 1981

Following the detailed consideration of the Act and, as noted previously, it would appear that s.1A is the key provision through which welfare standards are understood and delivered. The mandatory nature of s.1A and the corresponding sanctions for failure to comply with it suggest that zoos which persistently fail to provide adequate standards of care will be either fully or partially closed. The broad provisions of s.1A are supplemented by detailed (and sometimes species-specific) guidance contained within the Secretary of State's Standards of Modern Zoo Practice. This is, in turn, supplemented by further guidance contained in the Zoo Expert Committee Handbook. Enforcement of the Act is supplemented and supported by the guidance to the Act's provisions. The Act is underpinned by a system of inspection which seeks to assess and further advice on compliance with the Act.

When we compare the welfare provisions included in the ZLA 1981 with those outlined as part of the AWA 2006, it would appear that the demands on zoos are more rigorous and they have the potential to accommodate the specialized needs of wild animals more effectively. While there is a caveat in s.1A of the ZLA in that zoos are asked to "aim to satisfy" the biological needs of the animals, which suggests that no explicit demand to meet needs in full is placed upon the zoos, the criteria by which zoos are measured use the needs of the animals, rather than the limitations of the industry as their starting point. The "good practice" caveat incumbent on any assessment of animal welfare made under s.9 of the AWA 2006 does not apply in the context of the ZLA 1981.

For example, zoos "must" implement the following measures:

> accommodating their animals under conditions which aim to satisfy the biological and conservation requirements of the species to which they belong, including—
>
> (i) providing each animal with an environment well adapted to meet the physical, psychological and social needs of the species to which it belongs; and

(ii) providing a high standard of animal husbandry with a developed program of preventative and curative veterinary care and nutrition.

Whereas the AWA 2006 demands that needs are met to the "extent required by good practice" within that particular industry. For zoos, then while recognizing that they are asked to "aim" to satisfy needs, rather than simply satisfy needs, the demand placed upon them still appears more stringent than those made under the AWA 2006.

This means that, in zoos, there is constant room for improvement in that there is no upper limit to the standard of care—an animal kept in a zoo could, theoretically, have all of their biological needs met which would, theoretically, be close (if not equivalent to) having all of their welfare needs met. On the other hand, as will be explored in Chap. 8 on the regulation of circuses, standards of welfare based in the limitations of the circus industry as their starting point are assessed only in relation to other circuses due to the "good practice" caveat. As such, the (now repealed) circus regulations did set an upper limit of welfare standards (whatever constitutes good practice within the traveling circus industry) which could, theoretically, be exceeded, but there is no demand placed upon businesses that they should do so. It would seem, therefore, that the potential for protection under the ZLA 1981—law not specifically focused on animal welfare—appears (somewhat ironically) to be greater than under legislation introduced under the overarching animal welfare statute in England and Wales.

5.10 Mobile Zoos and the Zoo Licensing Act 1981

The case of Tropical Inc., mentioned previously in relation to its attempt to establish a permanent zoo premises without a zoo license, presents a sobering case study for the growing trend of mobile zoos in the United Kingdom. In January 2013, following a tip-off to staff at a UK-based animal protection charity[34] by one former and one current employee, 74 animals were confiscated by the RSPCA and police from the premises belonging to Tropical Inc. for alleged breaches of the AWA 2006.[35]

According to the employees, some of the animals had been kept for up to two years in the conditions in which they were found. In November 2013, the owner of Tropical Inc. was convicted of 34 offenses under s.9 of the Animal Welfare Act.[36] He was, however, not banned from keeping animals, and continues to run his mobile zoo company today. The case raised serious concerns over the lack of effective regulation for this and similar businesses, as well as the need to address this problem as a matter of urgency in the interests of animal welfare.

5.10.1 Mobile Zoos in England

A mobile zoo is a business which usually operates from a permanent base and takes animals to events so that they can be exhibited to the public and, more often than not, be used in handling sessions. The businesses may take animals to schools, fairs, parties or corporate events. Most mobile zoos claim to deliver educational and/or conservation goals as part of their work. The animals used by mobile zoos tend to be small in size (for ease of transport) and belong to both wild and domesticated species of animal. Numbers of animals used by each business varies from a small handful of individuals to over a hundred animals. All businesses must comply with the provisions of the AWA 2006 for animals fitting the description of "protected animal" kept but there is no associated licensing or inspection regime imposed on these businesses at the current time. This is despite the fact that mobile zoos impose a specific set of circumstances on the animals, such as regular transportation and handling, which presents recognized welfare concerns, particularly for wild animal species.

Research carried out throughout 2013 and 2014 and updated in 2016 suggests that there are over 187 mobile zoos in the United Kingdom, housing a minimum of 3500 individual animals.[37] These businesses are not currently licensed under the ZLA 1981 but, until recently, were theoretically subject to regulation under the Performing Animals (Regulation) Act 1925 (PAA 1925). While the PAA 1925 does not impose explicit animal welfare obligations upon those using animals in performance (beyond restricting infliction of cruelty during performance), it does impose a number of measures which should allow the extent of the use of animals to be ascertained if properly applied and enforced. For example, those animals used in performance must be entered onto a register, which includes basic details about the company or individual, the animals used and the way in which they are used. However, for various reasons (lack of renewal obligations and the absence of any associated regime of inspection or licensing, amongst other things), it has been widely agreed for some time that the PAA 1925 serves no meaningful purpose in the protection of animal welfare and government officials have confirmed that it "is not, however, intended to promote welfare and its provisions are widely regarded to be ineffective".[38] In addition to the inadequacy of the legislation itself, of the 169 businesses operating as mobile zoos in 2014, 67% of them were not registered with any local authority and therefore had failed to comply with even these minimal legal obligations placed upon them.[39]

Despite its limited regulatory impact, one benefit in relation to the application of the PAA 1925 to mobile zoo businesses is that it grants powers of inspection to the local authority. This is regardless of whether or not the business has registered under the PAA 1925 and therefore could be used in relation to businesses which had failed to register. Unfortunately, legal advice issued in 2014[40] to a local authority by a DEFRA lawyer and subsequently circulated widely has suggested that registration under the PAA 1925 is no longer deemed necessary by the government department for mobile zoo businesses. This is a worrying prospect for those concerned about the current lack of regulation in place for this industry. If councils follow this advice, the powers of entry and inspection granted to them by the PAA 1925 would no longer be applicable and inspection of mobile zoo premises would be restricted to those carried out with a warrant under the AWA 2006. Warrants are granted under the AWA 2006 only if there is reason to believe that an offense has been committed (in comparison to the spot-check inspections permitted under businesses which fall within the remit of the PAA 1925). If mobile zoos no longer have to register with local authorities and these powers of inspection are taken away, both the identification of businesses using animals in this way and the ability to scrutinize them are severely limited by DEFRA's legal analysis. Hundreds of businesses, housing thousands of animals, may effectively fall "below the radar". At the time the advice was released by DEFRA, queries were raised by the author surrounding the government department's jurisdiction to interpret legislation as this role falls to the judiciary. It was confirmed by DEFRA in correspondence that despite their legal advisor's views, "it is for the Courts to provide an authoritative interpretation of the legislation. DEFRA's view is not conclusive and, clearly, local authorities should reach their own view as to how the law applies to their regulatory activities".[41] Thus, while the DEFRA opinion may be persuasive to local authorities seeking guidance, it should not be considered to provide a definitive interpretation of the law. That said, it is worth reiterating that, whether DEFRA's interpretation of the law is correct or incorrect, it is unlikely to be decided one way or another in the courts for the reasons outlined previously with regard to challenging decisions relating to pet shop licenses. That is, that the organizations and individuals raising concerns over these practices are largely NGOs or charitable organizations which do not have the resources or expertise to bring these cases before a court with a view to establish precedent.

Despite the confusion surrounding the applicability or otherwise of the PAA 1925 to mobile zoos, as a result of the lack of regulation, mobile zoos are set apart from most other animal-use industries which, as a general rule, are subject to some form of control above and beyond the general provisions of the AWA 2006. This is in spite of the fact that the mobile zoo industry uses many animals of wild species which would be subject to zoo licensing regulations if the businesses using them were classified as zoos in the traditional sense.

5.10.2 Why Are Mobile Zoos Not Subject to Specific Legislation?

At the time that the ZLA 1981 was introduced, mobile zoo businesses were largely unheard of. Following the introduction and subsequent widespread use of the internet, hobbyists with animal collections began to seek commercial recompense by hiring out their animals as part of educational or recreational activities, with many using the internet as a means to advertise and promote their new ventures. Some of these businesses have now developed into sophisticated operations which offer a large number of activities to a range of different audiences. As noted above, research carried out in 2013/2014 and updated in 2016 suggested that there were at least 187 individual mobile zoo businesses operating in the United Kingdom. That there is no evidence to suggest that mobile zoo businesses were in widespread operation when the ZLA 1981 was introduced suggests that these businesses were not assessed and then deliberately excluded from regulation, but that they are newly developed operations which were simply not in existence when the law was introduced. Absence in Hansard records of discussion surrounding mobile zoo operations during the passage of the ZLA 1981 supports this theory, as does the fact that, unlike circuses and pet shops, no explicit exemption is granted to mobile zoos in the legislation. It is argued that the lack of regulation for mobile zoos represents a failure in law to protect animals whose welfare is offered protection in other, similar, circumstances. In order to remedy this gap in legislation, it is suggested that the operation of these businesses should be brought under regulatory scrutiny. It is further maintained that, due to the similarities between mobile zoos and traditional zoos, the ZLA 1981 can be interpreted as encompassing mobile zoo business without need for amendment.

5.10.3 The Potential for Application of the Zoo Licensing Act 1981 to Mobile Zoos Businesses

Mobile zoos have arguably been considered to fall outside of the definition of a "zoo" (as defined by s.1(2) of the ZLA 1981) by virtue of the fact that their premises are not open to the public. Instead, the animals are taken from the premises to different locations around the country in order to facilitate their displays and events. Other than this, mobile zoo businesses house many of the same wild animals that zoos hold, they make claims that they serve both educational and conservation purposes and, in some instances, explicitly refer to themselves as zoos, for example, Zoo2U,[42] ZooLab,[43] Kimmy's Mobile Zoo,[44] among others.

As previously noted, s.1(2) of the ZLA 1981 defines a zoo as follows:

> In this Act "zoo" means an establishment where wild animals (as defined by section 21) are kept for exhibition to the public otherwise than for purposes of a circus (as so defined) and other than in a pet shop (as so defined); and this Act applies to any zoo to which members of the public have access, with or without charge for admission, on more than seven days in any period of 12 consecutive months.

The EC Zoos Directive (1999/22/EC), from which the definition in the ZLA 1981 is derived, is as follows:

> '[Z]oos' means all permanent establishments where animals of wild species are kept for exhibition to the public for 7 or more days a year, with the exception of circuses, pet shops and establishments which Member States exempt from the requirements of this Directive on the grounds that they do not exhibit a significant number of animals or species to the public and that the exemption will not jeopardize the objectives of this Directive.

The EC Directive mandates that establishments should be permanent and does not explicitly demand that the public "have access" to the establishment, but merely that the animals are kept by the establishment for the purpose of exhibition to the public for seven days a year or more. The relevance of this will be explored shortly.

In s.1 of the ZLA and the EC Directive definition, the term "establishment" is not defined. The common definition of the word "establishment" is "an organization, institution or hotel[45]". Elsewhere in the ZLA 1981, the terms "zoo premises"[46] and "premises of the zoo" are referred to with "premises" given its ordinary meaning of "the building or land occupied by a business".[47] If a zoo is an "establishment", then it stands to reason that the legislature did not intend for the word "zoo" to relate specifically to "premises"; otherwise, the use of the terms "zoo premises" or "premises of the zoo" would be superfluous as they would be one and the same thing.

The zoo is, therefore, presumed to be something more than the premises itself. Indeed, when we consider s.1A of the ZLA 1981, it becomes clear that the zoo cannot be considered to be simply the premises of the business as the zoo is required to take part in conservation programs and education programs. It is required to keep records, and it is recommended that it is involved in the release of animals, amongst other things. It is, of course, not possible for a premise to do such things, but it is possible for an organization or institution to do these things. It stands to reason, therefore, that references to a "zoo" under the ZLA 1981 refer to the organization itself and extend beyond the static premises of the zoo. This theory is supported by the fact that this interpretation would give the term "establishment" as used in the legislation its ordinary meaning.

With the above analysis in mind, when considering s.1(2) of the ZLA 1981 and the demand that members of the public must have access to the zoo for seven days a year or more for a business to fall within the zoo definition, we can interpret this to mean that members of the public must have opportunity to see the animals exhibited by the zoo for seven days a year or more, but not necessarily the physical premises where the animals are kept as access is required to the "establishment", not the premises. This view is supported by the definition within the EC Zoos Directive, upon which the definition within the current ZLA 1981 derives its meaning. The EC Zoos Directive demands that the establishment (already defined as something more than simply the zoo premises) must keep animals for exhibition to the public for seven days a year or more. The EC Directive is silent upon the need for members of the public to access the premises in order to see those animals exhibited.

Of course, some static zoos are assessed and found to be eligible for a s.14(1)(a) dispensation which exempts the business completely from licensing (but nonetheless requires both initial assessment and ongoing monitoring to ensure that the dispensation continues to apply) or a 14(2) dispensation. These might apply to collections which are not made up of wild mammals (and do not exceed 120 individuals (potential 14(1)(a) exemption)) or those which have no more than 50 conservation sensitive wild mammals in the collection (14(2) dispensation). Alternatively, collections which contain non-conservation sensitive, non-hazardous wild species (not including wild mammals) that do not exceed 200 individuals might be granted a 14(1)(b) dispensation. In practice, a number of mobile zoos would be likely to fall under some form of dispensation, but it seems unlikely that all of them would.

When interpreted in this manner, it stands to reason that mobile zoos keep animals for exhibition to the public for more than seven days a year and the public are given access to the establishment's services in that the animals are transported to the events on request. It could be argued that only a small number of the animals in the mobile zoo are accessed by the public at any one time, but this is of no concern. There is no stipulation in the legislation that the public need access to all of the animals in the zoo and, in fact, it will regularly be the case that members of the public visiting a static zoo will not have access to all the animals on site. For example, a sanctuary for ex-pet primates, the Monkey Sanctuary in Cornwall, is licensed as a zoo, but some of the animals, due to traumas that they suffered in the past, are kept "off show" in order to meet their welfare needs.[48] That some of the animals are permanently "off show" does not exempt the sanctuary from the rigors of zoo licensing.

Section 2(c) refers to references to closure of the zoo to the public, but this can also be read in line with the interpretation above even if the premises themselves are not open to the public in that s.2(c)(ii) allows for "ceasing to exhibit animals of a particular description to the public" can be read so as to include the exhibition of animals off the zoo premises.

It is suggested that the current absence of specific regulation for the expanding mobile zoo industry can be remedied in part by clarifying the interpretation of the existing ZLA 1981 in such a way that the term "zoo" is understood to refer to the wider organization, of which the premises where the animals are normally kept form just one part. The ZLA 1981 and the EC Directive, from which the amended version of the Act derives, both allow for this interpretation and, indeed, in parts rely on this interpretation in order for the zoos to deliver upon their licensing obligations.

Of course, it must be accepted that, on inspection for compliance with the standards of the ZLA 1981, it may be found that due to the very nature of mobile zoos, some mobile zoos are simply unable to meet the relevant legal requirements. If this is the case, then those businesses would fail to gain a license to operate and thus be forced to end operation. If it were found that the welfare concerns for the animals used by mobile zoo businesses could not be remedied by regulation, there is the possibility of prohibiting the operation of mobile zoos under either primary legislation or regulations introduced under powers granted by s.12 of the AWA

2006. Failure to take any action at all to regulate mobile zoo business could reasonably be considered to fall within the scope of "jeopardizing the objectives"[49] of the EC Zoos Directive. Given its aims, there seems to be no logical reason why mobile zoo businesses should be given a blanket exemption because the animals are moved around. Indeed, many would agree that the regular transport of animals and the regular handling of them by members of the public (something not normally carried out in traditional zoos) present both animal welfare and public safety concerns that might not be relevant in the traditional zoo environment.

Notes

1. Draper, C. and Glanville, G. (2013). Application and enforcement of the Zoo Licensing Act 1981 by local authorities. [online] Horsham: The Born Free Foundation. Available at: http://www.bornfree.org.uk/fileadmin/user_upload/files/zoo_check/publications/enforcement-of-the-zoo-licensing-act.pdf [Accessed 24 Nov. 2017].
2. AHVLA (2012). AHVLA list of zoos operating in England (November 2012). [online] Bristol: DEFRA. Available at: http://webarchive.nationalarchives.gov.uk/20140708225757/http://www.defra.gov.uk/ahvla-en/files/cites-zoo-list-england.pdf [Accessed 24 Nov. 2017].
3. Ibid.
4. Casamitjana, J. (2012). Inspecting Zoos: A study of the official zoo inspection system in England from 2005 to 2011. The Captive Animal's Protection Society, Manchester.
5. Source: http://www.DEFRA.gov.uk/ahvla-en/imports-exports/cites/zoos-inspectorate/ [accessed 6.5.2013].
6. Draper, C. and Glanville, G. (2013). Application and enforcement of the Zoo Licensing Act 1981 by local authorities. [online] Horsham: The Born Free Foundation. Available at: http://www.bornfree.org.uk/fileadmin/user_upload/files/zoo_check/publications/enforcement-of-the-zoo-licensing-act.pdf [Accessed 24 Nov. 2017].
7. Pers. Corr. between author and local authorities.
8. BBC News. (2012). Tortoise sanctuary given 24 hours. [online] Available at: http://www.bbc.co.uk/news/uk-england-cornwall-15019104 [Accessed 24 Nov. 2017].

9. Pers. Corr. between the author and the local authority.
10. HL Deb, 20 May 1970, vol. 310 cc1049–52.
11. Ibid.
12. *HL Deb 21 March 1972, vol. 329 cc634–68 and HL Deb, 15 June 1973, vol. 343 cc986–1013.*
13. House of Commons Library (2005). Research Paper 05/87: The Animal Welfare Bill. London: House of Commons Library.
14. Introductory Text, The Zoo Licensing Act 1981.
15. S.10(5) The Zoo Licensing Act 1981.
16. DEFRA (2013). Secretary of State's Standards of Modern Zoo Practice. London: DEFRA. p. 1.
17. The Zoo Licensing Act 1981 s.16E.
18. Defra.gov.uk. (n.d.). Biodiversity and ecosystems—GOV.UK. [online] Available at: http://www.DEFRA.gov.uk/wildlife-pets/zoos/ [Accessed 24 Nov. 2017].
19. The Zoo Licensing Act 1981 s.9.
20. HC Deb 02 July 1984 vol 63 cc121–8.
21. See Sect. 5 in Chap. 2 for background on the Five Freedoms.
22. DEFRA (2012). The Zoo Expert Committee Handbook. London: DEFRA. p. 3.
23. BBC News. (2013). Zoo owners fined over breaches. [online] Available at: http://www.bbc.co.uk/news/uk-england-suffolk-20910877 [Accessed 4 Nov. 2017].
24. DEFRA (2013). Secretary of State's Standards of Modern Zoo Practice. London: DEFRA, p. 4.
25. With the exception of those Acts outlined in ss.5–8 of the AWA 2006.
26. Defined by s.2 of the Animal Welfare Act 2006.
27. DEFRA (2013). Secretary of State's Standards of Modern Zoo Practice. London: DEFRA. pp. 10, 24, 52.
28. Ibid., p. 55.
29. Ibid., p. 45.
30. DEFRA (2013). Secretary of State's Standards of Modern Zoo Practice. London: DEFRA, p. 4.
31. DEFRA (2013). The Zoo Expert Committee Handbook. London: DEFRA, p. 1.
32. DEFRA (2012). The Zoo Licensing Act 1981: Guide to the Act's Provisions. [PDF] London: DEFRA. Available at: https://www.gov.uk/

government/uploads/system/uploads/attachment_data/file/69595/zoo-licensing-act-guide.pdf [Accessed 4 Nov. 2017].
33. Ibid., p. 5.
34. The Captive Animals' Protection Society (CAPS).
35. BBC News. (2013). Exotic animals seized by RSPCA. [online] Available at: http://www.bbc.co.uk/news/uk-england-hereford-worcester-20908636 [Accessed 28 Dec. 2017].
36. Mail Online. (2013). TV wildlife expert kept 70 exotic animals in 'unspeakable' conditions. [online] Available at: http://www.dailymail.co.uk/news/article-2507986/Wildlife-expert-appeared-Alan-Titchmarshs-chatshow-kept-70-exotic-animals-unspeakable-conditions.html [Accessed 28 Dec. 2017].
37. Captive Animals Protection Society. (2016). Travelling zoos on the rise and animals increasingly at risk says animal protection charity. [online] Available at: http://www.captiveanimals.org/news/2016/03/travelling-zoos-on-the-rise-and-animals-increasingly-at-risk-says-animal-protection-charity [Accessed 4 Sep. 2016].
38. Radford, M. (2007). The Report of the Chairman of the Circus Working Group (The Radford Report).
39. Mobile Zoos. (2013). An unregulated industry—Mobile Zoos. [online] Available at: http://mobilezoo.org.uk/unregulated/ [Accessed 4 Sep. 2016].
40. Confirmed in correspondence between the author and DEFRA official in January 2014.
41. Pers. Corr. between the author and DEFRA.
42. More information: http://zoo2u.co.uk.
43. More information: http://www.zoolabuk.com.
44. More information: http://www.kimmyszoo.co.uk/.
45. Oxford English Dictionary, 10th Edition.
46. For example, S.1(2)(c), S.1A and others.
47. Oxford English Dictionary, 10th Edition.
48. Monkeysanctuary.org. (n.d.). FAQs | Monkey Sanctuary. [online] Available at: http://www.monkeysanctuary.org/plan-your-visit/faqs/ [Accessed 4 Nov. 2017].
49. Article 2, Council Directive 1999/22/EC.

6

Enforcing the Zoo Licensing Act 1981

6.1 The Operation of the Zoo Licensing Act 1981[1]

Any business which meets the definition outlined in s.1(2) of the ZLA 1981 (a definition discussed in some detail in the foregoing chapter) must either be in possession of a license issued by the relevant local authority in order to operate[2] or be granted a dispensation under s.14(1)(a) of the Act which exempts the business from licensing obligations. The application for a license must be made in line with the requirements of s.2 of the Act. The local authority must then consider the license in light of the requirements outlined in s.3 and the decision to grant or refuse the license is governed by s.4. Under s.4, the local authority is obligated to refuse a license if it is believed that the grant of a license would "injuriously affect the health or safety of persons living in the neighborhood of the zoo, or seriously affect the preservation of law and order" or if it is believed that the mandatory provisions of s.1A[3] will not be met. A license must also be refused, or the grant of a license postponed, if planning decisions remain outstanding.

E. Tyson, *Licensing Laws and Animal Welfare*, The Palgrave Macmillan Animal Ethics Series, https://doi.org/10.1007/978-3-030-50042-9_6

The local authority has discretion to refuse to grant a license if the applicant (or a keeper at the zoo) has been convicted under relevant animal welfare-related legislation or if "they are not satisfied that the standards of accommodation, staffing or management are adequate for the proper care and wellbeing of the animals or any of them or otherwise for the proper conduct of the zoo".[4]

Under s.14, the local authority[5] or the zoo itself[6] has the ability to apply to the Secretary of State for a dispensation for the zoo if the zoo is particularly small, has few animals or has animals of few species. If granted, a dispensation may have the effect of exempting the zoo from the provisions of the Act altogether,[7] limiting the number of inspectors required during inspections[8] or limiting the number and type of inspections required under the Act.[9] DEFRA guidance states that, while each case is considered on its merits, zoos that have more than 50 "conservation-sensitive"[10] or "hazardous"[11] animals in their collection should not normally be granted a dispensation.[12]

Local authorities are responsible for the enforcement of the Zoo Licensing Act,[13] supported by guidance from DEFRA[14] and advised periodically by government-appointed inspectors.[15] Acts or omissions which constitute offenses under the Act are outlined in ss.19 (1), (2) and (3) as follows: operating without a license, failing without reasonable excuse to comply with a license condition and intentionally obstructing an officer acting pursuant to the Act. Sections 19(3A)–(3G) outline offenses for failure to comply with directions issued under s.16 of the Act (see below) and other related offenses, including failure to display the zoo license at the entrance to the zoo. At the time of writing, offenses under ss.19(1), (2), (3A), (3B, (3C), (3E) or (3F) are liable on summary conviction to a fine of no more than level 4 (currently £2500) on the standard scale. Offenses under subsections (3), (3D) or (3G) are liable on summary conviction to a fine of no more than level 3 (currently £1000) on the standard scale.

Section 1A of the Act incorporates the provisions of the EC Zoos Directive,[16] compliance with which is mandatory for all zoos. Despite their mandatory nature, failure to comply with the provisions of s.1A does not constitute an offense under the Act. Instead, the obligation is placed upon the local authority to ensure that the zoo is licensed in accordance with the provisions of s.1A, rather than the legislation itself making a direct demand on the zoo that the provisions of s.1A be met. As seen above, failure to comply with conditions without reasonable excuse is an offense under s.19(2) of the Act and failure to comply with conditions within an agreed timescale can lead to zoo closure under s.16A of the same. As such, it is therefore by adding conditions to the zoo's license that the provisions of s.1A (and other sections which are not directly enforceable) are given legal force. In order to fulfill their obligation under the Act, local authorities must attach conditions to the license of every zoo which demand compliance with s.1A. As outlined in previous chapters, it is s.1A(c) whose provisions impact most upon animal welfare.

In order to encourage the inclusion of the mandatory conditions in zoo licenses, DEFRA included suggestions for wording of the relevant conditions in a circular issued in 2003 to all local authorities.[17] Zoos found to be non-compliant with any one of these license conditions at the time of inspection must be issued with a "Direction"[18] and given a timeframe within which they must meet the required standard. That timeframe can be up to, but not exceeding, two years.[19] If the zoo continues to fall below standard after the agreed timeframe, the local authority must close the zoo (or the relevant part of it) permanently to the public.[20]

Local authorities have the discretion to add conditions to zoo licenses which do not relate to the provisions of s.1A but they cannot include any conditions which relate solely to the health, welfare and safety of persons working at the zoo[21] or any condition which is inconsistent with the provisions of s.1A.[22]

Failure to meet conditions other than those relating to the delivery of provisions outlined in s.1A also leads to consequences for the zoo but, in the case of failure to comply with a non-s.1A condition, the local authority has some discretion to decide timeframes for compliance and can choose whether to close the zoo or not in the event of failure to comply.[23] With s.1A conditions, the local authority does not have this flexibility due to the mandatory nature of enforcement action required by local authorities in the event of a s.1A condition being breached.[24]

6.2 The Inspection Process

In order to assess compliance, the standards outlined in the Act are underpinned by a system of inspection which can be broadly summarized as follows:

> Zoos are inspected by inspectors from both the local authority and from two lists which are drawn up and maintained by DEFRA, on advice from the British and Irish Association of Zoos and Aquaria (BIAZA) and the British Veterinary Association (BVA), by DEFRA.[25] One DEFRA list is made up of government-appointed (DEFRA) inspectors with expertise on managing zoos and the other is made up of government-appointed (DEFRA) inspectors who are qualified vets. DEFRA inspectors (accompanied by local authority inspectors) carry out what are known as 'formal' inspections. These comprise first inspections for new zoos, periodical inspections at around the midway point of the zoo's license and renewal inspections prior to the license expiration.[26] The local authority carries out what are known as 'informal' inspections unaccompanied by a DEFRA representative in each intervening year when a formal inspection is not carried out.[27] If a specific concern has been raised with regard to the operation of the zoo, a 'special' inspection might be carried out in addition to, or instead of, an informal inspection.[28] The process of inspection is what leads to the grant, refusal, amendment or confirmation of compliance with conditions of a license. Specific details regarding each type of inspection are as follows:

1. First Inspections[29] are carried out to assess whether a new zoo meets the standards laid out in the Act. If it is deemed that the zoo is likely to meet the standards (which is often a hypothetical decision at this point because the zoo should apply for the license before it starts to operate as such), then it will be recommended that the license is granted. When a license is granted for the first time, it lasts for four years.[30] Subsequent licenses are granted for a period of six years.[31]
2. Periodical Inspections[32] are carried out during the first year of a new license (a four-year license)[33] and during the third year of a renewed or fresh license (a six-year license).[34]
3. Renewal Inspections are carried out no later than six months before the expiry of a license.[35]

4. Informal Inspections—must be carried out in every year that no other type of inspection is carried out.[36] They are carried out by the local authority only, with no DEFRA representative in attendance. Special inspections sometimes (but not always) replace an informal inspection.
5. Special Inspections[37]—usually carried out to assess a specific issue or concern, which has arisen outside the normal inspection timetable. This might include a complaint or concern raised about the zoo in question, it might be carried out to confirm compliance with existing license conditions or for any other reason as the local authority sees fit. These inspections can be carried out without giving the zoo proprietor notice, unlike formal inspections, which are arranged in advance. These inspections can be carried out by the local authority inspectors alone or can be accompanied by DEFRA inspectors. If the issues to investigate are related to animal welfare, a vet must be in attendance.

In order to assist inspectors in their assessment of zoos, a number of forms have been devised by DEFRA, which can be filled in during an inspection. The forms differ slightly, depending on whether the inspection is for a first license (form ZOO3[38]) or for a renewal or periodical inspection (form ZOO2[39]) but, as a general rule, the forms ask specific questions, which relate directly back to the legislation.

The forms are designed to offer a Yes/No/Not Applicable answer in relation to legal standards, with an area for notes, recommendations and comments, an area to include any additional license conditions which the DEFRA inspector believes should be attached to the zoo's license, a check to see if existing license conditions have been met and a tick box to say whether the inspector recommends that a license is granted, granted with additional conditions, amended or refused. The majority of formal inspection reports are completed using the DEFRA forms. See Figs. 6.1 and 6.2 for excerpts from form ZOO2.

The ZOO2 form, which was subject to some minor changes in 2012, with further changes mooted for 2020, is currently made up of 100 questions to be answered by the inspector. Of those 100 questions, 63 questions relate to compliance with s.1A of the Act (made clear by the inclusion of a reference to the relevant s.1A subsection next to the relevant question, see Fig. 6.1), 1 question relates to compliance with s.19 (3G) of the Act (regarding public display of license) and 1 question helps

Findings at inspection

Guidance note: Where possible a Yes, No or Not Applicable (N/A) answer should be given. Where not all criteria are met for a particular question, comments and clarification should be made indicating where any deficits occur. If appropriate, means of correction or improvement should be included as Conditions or Recommendations under 'Additional conditions' or Additional space' towards the end of the form.

1. Provision of food and water	Marking Yes No N/A	Comments/clarification
Section 1A(c)(ii) ZLA 1981: 1.1. Are animals provided with a high standard of nutrition?	Select	
1.2. Is food and drink that is supplied appropriate for the species/individual?	Select	
1.3. Are supplies of food and water: (a) kept hygienically?	Select	
(b) prepared hygienically?	Select	
(c) supplied to the animal hygienically?	Select	
1.4. Has natural feeding behaviour been adequately considered to ensure that all animals have access to food and drink?	Select	
1.5. Are feeding methods safe for staff and animals?	Select	
1.6. Is feeding by visitors permitted?	Select	
(a) if 'yes', is it properly controlled?	Select	
2. Provision of suitable environment		
Section 1A(c)(i) ZLA 1981: 2.1. Are the animals provided with an environment well adapted to meet the physical, psychological and social needs of the species to which they belong?	Select	
2.2. Are the following environmental parameters appropriate: (a) temperature?	Select	
(b) ventilation?	Select	
(c) lighting?	Select	

Fig. 6.1 Column 1: Assessment criteria and relevant section of the Act; Column 2: Answer area; Column 3: Notes

Inspecting team's recommendation to the local authority

Having inspected (name of zoo) ____________________

on: ____________________

the inspecting team make the following recommendation: *Please tick appropriate box*

- it is recommended that a licence be refused.. ☐
- it is recommended that the above collection be licensed in accordance with the ZLA 1981 subject to the conservation measures in section 1A .... ☐
- it is recommended that the above collection be licensed in accordance with the ZLA 1981 subject to the conservation measures in section 1A and the following Additional Conditions (N.B Additional Conditions must be clearly worded so as to be enforceable and a timescale applied for compliance) .... ☐
- it is recommended that the following alterations be made to the above collection's licence conditions .... ☐

Additional Conditions (if appropriate)

Inspector(s) signature(s)	Date signed

Fig. 6.2 Recommendation to local authority and suggested license conditions

to inform understanding of compliance with s.19(2) (regarding failure to comply with conditions without reasonable excuse) as well as indicating a need for action under s.16A (1) (the need for a direction to be issued in the event of non-compliance with a license condition). The remaining questions help to inform compliance of the zoo with other important standards, including animal welfare and safe transport of animals. Unlike the provisions of s.1A, it is not mandatory for conditions in relation to these other standards to be attached to the license. Thus, while the local authority is advised that, in deciding what conditions to attach to a license, it must have regard to the standards outlined by the Secretary of State in the Standards of Modern Zoo Practice, it is not subject to any absolute requirement to add license conditions other than those relating to s.1A.

Formal inspection rules include a requirement for a report to be completed and submitted to the local authority,[40] as do special inspections (albeit an abridged version).[41] Legally, reports do not need to be completed following informal inspections, but it is strongly recommended in DEFRA guidance that a report is completed regardless.[42]

Issues or concerns identified during an inspection and recorded in inspection reports do not create any legally binding obligations on the zoo as it is the local authority, and not the inspector, which has jurisdiction to impose license conditions. As such, the reports act as guidance and offer recommendations to the local authority as to what, if any, conditions the inspectors believe should be attached to the zoo's license and what, if any, improvements might need to be made. As a general rule, and with the exception of those acts or omissions which constitute an offense under s.19 of the Act, it is only when the local authority adds conditions to the license of the zoo that the inspector's recommendations become legally binding upon the zoo.

As the DEFRA inspector acts in an advisory capacity, the local authority must choose whether to act on the advice given and must refer to the legislation to ensure that any amendment to the license is in line with what the Act says the authority must do. If the condition relates to a failure to meet s.1A provisions,[43] the local authority must also issue a direction under s.16A of the Act. If the condition relates to a non-s.1A provision, then a direction is only necessary if the zoo has already been notified of the issue and it already has a condition attached to its license. As well as giving rise to action under s.16A, failure to comply with a condition is also an offense under s.19 of the Act.

If a direction has been issued and not complied with, the zoo (or part of it) must be closed (if the condition relates to s.1A) or can be closed (if the condition relates to something other than s.1A) at the local authority's discretion.

6.3 Assessing the Extent to Which the Zoo Licensing Act 1981 Is Enforced with Respect to Non-compliant Zoos

As outlined in the previous section, there are two main mechanisms by which enforcement action can be carried out against zoos found during inspection to be non-compliant with the provisions of the ZLA 1981. The first is by identifying that an offense has been committed for the purposes of s.19 of the Act and bringing charges against the zoo, for example, for failing to comply without reasonable excuse with a condition attached to the license or failing to display the license and conditions at the public entrance. If found liable on summary conviction of an offense under s.19, the zoo (both the body corporate and individuals acting in the relevant capacity) may be fined in line with the penalties outlined earlier. In practice, prosecution of zoos under s.19 is rare, and no data was provided relating to evidence of prosecution under s.19 of the Act by local authorities as part of this research.

The second mechanism for enforcement is the addition of conditions to the zoo's license and, in the event that the zoo is found non-compliant with such conditions within the agreed timeframe, the issuance of a direction under s.16A of the Act. The direction will outline a clear timeframe by which action needs to be taken and, in the event that the terms of the condition are still not met within this timescale, all or part of the zoo must be closed to the public.

These two approaches combined, if properly applied, provide remedies which see non-compliant zoo operators fined for failure to meet standards under s.19 and a process, via s.16A and associated sections of the Act, which provides a long-term solution for the animals held by the zoo should the establishment persistently fail to meet standards and the zoo be mandatorily closed (as outlined in s.16E of the Act).

In order to assess the extent to which enforcement action is carried out against non-compliant zoos, it is therefore essential to establish the extent to which the enforcement tools available to local authorities are used when non-compliance is recognized.

6.4 Data Collection

Data was collected as part of the initial research for this project for the period from 1 January 2008 to 10 July 2014. The data was updated in 2019 to encompass the dates 11 July 2014–10 June 2019. As such, the complete period examined in this book is from 1 January 2008 to 10 June 2019, the most comprehensive study of zoo licensing in England carried out to date.

Only zoos in England were considered because, while the ZLA 1981 applies to England, Scotland and Wales, other parts of this research consider interplay between various pieces of legislation[44] which apply only in England.

As outlined in Sect. 1 of Chap. 5 on the size and shape of the zoo industry, the list held by DEFRA of zoos in England is not kept up to date and, indeed, by the time the data was updated in 2019, the list seemed to have fallen out of circulation altogether. At the time of writing (March 2020), the most recent publicly available list dated back to 2012. As a result of this, all councils were contacted to request information on zoos currently operating in their jurisdiction, regardless of whether they had a zoo listed on the most recent DEFRA list.

In the first research period, emails were sent to 326 English councils: 318 councils responded to the request for information, representing a 98% response rate. Three councils refused to provide information on grounds of exemptions to Freedom of Information requirements. These refusals were challenged and pursued to internal review stage on the grounds that the information had been erroneously withheld. One complaint was upheld, and the information subsequently released, the other two were not. Due to the periodic restructuring of councils, the total number of councils in England changed from 326 to 315. As such, for the second research phase, emails were sent to 315 relevant councils in England: 293 responses were received, representing a 93% response rate for the second period. In the second research period, 22 councils failed to respond to the Freedom of Information request.

In total for the complete research period, information was received relating to 237 zoos. This information was contained within 564 separate inspection reports, spanning over a decade, and accompanying documentation.

6.5 Data Entry

Only formal inspection reports (using the DEFRA ZOO2 form), excluding those for first inspections, were used in the data input stage as it is the formal inspections which are completed by government officials and it is formal inspections which generally give rise to license renewal, new conditions being added to the license and alteration of the license. First inspection reports, as noted previously, provide predictions as to whether standards will be met when the zoo is opened in the future and therefore cannot be considered to be assessing compliance with the legislation at that time. Informal inspection reports provide useful supplementary information but follow no specific format and do not necessarily inspect all elements of the zoo's operation or its compliance with the legislation. As such, informal inspection reports are not deemed to be reliable indicators of compliance with the legislation.

As noted above, the ZOO2 form used by inspectors to assess zoos was updated in late 2012 and came into proper use during 2013 (though some inspectors continued to use the old form throughout 2013 and beyond). Relevant adjustments have been made in the data input stage of this research in order to ensure that changes in the form, and the potential impact upon the data, have been properly accounted for.

DEFRA was carrying out work to further update the ZOO2 form in 2019, with a view to publish the updated form in January 2020. While the new form was not in use during the second research period, one council was using the new form, seemingly erroneously as DEFRA officials informed the author that the form had not yet been approved.

In total, 564 formal inspection reports relating to 237 zoos located across 143 different local authorities were analyzed. The maximum number of reports provided for any zoo was five (one zoo), four reports were provided for 39 zoos, three reports were provided for 65 zoos, two reports were provided for 65 zoos, and one report was provided for 67 zoos. As such, it should be noted that adding up the number of zoos in each year will not give the total number of zoos, but the total number of reports, as some zoos are represented in more than one year.

The reports provided by local authorities were distributed across the years as given in Table 6.1.

All data from all formal inspection reports provided was entered into a Microsoft Excel workbook. Each zoo was allocated its own sheet within the Excel workbook and all data for each zoo was recorded on the same sheet. Data was inputted by noting whether the inspector answered "Yes", "No", "N/A" or provided no answer to questions with regard to compliance with standards (both legal and otherwise).

Where a "No" answer was recorded by the inspector, this was deemed to indicate non-compliance with the criteria to which the question related. Where a "Yes" answer was noted by the inspector, this was deemed to indicate compliance with the criteria to which the question related. This was the case even when the accompanying notes suggested that the "Yes" answer was incorrect. For example, if an inspector marked "Yes" to the question "Do animals on display to the public appear to be in good health?" before going on to list a number of animals with physical ailments which needed treatment, it would appear that despite the "Yes" answer, the zoo is, in fact, non-compliant with the criteria to which the question corresponds. This issue relating to interpretation of inspection reports has been identified in other studies (i.e., CAPS/Casamitjana 2012[45] and Draper 2012[46]) and was labeled by Casamitjana in 2012 as the "Yes, but" problem. For the purposes of this study, the tendency

Table 6.1 Reports used as part of this study

	2008	2009	2010	2011	2012	2013	2014	2015	2016	2017	2018	2019
# of zoos per year/reports	32	45	55	54	38	68	56	35	65	48	59	14

toward answering "Yes, but" is recognized as a recurring phenomenon, but given the need of this research to identify recognized non-compliance and action taken to remedy that non-compliance, "Yes, but" answers have been classed as "Yes" and therefore deemed compliant with the legislation to avoid introducing elements of speculation into the research. As such, only "No" answers have been considered to indicate non-compliance. Answers of "N/A" or no answer provided were also discounted for the purposes of establishing compliance (or otherwise) with standards.

In two cases, the giving of a "No" answer to a question on the form was not treated as indicating non-compliance. Firstly, the giving of a "No" answer to the question "Is feeding permitted by visitors?" was treated as a simple statement of fact rather than an indication of non-compliance. Secondly, a zoo was only treated as being non-compliant with the conservation measures outlined in question 7 of the ZOO2 form if all five of questions 7.1(i)–7.1(v) received a "No" answer (the zoo is only required to fulfill one of the five measures in order to be considered compliant with the relevant section[47] of the ZLA 1981). Data analysis took this into account following the input phase.

Using the "Yes" and "No" answers as key indicators of perceived legal compliance in the view of the inspector and discounting "N/A" or no answer, the data was then analyzed for overall compliance with the legislation. Evidence of non-compliance was then cross-referenced with information provided by local councils with regard to carrying out of enforcement action under s.16A of the Act and prosecutions brought for offenses committed under s.19 of the Act.

A simple analysis which considered the number of times non-compliance which should give rise to action under s.16A and/or constitute an offense under s.19 was met with the correct enforcement action was carried out. This gave rise to the main quantitative results.

6.6 Interpretation: When Does a "No" Answer Indicate Non-compliance with the Law?

There are two questions on the form for which a "No" answer indicates clearly that an offense under s.19 of the Act may have been committed. Those are questions 12.1 (Is the current license or a copy on public display at each public entrance?) and 12.3 (Have any additional license conditions been met?). An answer "No" to either of these questions has been deemed to be indicative of an offense under s.19 of the Act.

With regard to the need for action under s.16A of the Act (the issuance of a direction to enforce license conditions, after giving the operator an opportunity to be heard), the interpretation is slightly more complex. Section 5(2A) of the Act confirms that "A license under this Act shall be granted subject to conditions requiring the conservation measures referred to in section 1A to be implemented at the zoo". This means that all licenses correctly issued will already be subject to license conditions relating to compliance with s.1A of the Act. Consequently, any recognition during inspection that any area of s.1A of the Act has not been met would constitute a failure to comply with a license condition and thus give rise to action under s.16A of the Act. The need for action under s.16A may also indicate an offense under s.19; this will be explored in more detail below.

As noted above, the criteria which are deemed to relate to s.1A of the Act are easily recognized in the ZOO2 form, as the relevant s.1A subsection is clearly listed against the question which the inspector is answering (see Fig. 6.1). Around 63 of the 100 questions in the ZOO2 form relate to compliance with s.1A. With this in mind, any instance in which the inspector, during the inspection process, has noted a "No" answer next to a question which relates to the implementation of s.1A suggests that the inspector considers the zoo to be non-compliant with an element of s.1A of the Act.

Unlike the interpretation of questions 12.1 and 12.3, for which a "No" answer appears to clearly constitute an offense under s.19 of the Act, the need for enforcement action under s.16A (and any offenses under s.19

which flow from that need) cannot be determined by considering the answers on the form alone. This is because action under s.16A is only required if the mandatory conditions have been correctly attached to the license. If the license has not been issued subject to the mandatory conditions contained within s.1A in the first instance, then there is no requirement for action under s.16A, nor does the non-compliance with standards included in the form constitute an offense under s.19.

Further, even if the correct conditions have been added to the license, it cannot be assumed that each instance of non-compliance with s.1A should result in the making of a direction under s.16A nor that it constitutes an offense under s.19. This is because the conditions may be worded so as to incorporate a number of different criteria from the form. Consequently, multiple "No" answers on the form may relate to just one condition and thus one single "No" response might not equate to a clear cut and easily identifiable breach of a condition. With this in mind, it is important to recognize that the analysis carried out below recognizes non-compliance with s.1A which *could* give rise to both action under s.16A and offenses under s.19, but the extent to which action is required can only be determined properly by further analysis of the licenses themselves and the conditions attached to them. This matter is explored via a series of case studies in Sect. 6.10.3 of this chapter, and it is for this reason that clear and quantifiable offenses under s.19 and potential action being required under s.16A resulting from non-compliance with s.1A provisions have been dealt with as separate concerns.

For those questions which do not relate directly to compliance with s.1A or for which a "No" answer recognizes an offense under s.19 of the Act, a "No" answer only implies non-compliance with the law (and thus the potential for enforcement action to be taken) if the criteria under question are already included in an additional condition attached to the zoo license. Given that non-compliance with additional license conditions is explicitly addressed in question 12.3 of the form, then any non-compliance with conditions relating to sections other than s.1A should be captured by the answer to this question. For this reason, the only "No" answers taken into account in the research besides answers to questions concerning compliance with s.1A are answers to questions 12.3 and 12.1

(which deal with display of an establishment's license at its public entrance).

Of the 564 reports analyzed, 31,213 individual answers to questions were considered relevant for this part of the research.

6.7 Results

Between 2008 and 2019, 1882 instances of non-compliance which should (if licenses are correctly administered) give rise to enforcement action being carried out under s.16A were noted by inspectors. Just 18 directions were issued by local authorities under s.16 during the same period, with the very first direction being issued in 2016. There was no evidence of directions being issued prior to this time. One local authority provided one zoo with "an opportunity to be heard" as an apparent preliminary to issuing a direction in 2008, but no direction was subsequently issued and no evidence of the zoo's response to the "opportunity to be heard" was made available.

6.8 Instances of Non-compliance Indicating Potential for Action Under s.16

6.9 Offenses Committed Under s.19

For the complete study period, there were 106 recognized offenses committed under s.19. During the first research period, news reports suggested that a prosecution had been carried out against a zoo, but the council responsible for the prosecution did not respond to either initial or follow-up Freedom of Information requests. As such, the zoo to which this prosecution relates is not included in this dataset (Tables 6.2 and 6.3).

According to the information provided, and other than the case noted above, no prosecutions under s.19 were carried out by responding local

Table 6.2 Instances of non-compliance indicating potential for action under s.16

	2008	2009	2010	2011	2012	2013	2014	2015	2016	2017	2018	2019	Total
# reports/zoos per year	32	45	55	54	38	68	56	35	65	48	59	14	564
# of zoos non-compliant with s.1A (thus giving rise to potential for action under s.16A)	24	31	23	29	25	37	44	22	47	36	39	11	368
% zoos found to be non-compliant	75	69	42	54	68	54	79	63	72	66	79	65	66 (Avg.)
# of instances of non-compliance potentially requiring action under s.16	104	149	77	116	94	161	221	95	218	174	298	115	1882

Table 6.3 Offenses committed under s.19

	2008	2009	2010	2011	2012	2013	2014	2015	2016	2017	2018	2019	Total
# reports/zoos per year	32	45	55	54	38	68	56	35	65	48	59	14	564
# of zoos committing an offense under s.19 per year	4	11	10	10	7	6	11	6	7	9	13	3	97
% of zoos committing an offense per year	13	24	18	19	18	9	20	17	11	19	22	21	17.5 (Avg.)
# of instances of non-compliance considered an offense under s.19(3)(g) of the Act	1	3	3	2	1	2	5	1	2	1	3	2	26
# of instances of non-compliance considered an offense under s.19(2) of the Act (also warranting action under s.16)	3	9	8	10	7	5	7	4	5	9	12	1	80
Total # of offenses under s.19	4	12	11	12	8	7	12	5	7	10	15	3	106
% of zoos committing offenses under s.19	12.5	27	20	22	21	10	21	14	11	21	25	21	18.9 (Avg.)

authorities against zoos included in this study despite the fact that the 1822 instances of non-compliance warranting action under s.16A noted in the zoos to which the responses relate might also indicate associated offenses under s.19 of the Act. Explicit failure to comply with conditions (determined by an answer "No" to question 12.3 "Have any additional conditions been met?"), which is considered an offense for the purposes of s.19(2) of the Act, was noted 79 times. An offense under s.19(2) of the Act also warrants action being taken under s.16 and so is both an offense and a trigger for enforcement action under s.16A.

A further 24 offenses were noted under s.19(3)(g) of the Act for zoos for which responses were received with regard to prosecution failing to publicly display their license. This offense does not correspond with the need for action under s.16A of the Act unless a condition has been attached to the license requiring that the license be displayed (Table 6.4).

Of the 237 zoos analyzed, 201 zoos should have been faced with action under s.16A of the Act at some stage during the ten-year period, some more than once. This represents 85% of all zoos. Of the 237 analyzed, 79 zoos were noted to have committed offenses under s.19 of the Act, some more than once. This represents 33.4% of all zoos. Despite this, there is evidence of just four local authorities taking action against five zoos using enforcement tools provided by s.16 of the Act over the entire decade under consideration. A total of 18 directions were issued during the study period to these five zoos and no enforcement action at all was taken under s.16 prior to 2016. Eleven of the directions correctly issued were against the same zoo in 2019. No evidence of prosecutions under s.19 of the Act was provided. It is clear from these results that, even with the negligible and sporadic use of correct enforcement tools in recent years, there remains an almost complete lack of formal enforcement action being

Table 6.4 Non-compliance with ss.16 and 19 of the ZLA 1981 between 2008 and 2019

Non-compliance	2008–2019
# zoos non-compliant for purposes of s.16	201
% zoos non-compliant for purposes of s.16	85
# zoos committed offenses under s.19	79
% zoos committed offenses under s.19	33.4

carried out against zoos under the ZLA 1981, despite widespread and explicitly recognized non-compliance with statutory standards.

6.10 Discussion

6.10.1 Considering the Extent to Which Animal Welfare Is Impacted by Recognized Breaches

As outlined previously, it was the inclusion of s.1A in the ZLA 1981 which imposed statutory animal welfare demands on zoos, with the subsections of s.1A having varying degrees of impact upon animal welfare. Section 1A(c) is the subsection of the Act which deals specifically with animal welfare demands and therefore breaches of this particular subsection are likely to indicate that animal welfare is being compromised. Almost half of the breaches (42%) noted as part of this research do, in fact, relate to s.1A(c) (763 noted instances of non-compliance)—more than found in relation to any other subsection of the Act. Section 1A requires a number of measures to be implemented which do not have a bearing on animal welfare namely those required to be implemented under s.1A(a) and 1A(b). About 132 instances of non-compliance were of failure to implement such measures. The other parts of s.1A have an indirect bearing on animal welfare in that if they are not met, it is likely that poor welfare will be the knock-on effect (s.1A(d), 1A(e) and 1A(f)). Around 762 instances of non-compliance in the results were of failure to implement the measures which these subsections require. Section 16A may have a bearing on animal welfare, dependent on which conditions have been breached, but this can only be found by considering each instance of non-compliance against the conditions. In any case, failure to meet existing license conditions is also an offense under s.19 of the Act. In total, there were 1525 instances of non-compliance which appeared to have either a direct or indirect impact on animal welfare (or are strong indicators that welfare is being compromised) and a further 165 instances which may have a bearing on animal welfare, depending on what conditions were attached to the relevant license.

While it appears, therefore, that the majority of instances of non-compliance can be considered to have, in theory, a direct or indirect impact on animal welfare, the extent to which animal welfare may be impacted in practice by these breaches will be considered in this section.

The five questions on the form with the highest level of non-compliance were given in Table 6.5.

The first most common breach is one which relates to escape drills. This was a point which was specifically added to the form in 2013 and so was not part of the inspection report prior to that time. Despite only having become a formalized requirement since 2013, there have been more breaches of this demand than any other. This may suggest that DEFRA, local authorities or inspectors need to actively highlight any new or amended demands as they change. If they are simply added to the form, it seems that they are not necessarily internalized and followed by the zoos themselves. Breach of this condition does not directly impact animal welfare.

The second most common breach noted relates to the review of veterinary records. Non-compliance with this criterion suggests a lack over veterinary oversight and monitoring of health, but does not necessarily indicate an animal welfare problem in itself.

The third most common point of non-compliance relates to arrangements for post mortems. Again, of course, once an animal is dead, then there can be no welfare concerns for that animal, but if deaths are occurring and no attempts are being made to understand why, then there may be welfare concerns within the zoo which are not being properly identified or addressed. If deaths are being caused by disease or poor husbandry, the failure to carry out post mortems could mean that preventable deaths continue to occur.

The fourth most common breach relates to the provision of a documented program of veterinary care and nutrition. As veterinary care is one of the major influences on animal welfare, failure to meet this criterion suggests possible failure to meet animal welfare needs. That said, lack of vet care will only have a direct impact upon welfare if an animal requires treatment but that treatment is not provided. A healthy animal will not suffer poor welfare simply because he or she is not seen by a vet. In addition, the lack of a written program of veterinary care and nutrition

Table 6.5 The five questions on the form with the highest level of non-compliance

Section		2008	2009	2010	2011	2012	2013	2014	2015	2016	2017	2018	2019	Total
1A(d)	8.3. Are escape drills carried out four times a year, recorded and regularly reviewed (at least two drills should include the escape of a category 1 animal where present)?	N/a	N/a	N/a	N/a	N/a	8	21	12	24	20	16	7	108
1A(c) (ii)	3.10 is there a system for the regular review of clinical and pathological records?	8	9	2	5	8	10	10	5	11	9	10	2	89
1A(c) (ii)	3.15 are post mortem examination arrangements satisfactory?	4	9	2	4	5	10	5	4	9	11	15	5	83
1A(c) (ii)	3.9 are the animals provided with a documented and maintained program of preventative and curative veterinary care and nutrition?	5	9	2	6	5	10	12	3	9	8	11	3	83
16(1)	12.3. Have any additional license conditions been met?	3	9	8	10	7	5	6	4	5	9	12	1	79

does not necessarily indicate that no veterinary oversight exists, simply that it is undocumented.

The fifth most common breach—failure to meet additional license conditions—relates to a clear offense under the Act as failure to meet conditions is an offense under s.19 and also a reason to take action under s.16A. This may or may not impact upon animal welfare, depending upon what the breached conditions relate to.

It is perhaps worth noting that the nature of the breaches and their potential to impact upon animal welfare are not necessarily relevant given the almost complete absence of enforcement action. If it were the case that very few breaches which impact upon animal welfare were occurring but, when they did, correct enforcement action was being taken, it might be reasonable to conclude that, even in the absence of overall effective enforcement, animal welfare needs were being prioritized and met. As there appears to be no difference in the way breaches which impact upon animal welfare are treated compared to those that do not, or only impact upon animal welfare indirectly, then it can be inferred that the lack of enforcement persists regardless of whether the breaches impact upon animal welfare or not.

6.10.2 Corroborating Evidence and Potential Reasons for Non-compliance

This book has, so far, identified a significant number of instances of non-compliance with the legislation and an almost complete absence of formal enforcement action to aid compliance. The extent to which this non-compliance (and subsequent failure to take action to remedy breaches) affects animal welfare is difficult to ascertain, but it is reasonable to conclude that there must be some impact on animal welfare due to the context of some of the breaches and the almost absolute absence of enforcement action. The findings of this work are corroborated to a greater or lesser extent by previous research into compliance with the ZLA 1981. A number of studies (e.g., Draper 2012,[48] FFA/Casamitjana 2012[49] and ADAS 2010[50]) have been carried out in the past which considered the way in which the ZLA 1981 is implemented. Some, such as Draper's work, uses formal inspection report data to assess the delivery of welfare standards, rather than enforcement of the Act per se.

The ADAS report, which was commissioned by government and published in 2010, considered enforcement of the Act from the perspective of the local authorities charged with delivering it. Findings were based on questionnaires filled in by local authority officials answering questions on how well they felt the ZLA 1981 was being delivered. No empirical evidence of enforcement action was gathered as part of the ADAS study. Finally, the CAPS report considered enforcement in a broad sense (among other elements of the system) but did not carry out detailed analysis surrounding legal compliance and enforcement.

Notwithstanding the fact that none of the aforementioned research focused specifically on empirical evidence of compliance and enforcement action being carried out with regard to the ZLA 1981, every one of the reports on this issue recognized, to some extent, concerns over either compliance of zoos with standards or enforcement of the Act itself. Specific concerns, taken from the aforementioned reports, are reproduced below:

> *We highlight a number of concerns about the inspection process itself, and identify areas where changes would lead to improvements in both the inspection process and our ability to monitor animal welfare standards in zoos.*[51]

> *The zoo licensing system in England does not work and, in its present form, is both unreliable and unworkable; therefore rendering the effective guarantee of protection of all animals held in zoos impossible.*[52]

> *The initial review provided some evidence for a number of issues raised in connection with the implementation of the Act, particularly prior to 2008, such as missed or late inspections, incomplete inspection teams and license conditions not being enforced. However, there was also evidence of significant improvements in these areas in recent years".*[53] In addition, *"Inspectors commented that while they had seen improvement in local authorities' management of the inspection process, there was room for further improvement.*[54]

The ADAS report went on to discuss local authority and inspector views with regard to the efficacy of the legislation and a key finding was that local authorities and inspectors suggested that more enforcement powers, in addition to license refusal, should be made available to them.[55] They suggested powers equivalent to "enforcement notices" which are available under the AWA 2006. In fact, directions issued under s.16A operate in almost exactly the same way as improvement orders under s.10 of the AWA 2006, with the exception that improvements notices under the AWA 2006 can be effectively extended indefinitely, whereas directions under s.16 are subject to a maximum of two years when associated with breaches of s.1A. One of the report's final recommendations was that these "extra" enforcement powers should be added to the Act. This report was written in conjunction with BIAZA and commissioned and published by the government. The fact that the powers proposed already exist for local authorities suggests that, in 2010 at least, there was a clear lack of understanding among key stakeholders of what enforcement measures were available to local authorities under the existing legislation under consideration when dealing with non-compliant zoos. This pointed toward poor understanding of the existing legislation on the part of the local authorities, BIAZA and the government itself.

The lack of understanding (and thus failure to apply) enforcement measures under s.16A appeared to be corroborated by the FFA study in 2012. In order to explore this issue further, in 2012, the author of this book carried out a brief study of the implementation of s.16A of the Act, using data gathered by Casamitjana as part of the 2012 FFA study. The study collated "No" answers given in relation to questions relating to compliance with s.1A of the Act from formal inspection reports for 124 zoos examined between 2005 and 2011 (using similar, but less rigorous, methodology to that employed in this research). The study found 1003 instances of non-compliance with elements of s.1A across 124 English zoos and just one instance of action being taken under s.16A. The study, which remains unpublished, formed the basis of a formal complaint made to the European Commission over the apparent failure of the UK government to ensure the correct enforcement of the EC Zoo Directive (EC 1999/22) and was also used to support discussions with government department, DEFRA, to discuss ways in which the apparent lack of enforcement action could be addressed. In addition, it was the results of this pilot study from which the proposal for the present research surrounding licensing as an effective regulatory framework arose.

In May 2012, the author of this research met with DEFRA officials specializing in zoo policy. Concurring with the results of the pilot study presented to them, the DEFRA team agreed to update government guidance[56] to local authorities with regard to their obligations under s.16 of the Act and to make clear the mandatory nature of the action to be taken where non-compliance is found. This guidance was published in late 2012 and information, including a letter specifically outlining the mandatory nature of enforcement action,[57] under s.16A in the event of non-compliance was sent to local authorities in November 2012. This letter effectively confirmed to local authorities that they did have an enforcement tool available to them which was very similar to the "improvement orders" which had been raised in the past as potentially useful (particularly as part of the aforementioned ADAS report) and were erroneously believed to not form part of the legislation.

In November 2013, the complaint which had been raised by the author of this work with the EC with regard to compliance was answered by way of the relevant EC officials forwarding a letter written by DEFRA to the EC in response to a different, but similar complaint on the issue. The letter stated that it was now DEFRA's belief that there was no failure to use enforcement powers under s.16A and, instead, powers were being used to effectively resolve issues.

The section of the letter, which was made public by DEFRA following a Freedom of Information request, dealing with the previous failure to use powers of enforcement under s.16A of the Act stated:

> *The UK authorities do not accept that analysis of the documents alone gives an accurate or complete picture of the operation of the zoo licensing system. The legislation provides that before a local authority makes a direction specifying which condition has not been met (and the section of the zoo to which it relates, and the action to be taken to comply, and by when (section 16A(2)), and before it issues a zoo closure direction (section 16B(1)), it must give the zoo operator an opportunity to be heard. The Government would expect the majority of non-compliance incidents to be resolved quickly between the local authority and the*

zoo, which could obviate the need for the formal compliance procedures provided for in the Act. The prompt resolution of compliance problems in this way may not be captured through the analysis of documents alone.[58]

While the point that all relevant information in all cases might not be captured by inspection reports is a valid one, it is clear from the information contained within them that instances of non-compliance range from minor (e.g., minor repair works) to major (failure to implement a program of veterinary care) with varying degrees of seriousness in between. Arguably, some of the simpler problems could perhaps be both recognized and solved on the day of the inspection or shortly afterwards, but it is abundantly clear from the reports that this does not always occur. This letter also suggests that, in being given an "opportunity to be heard" (the necessary precursor to a direction being issued), the zoos would be able to explain their failure to comply with conditions or prove the inspector's initial assessment to be incorrect. If it were the case that all breaches noted could be remedied simply by giving the zoo an "opportunity to be heard", that would suggest that there are serious deficiencies in the inspectors' understanding of the law and breaches were being identified where, in fact, they were not in fact occurring (or reasonable excuse could be provided for them on each occasion). This seemed somewhat unlikely, given the 783 instances identified during the first research period and the total of 1882 during the entire decade under consideration when s.16 sanctions potentially should have been imposed. If it is true, it raises concerns over the expertise of the inspectors.

It is thus unclear why the government believed that the "majority of non-compliance incidents to be resolved quickly between the authorities and the zoo"[59] and, indeed, via what mechanism this informal resolution would be carried out, given that there are clear guidelines for how to deal with non-compliance and the legislation does not grant discretion to local authorities to deal with breaches in any way other than that outlined within the statute. DEFRA confirmed in conversation with the author of this book in 2019 that it has not carried out its own research into compliance or the nature of non-compliance following the publication of its 2010 report (commissioned to ADAS and mentioned previously), so this statement represents a matter of opinion which contradicts the findings of both the 2012 pilot study and the present research. It is difficult to believe that the numerous instances of non-compliance requiring action under s.16 identified as part of the current research were, in fact, misunderstandings and were all resolved without recourse to formal enforcement action.

In fact, as directions are issued in the first instance in tandem with license conditions (indeed, they are issued in order to enforce license conditions), then if DEFRA's view were true that issues were resolved swiftly without recourse for formal action, we would expect to see a significant drop in license conditions being added to the licenses of zoos as a result of this swift, informal resolution process, and particularly those conditions which relate to s.1A (as if they become conditions attached to the license, they should always necessitate a direction too, as long as the original license was correctly issued subject to the s.1A provisions). If there are a high number of license conditions being added to licenses, then it follows that there should be a high number of directions. If the operators have been given opportunity to be heard and convinced the local authority that formal compliance action is unnecessary under s.16A, then they would be issued with *neither* license conditions nor directions.

In the aforementioned letter with regard to the EC complaint, the government department also made the point that the data relating to the 2012 complaint covered 2005–2011 and the majority of it was therefore not reflective of improvements in compliance. The government suggested that they expected there to be significant improvements in enforcement from 2008 onward (though this was not found to be the case in the 2012 pilot study nor for the remainder of the ten-year study period to 2019). In addition, it seems reasonable to assume that, as a result of the specific instructions sent to local authorities in late 2012 as a result of the work of the present author via her role in FFA, whatever reason there was for the lack of enforcement being carried out prior to that date, an improvement should be seen beyond that date.

The government letter stated:

> *The Government has, however, already taken action to clarify and strengthen its published guidance relating to the compliance and enforcement provisions of the Act (see paragraph 10 and Annex E: flowchart 12. See also Annexes J-M of*

the guidance relating to compliance and enforcement issues). We believe that the amended guidance ***removes any possible doubt about the compliance and enforcement provisions of the Act.*** [My emphasis]

Given the government's apparent acceptance that there was a need for clarification of the law in 2012 and its subsequent statement in 2013 that it felt its clarification had removed "any possible doubt" with regard to the way in which the law should be applied, one would expect to see that enforcement in 2014 onward meeting the standards required or, if not, the government taking action to remedy this.

While questions remain over the government's position, it is important to explore the suggestion that enforcement may have been being carried out informally, as suggested. In order to establish whether this was indeed the case, the 27 reports relating to 2014 in the initial study period used as part of this analysis were revisited. An assessment was carried out to consider non-compliance and the theory put forward by DEFRA—that compliance had improved in recent years and that issues were being resolved informally—was tested. This was done by considering the number of instances of non-compliance noted during inspection, the conditions subsequently added to licenses (if DEFRA's view was founded, we would expect to see few conditions added to licenses as issues were being resolved informally). If licenses had been correctly issued and conditions relating to s.1A of the Act were correctly attached to the license at the outset, then any non-compliance with s.1A should lead to a condition *and* a direction.

6.10.3 Case Studies

Of the 27 zoo inspection reports completed in 2014, 18 of them noted non-compliance with areas of s.1A or offenses under s.19.

These 18 zoos were assessed in order to consider DEFRA's assertion that s.16 action was not being taken because issues noted on the day of inspection were being dealt with informally (thus negating the need for formal action, and without the need to add conditions to licenses or implement formal enforcement action by way of issuing a direction).

Inspection reports for the 18 zoos were considered and it was found that there were 104 instances of non-compliance recorded against those zoos during 2014: 75 of the instances of non-compliance should have given rise to action under s.16 of the Act; 5 of the instances of non-compliance noted constitute offenses under s.19 of the Act. If issues were noted during inspection but then not added as license conditions subsequently, this may support DEFRA's suggestion that issues were dealt with informally. It may also support other interpretations, which will be explored in this section.

Of the 18 zoos for which instances of non-compliance were noted, the most recent license was also provided by the relevant councils for three of the zoos. One would expect the license to be amended following an inspection where conditions were recommended and in the event that conditions relating to s.1A were added to the license following the inspection, one would expect to see accompanying s.16A directions if the law is being properly enforced. These licenses provided had 23 conditions attached (combined) in order to remedy the issues noted during the previous inspections. It should be noted that 23 conditions do not necessarily equate to 23 separate instances of non-compliance. Indeed, between the three zoos, one zoo showed eight instances of non-compliance which would give rise to action under either s.16 or s.19 and had 13 new conditions added to the license. One zoo had one instance of non-compliance which would give rise to action under s.16 and one instance of non-compliance which would not give rise to action under s.16 (unless the non-compliance involved breach of an existing condition). One condition was added to the license following inspection. The non-compliance with s.1A was not dealt with by this condition, yet the minor non-compliance was. The report on the final zoo noted one area of non-compliance with s.1A and suggested nine conditions added to the license, none of which addressed the recognized failure to comply with s.1A. The license that was issued following this inspection included the nine suggested conditions and none implementing s.1A or other standard conditions. As licenses must be issued subject to the provisions of s.1A, it is clear that the license was issued incorrectly.

The case of these three zoos highlights that, at least in these cases, it is not true that all issues are dealt with informally, thus doing away with the need to add formal conditions and take action under s.16. As these conditions have been added to the license, and they relate to s.1A, they should be accompanied by a direction under s.16. This is simply not happening. However, with just three zoos in this sample, it is important to consider whether or not this means that DEFRA's position is supported by the other 15 zoos under consideration.

As with the three already considered, there does not appear to be evidence that the reason conditions are not being added to licenses is as a result of swift compliance with concerns.

One zoo (Mainsgill Farm) has 23 instances of non-compliance with s.1A noted during 2014. This inspection followed a period of two years during which, according to council correspondence, the zoo had been operating without a license at all. Rather than use the enforcement tools available within the ZLA 1981 (i.e., directions under s.16 or prosecution under s.19), prior to 2014, the council sent repeated letters to the zoo, demanding compliance. No legal action was taken and, ultimately, the license issued in 2014 simply added the pre-existing conditions as part of a new license. Under the question "have existing license conditions been met?" it was answered that this was inapplicable as this was a "first license". The two years of operating in contravention of the law and clear breach of license conditions from previous reports were not acknowledged and the new license served the purpose of "wiping the slate clean" for the zoo.

A similar situation occurred with the Yorkshire Dales Falconry and Wildlife Centre, whose license lapsed. The local authority first attempted to backdate the license before realizing, following advice from DEFRA, that this was not possible. They then asked the zoo to reapply for a new license. This was treated as a new license inspection and the non-compliance noted in 2014 was not connected to the previous license and therefore does not appear to be deemed a breach of condition. No action was taken against the zoo for operating without a license—an offense under s.19 of the Act.

Another zoo (York Bird of Prey) was noted to have failed to meet existing conditions (an offense under s.19 of the Act and a trigger for action under s.16) in 2014. Rather than take the relevant action, the council extended the timescale allowed for both conditions and took no other enforcement action to remedy non-compliance.

Local authorities failed to provide a license for three of the zoos under consideration (Porfell, The Owl and Falconry Centre and National Marine Aquarium) and so action taken with regard to noted non-compliance post-inspection could not be ascertained.

For the remaining ten zoos under consideration, the licenses provided all pre-dated the inspection reports, suggesting that no update had been made to the license following the inspection and no new conditions had been added. This may support DEFRA's view that the majority of issues are dealt with without the need for new conditions and action under s.16. However, the nature of some of the instances of non-compliance makes it difficult to see how this could be the case. For example, for one zoo (Kirkleatham Owl Centre), a condition recommended during the inspection was included in the report as follows:

> *A program of preventative and curative veterinary care must be developed and recorded. This must include two recorded routine visits annually and must include a program for the regular review of clinical and pathological records.*

This condition seeks to remedy noted non-compliance with the need to provide veterinary care and the need to have in place a system to review pathological and clinical records. Both of these points relate to s.1A of the Act and failure to comply would be a trigger for action under s.16.

In this instance, it would be impossible for this issue to be remedied informally without need for the condition (and direction under s.16) to be issued on because the condition demands action to be carried out over a period of 12 months. This cannot be remedied quickly between the zoo and the local authority, and so this would suggest that the failure to add the condition to the license (and failure to issue the direction) was less a recognition of the non-compliance being dealt with, but a failure to carry out the necessary enforcement action on behalf of the local authority. A further three zoos (Avon Valley, Beale Park, Rutland Falconry) were found to not be providing a "program of preventative or curative veterinary care" and, in the inspection reports, it was recommended that a condition requiring that they do so be added as a condition to the license.

No conditions mandating the provision of a program of preventative and curative veterinary care were added to any of the licenses (despite this being a mandatory s.1A condition), and no direction was issued to any of the three zoos. The absence of a veterinary program is not something which could be considered a minor infraction and is not something which could be resolved informally between the zoo and the authority as it would require assessment and monitoring once implemented. As such, these three case studies do not support DEFRA's view that enforcement is adequate.

Other conditions recommended during the Kirkleatham 2014 inspection could feasibly have been dealt with quickly, and therefore, as there is a lapse in time between the inspection being carried out and the final report (and any subsequent changes to the license) being issued, some minor issues could have been remedied. For example, it was demanded that risk assessments were produced for certain activities, a relatively simple exercise on paper which could be done immediately following the inspection. It seems highly feasible that risk assessments could have been provided to the council and the condition recommended in the inspection report be rendered irrelevant.

For Avon Valley, one of the areas of non-compliance with s.1A was that it was found that the conservation efforts for the collection were inadequate. Again, it is difficult to envisage how this point could be remedied quickly and easily on the day of inspection or after giving the proprietor an "opportunity to be heard" as it is something which would need to be demonstrated and assessed again over a period of time.

Blue Reef Aquarium had a recommended condition that "running hot and cold water to be supplied in the vet room" which was not then added to the license, despite the lack of running water being deemed, by the inspector, as a breach of s.1A. As this would require plumbing work to be carried out, it stands to reason that this is, again, not a point which could simply be remedied informally on the day of inspection, but something which would require planning, work and assessment afterward for compliance. The condition in question was a pre-existing condition which the zoo had already failed to meet at the time of the 2014 inspection. Despite this, no enforcement action was taken when the non-compliance was found and no changes were made to the license to reflect the failure to meet the condition.

Pensthorpe zoo inspection report noted two instances of non-compliance with s.1A, indicated by the inspector marking "No" in response to two separate questions relating to s.1A on the ZOO2 form. However, no notes, recommendations or suggested conditions were then added to the form by the inspector, and it did not appear that the local authority followed the issue up. No conditions were added to Pensthorpe's zoo's license in order to either clarify the breaches or to bring the zoo into compliance.

The final two zoos in this sample were noted to have breached s.1A with regard to failing to document animal escapes. Again, as compliance with this could only be tested over time, then it seems illogical to issue the license without this condition as it is not something that the inspector could assess on the day of inspection as it relates to events that have not (and indeed may not) happen until a future date.

From these 18 case studies, which represent just a small handful of all of those zoos and reports considered, it becomes clear that the suggestion from DEFRA that the lack of enforcement action being carried out against non-compliant zoos could not be attributed to non-compliance being dealt with quickly and informally is not borne out in evidence. Instead, there appear to be a number of different reasons for the lack of enforcement action. In some cases, it seems that the local authority is confident in adding conditions to licenses but does not either understand or comply with the obligation to also take action under s.16, much less even consider taking action under s.19. There is no suggestion in correspondence which would support the idea that issues noted during inspection were being remedied before the issuance of the new/amended license—and instead it appears that, in many cases, no changes are made to licenses over a number of years, despite recognized breaches which logically could not be remedied quickly as compliance would require assessment after a period of time. For example, demanding that four vet visits are carried out each year can only be assessed for compliance after the year has passed. The failure to amend the licenses means that no binding timescale is placed on the zoo to enforce the standards.

There is some evidence to show that, when licenses are allowed to expire, the local authorities do not take action to either prosecute or close the zoo down and, instead, allow for a new license to be issued, which has the effect of "wiping the slate clean" for the zoos in question with regard to previous instances of non-compliance as happened with Mainsgill Farm.

Overall, there is no conclusive evidence which supports DEFRA's assertion that local authorities understand and are delivering their enforcement obligations under the Act. There is a lack of consistency in application of the Act across local authorities and sufficient evidence that the Act is poorly understood.

It seems clear that, on the one hand, there is a lack of understanding of the mandatory nature of action under s.16 of the Act or at least this was the case historically. Since 2012, the local authorities have been explicitly informed of the operation of s.16 and yet there is hardly any evidence of it being used whatsoever. The government's suggestion that directions are not being issued as a result of problems being resolved following local authorities giving zoo operators an opportunity to be heard does not stand up. If it were the case that all issues noted during inspection were resolved without the need for a direction, this would also mean that conditions were not being added to licenses, a theory not borne out in the evidence considered as part of the 18 case studies discussed above.

6.11 South Lakes Safari Zoo

While there has been a distinct lack of evidence to demonstrate how the ZLA 1981 might bring non-compliant zoos into line due to the almost complete absence of enforcement action, there is one case study which may serve to provide important information on this point.

In 2017, the license holder of South Lakes Safari Zoo, which is based within the jurisdiction of Barrow-in-Furness council, applied for a renewal of his license under the ZLA 1981. Inspection reports had shown that South Lakes Safari Zoo had had a mortality rate of over 12%, with 486 animals dying in less than four years. This, plus concerns that the management structure of the zoo was inadequate and failure to follow two directions issued previously to the zoo, led the council to refuse the license under s.4(2A)(3), which states that a license may be refused if "[the council] are not satisfied that the standards if accommodation, staffing or management are adequate for the proper care and wellbeing of the animals or any of them or otherwise for the proper conduct of the zoo".

At that time, following inspections which had raised concerns over various elements of the zoo's operation, Mr. Gill., the license holder, had reportedly stepped down from the day-to-day running of the zoo but remained named as the license applicant.

While the decision to refuse was appealed, the zoo was allowed to stay open. After a somewhat protracted period of deliberation by the licensing committee, a fresh license was granted to a new license holder—Karen Brewer—in May 2017. By this time, the zoo was operating under the name of a new company: Cumbrian Zoo Company Ltd. Criticisms were leveled at the decision to grant a fresh license, in large part because Brewer, the CEO of the new zoo company, was also the previous CEO under Gill. While inspectors took into account the previous issues and conditions on the former zoo's license, what was granted from a legal perspective was a license such as that which would be granted to a brand-new zoo—it was a clean slate. Campaigners expressed deep concern that, while the name on the license had changed, it appeared to be "business and usual" as the management team of the new company was largely made up of the same people and, in particular, that the CEO had been expressly named by former employees are being directly involved in the prior animal welfare issues.[60] In addition, the new zoo company was leasing the land from Mr. Gill for a period of eight years from the time of the grant of the license, as he retained ownership of the land itself.

No charges were brought against the zoo itself under the ZLA 1981 or AWA 2006 and the entire process was dealt with by the council's licensing committee. This was despite suggestions from zoo inspectors that a prosecution should be mounted. Of some of the animals who died over the period in question, this included two baby snow leopards whose bodies were found partially consumed by the other leopards in their enclosure, a tortoise who died by electrocution, after becoming entangled in the electric fencing, a rhino crushed to death by her partner, lemurs and birds being run over by the zoo's miniature train, and rat poison killing at least two animals.

It is difficult to know how another council might have dealt with the same process and so this one case study might not be indicative of how a similar issue might play out at another zoo or in another jurisdiction. That said, it seems clear that, if a zoo where so many animals died, and where there were so many serious welfare concerns for the animals—not to mention prior history involving staff safety[61]—can avoid closure, the ability of the ZLA 1981 to protect animals in practice is questionable. In addition, that the zoo and its management also avoided prosecution under the AWA 2006 perhaps speaks to the reluctance of councils to pursue criminal prosecution in cases where animal welfare is compromised and where they have the opportunity to deal with it via administrative processes such as those laid out in the ZLA 1981. Taken as a whole, the case of South Lakes Safari Zoo appears to have been a process of ensuring continued operation of the business, in spite of very serious breaches of the ZLA 1981 and, likely, the AWA 2006, in place of securing meaningful protection for the animals.

6.12 Conclusion

Having considered in detail the operation, application and enforcement of the ZLA 1981, a number of weaknesses have been noted with lack of enforcement and understanding of the Act on the part of local authorities being the most conspicuous. It appears that reassurances made by government officials in 2013, that the Act is being adequately enforced, are not borne out in evidence. Indeed, despite insisting there was no problem with enforcement, the government itself took steps in 2019 to clarify again the legal enforcement tools available to councils by reinstating training and updating the ZOO2 form to include explicit instructions relating to directions.[62] Should enforcement be improved, the impact upon animal welfare might be significant. Notwithstanding the arguably flawed example of South Lakes, zoos that persistently fail to meet legal standards could be held accountable and forced to meet standards or otherwise face closure. As a result of this, the standards of the industry should, theoretically, improve as the worst performing businesses either improve or cease to operate. The animals in the case of zoo closure become the responsibility of the local authority, which would then take on the duty to ensure that they are properly cared for, rehomed or otherwise disposed of.[63]

Notes

1. Unless otherwise stated, reference to the Zoo Licensing Act 1981 from this point onward refers to the Act in its current form.
2. S.1(1).
3. Outlined in Sect. 4 of Chap. 4.
4. S.4(3).
5. S.14(1).
6. S.14(2).
7. S.14(1)(a).
8. S.14(2).
9. S.14(1)(b).
10. Defined as "any species listed in Appendix I of CITES and/or listed in the following categories of the IUCN Red List of Threatened species (Extinct in the wild; Critically Endangered; Endangered; Vulnerable)" (Zoo Licensing Act 1981: Guide to the Act's Provisions, DEFRA, 2012).
11. Defined as "any species listed in categories 1 and/or 2 of Appendix 12 of the Secretary of State's Standards of Modern Zoo Practice" (DEFRA (2017). Zoo Licensing Act 1981: Guide to the Act's Provisions. London: DEFRA. Annex C.
12. DEFRA (2017). Zoo Licensing Act 1981: Guide to the Act's Provisions. London: DEFRA.
13. S.1(3).
14. For example, Secretary of State's Standards of Modern Zoo Practice and Zoo Licensing Act 1981: A Guide to the Act's Provisions, DEFRA (2012).
15. S.8.
16. European Council Directive 1999/22/EC.
17. DEFRA. (2003). Government Circular 02/2003—Zoo Licensing Act 1981, London: DEFRA [Available at: (http://archive.DEFRA.gov.uk/wildlife-pets/zoos/documents/zoo-gc022003.pdf].
18. S.16A.

19. S.16A(2)(c).
20. S.16B.
21. S.5(7).
22. S.5(5A).
23. S.16B(4).
24. S.16A(2) demands that the authority **shall** make a direction in the event that a condition is breached and s. 16B demands that the authority **shall** make a zoo closure direction if the original direction is not complied with (my emphasis). Other parts of the legislation clearly state that the authority "may" take enforcement action. The use of the word "shall" makes it clear that the authority is required to act on breaches of conditions.
25. S.8(1).
26. S.10(3).
27. S.12.
28. S.11.
29. S.9A.
30. S.5(1).
31. S.5(2).
32. Legally, a Renewal Inspection is a type of Periodical Inspection and therefore is governed by s.10(3) of the ZLA. Practically, and in relation to inspection reports, DEFRA splits this type of inspection into two. For the purpose of this report, and for ease of interpretation of the data, any referral to a "Periodical Inspection" is made in reference to the inspections carried out during year 1 (for a four-year license) and year 3 (for a six-year license) and any referral to a "Renewal Inspection" is made in reference to the inspection carried out no later than six months before the expiry of a license. This differentiation has no bearing on the interpretation of the data or legal consequences flowing from them.
33. S.10(3)(a).
34. S.10(3)(b).
35. Either 10(3)(a) or 10(3)(b), dependent on the duration of the license to which it relates.
36. S.12(1).
37. S.11.
38. Available at: https://www.gov.uk/government/uploads/system/uploads/attachment_data/file/408849/zoo3-licence-inspection-report.pdf.

39. Available at: https://www.gov.uk/government/uploads/system/uploads/attachment_data/file/408848/zoo2-inspection-report-form.pdf.
40. S.10(5).
41. S.11(5).
42. DEFRA. (2003). Government Circular 02/2003—Zoo Licensing Act 1981, Annex to Circular, Clause 75. [Available at: http://archive.DEFRA.gov.uk/wildlife-pets/zoos/documents/zoo-gc022003.pdf].
43. On the proviso that the original license was correctly issued subject to the mandatory s.1A conditions.
44. For example, the Welfare of Wild Animals in Traveling Circuses (England) Regulations 2012.
45. Casamitjana, J. (2012). Inspecting Zoos: A study of the official zoo inspection system in England from 2005 to 2011. The Captive Animal's Protection Society, Manchester, p. 7.
46. Draper, C. & Harris, S. (2012), 'The Assessment of Animal Welfare in British Zoos by Government-Appointed Inspectors'. Animals, vol. 2, p. 507.
47. S.1A(a) Zoo Licensing Act 1981.
48. Draper, C. and Harris, S. (2012). The Assessment of Animal Welfare in British Zoos by Government-Appointed Inspectors. Animals, 2(4), pp. 507–528.
49. Casamitjana, J. (2012). Inspecting Zoos: A study of the official zoo inspection system in England from 2005 to 2011. The Captive Animal's Protection Society, Manchester.
50. ADAS (2010). Review of the implementation of the Zoo Licensing Act 1981 in local authorities in England and Wales. [online] London: DEFRA. Available at: http://randd.defra.gov.uk/Document.aspx?Document=ADASReviewoflocalauthorities%27implementationoftheZooLicensingAct.pdf [Accessed 4 Nov. 2017].
51. Draper, C. and Harris, S. (2012). The Assessment of Animal Welfare in British Zoos by Government-Appointed Inspectors. Animals, 2(4), pp. 507–528.
52. Casamitjana, J. (2012). Inspecting Zoos: A study of the official zoo inspection system in England from 2005 to 2011. The Captive Animal's Protection Society, Manchester, p. 9.
53. ADAS (2010). Review of the implementation of the Zoo Licensing Act 1981 in local authorities in England and Wales. [online] London:

DEFRA. p. i. Available at: http://randd.defra.gov.uk/Document.aspx?Document=ADASReviewoflocalauthorities%27implementationoftheZooLicensingAct.pdf [Accessed 4 Nov. 2017].
54. Ibid., p. 27.
55. Ibid., p. ii.
56. The aforementioned "Guidance to the Act's Provisions".
57. Confirmed in a meeting between the author and DEFRA officials in late 2012.
58. Letter available in full as part of FOI disclosure documents on DEFRA website: https://www.gov.uk/government/uploads/system/uploads/attachment_data/file/283424/6109-doc1.pdf.
59. Ibid.
60. Freedom for Animals. 2017. Council Grants Licence for South Lakes Safari Zoo to Remain Open. [online]. Available at: https://www.freedomforanimals.org.uk/news/council-grants-licence-for-south-lakes-safari-zoo-to-remain-open [Accessed 21 March 2020].
61. BBC News. 2016. Tiger Maul Death Zoo Fined For Breaches. [online] Available at: https://www.bbc.com/news/uk-england-cumbria-36501417 [Accessed 21 March 2020].
62. Pers. Corr. Author and DEFRA representatives, October 2019.
63. S.13(8) Zoo Licensing Act 1981.

7

International Perspectives: Snapshots of Zoos from Other Jurisdictions

7.1 Comparisons of Zoos in Other Countries

The ZLA 1981, while originally implemented as a result of domestic legislative policy, was updated in 2003 in order to incorporate the demands of the EU Zoo Directive 1999/22 (see Sect. 4 in Chap. 5 for more detail). The Directive created an obligation on all zoos within the European Union to implement a system of licensing. The Directive has been transposed to varying degrees in relevant member states. This chapter considers case studies from a handful of different European countries whose implementation may be considered either problematic or progressive.

Despite being implemented in April 2002, a number of member states delayed in its introduction with most member states having published their new or amended zoo legislation by 2005. At that time, implementation in Germany, Italy and Spain was delayed further due to the need for transposition at both national and then regional levels. Spain's continued delay in effective implementation led to a fine in 2008.[1]

E. Tyson, *Licensing Laws and Animal Welfare*, The Palgrave Macmillan Animal Ethics Series, https://doi.org/10.1007/978-3-030-50042-9_7

The 2011 *EU Zoo Inquiry*, a thorough analysis of implementation of the EC Zoos Directive, carried out by the Born Free Foundation, found that a number of member states had not fully transposed, or interpreted correctly, the EC Zoos Directive into National Law. Those countries were Austria, Belgium, Cyprus, Estonia, Latvia, Greece, Poland, Slovenia, Portugal, the Czech Republic and Malta. The various countries had failed in different areas of implementation, including incorrect interpretation of Article 1 of the Directive ("the role of zoos in the conservation of biodiversity"), incorrect interpretation of Article 2 of the Directive (the definition of a "zoo"), inaccurate and sometimes incomplete interpretation of Article 3 of the Directive ("requirements applicable to zoos"), omission of the requirement of Article 4(2) of the Directive to undertake on-site inspections, and omission of the requirements of Article 6 of the Directive concerning zoo closure and the implementation of contingency plans for the animals.

The following section explores the approaches—in some cases erroneous and in some cases progressive—of different countries in their implementation of the EC Zoos Directive as a means of comparison with the foregone research and analysis.

7.1.1 Greece

In 2017, the Pan-Hellenic Federation for Animal Welfare highlighted concerns over the Greek government's failure to implement the EU Zoos Directive. After an initial delay, Greece did implement the Directive but then in 2007 adopted a ministerial decision (Gov. 396/21.3.2007) which effectively ruled the majority of zoos in the country out of licensing obligations. On examination of the legislation in place, the Greek government appeared to have elected a somewhat bizarre and legally absurd interpretation of the EU Zoos Directive. While the Directive demands that any place that exhibits wild animals to the public for more than seven days a year must be subject to zoo licensing, there is no specific guidance as to how many animals need to be displayed in order to warrant a license. There is discretion granted to member states on this point, presumably to ensure, as guidance in England outlines, that, for example, doctor's offices with fish tanks are not captured by the legislation (which they could be if it was interpreted literally). This discretion is necessary but Greece appears to have taken it to absurd levels.

Attica Zoo in Greece is home to over 1600 animals and is the only licensed zoo in the country. This is despite dozens of establishments which appear to fit the EU's definition of zoo being in operation. The reason that these establishments avoid the need for licensing is because the Greek government have set an inordinately high number of animals (based on the number of animals in Attica Zoo) as the baseline. So, rather than zoo licensing applying to any establishment which displays wild animals to the public for seven days of the year or more, Greece has effectively mandated that any establishment which displays over the same number of wild animals (or more) than Attica Zoo, to the public for seven days of the year or more, required a license. Of course, most zoos do not meet this threshold. The Pan-Hellenic Federation for Animal Welfare are in the process of complaining to the EU on this matter with the hope that the EU will force the Greek government to amend the legislation and capture all relevant zoos in future.

According the Born Free EU zoo inquiry, completed in 2012, "the competent authorities are working to make the necessary changes to the zoo legislation". Despite this, the situation remains unchanged at the time of writing in January 2020.

7.1.2 Ireland

Following publicity surrounding the lack of regulation of "mobile zoos", brought about partly by a campaign run by the author in her capacity as Director of Freedom for Animals following successful prosecution of a mobile zoo in England under the Animal Welfare Act, a review of zoo legislation in Ireland led to the capturing of mobile zoos under the national zoo legislation. It had long been argued by this author to the Zoo Expert Committee and DEFRA that mobile zoos should be captured under the ZLA 1981 and a detailed legal analysis was submitted to Zoo Expert Committee members by the author of this book in 2014 to highlight the case. While DEFRA chose to pursue lesser licensing for mobile zoos in England, Ireland has now adopted a model which brings mobile zoos under the mantel of the EU Zoos Directive, making it significantly more comprehensive (and, arguably, progressive) than the English legislation.

7.1.3 Wales

Wales has, like England, chosen to exclude mobile zoos from its zoo legislation and is currently consulting on draft legislation which looks very similar to the AWR 2018. Like the English licensing legislation, while these new regulations explicitly exempt zoos from their remit, the new Welsh draft legislation appears to create a conflict with the ZLA 1981 in that the definition used to describe activities requiring a license for exhibition of animals is very similar and, arguably, indistinguishable, from the definition of a zoo.

The draft regulations define licensable activities as follows:

(a) *keeping animals in Wales where those animals are being used for exhibition for educational or entertainment purposes,*
(b) *training animals in Wales where those animals are being used for exhibition for educational or entertainment purposes, or*
(c) *exhibiting animals in Wales for educational or entertainment purposes.*

It is unclear, again, how one would differentiate between a standard zoo which is defined as "an establishment where wild animals (as defined by section 21) are kept for exhibition to the public otherwise than for purposes of a circus (as so defined) and otherwise than in a pet shop (as so defined)" and which is a "zoo, to which members of the public have access, with or without charge for admission, on more than seven days in any period of 12 consecutive months" and one of the establishments covered by the proposed licensing regulations.

Businesses which would clearly fall outside of zoo licensing would be those that only exhibit domesticated animals but, beyond that, it is difficult to see how the Welsh government intends to exempt businesses which, otherwise, look and are defined in almost identical terms as zoos, as something different (and thus give them lesser licensing demands).

The outcome of the consultation has not yet been published at the time of writing (January 2020) and so whether the legislation will move forward in its current form is not yet known.

7.1.4 Bulgaria

In Bulgaria, Varna dolphinarium is considered by the authorities to be a circus rather than a zoo. While it has been argued that dolphinaria are similar to circuses (as indeed, in the opinion of the author are zoos in general) in that they serve no real educational or conservation purpose, every other EU member state has interpreted the Directive as including dolphinaria, with the exception of Bulgaria. It is understood that this is the only case in the EU. This is problematic as, much like mobile zoos, there appears to be a line being drawn by authorities which looks to the intent of a business in place of the practicality of it. Put differently, the Bulgarian government considered that if the *intention* is to simply show dolphins for entertainment, then it can be considered to be a circus. This categorically fails as the EU Zoos Directive is worded in such a way that it demands that anywhere which displays wild animalsS to the public *must* fulfill conservation and education criteria. It is not acceptable for a place which displays wild animals for entertainment to simply state that it doesn't want or intend to be a zoo and thus effectively exempt itself from zoo licensing. If this were the case, the EU Directive would have no power and zoos in everything but name could simply exempt themselves from the rigors of licensing.

Note

1. 2012. THE EU ZOO INQUIRY 2011: An Evaluation of the Implementation and Enforcement of EC Directive 1999/22, Relating to the Keeping of Animals in Zoos. [online] Horsham: The Born Free Foundation. Available at: https://www.bornfree.org.uk/storage/media/content/files/Publications/FINDINGS%20%26%20RECOMMENDATIONS.pdf [Accessed 21 March 2020].

8

Secondary Licensing Legislation: The Regulation of the Use of Wild Animals in Traveling Circuses in England

Having considered the regulation of zoos in England and how licensing of zoos via primary legislation might serve to protect animal welfare, this chapter provides an introduction to the second piece of legislation under consideration as part of this research—the, now repealed, Welfare of Wild Animals in Travelling Circuses (England) Regulations 2012 (WWATC 2012), beginning with the history of the industry itself and the move toward its regulation in recent years.

The tradition of using animals in circuses in England dates back over 200 years. The "heyday" of the traveling circus was around the 1950s and 1960s. At this time, there were dozens of circuses traveling the country with menageries of animals totaling an estimated 200 individuals. Animal species included elephants, lions, tigers, bears, monkeys, zebras and camels.[1]

As a result of lobbying by animal welfare advocates, the use of wild animals in circuses came under scrutiny as it was claimed that the conditions in which the animals were kept, coupled with the training and performance elements of circus life for them, compromised their welfare to the extent that their use in these businesses should be prohibited.[2] The first attempt to see animal circuses outlawed was in 1965, when Lord

E. Tyson, *Licensing Laws and Animal Welfare*, The Palgrave Macmillan Animal Ethics Series, https://doi.org/10.1007/978-3-030-50042-9_8

Somers, then the president of Freedom for Animals (FFA), brought forward a Private Member's Bill to ban the use of wild animals in circuses. The proposal was defeated at the time by 45 votes against to 31 in favor. The Undersecretary of State said at the time that an investigation had been carried out in 1951 which showed no evidence of cruelty.[3] It should perhaps be noted at this point that the law at this stage, which was still the Protection of Animals Act 1911, did not make demands of those responsible for animals that they provide for the welfare of those animals. This only became law in 2007, on the introduction of the AWA 2006.

The parliamentary process which led to the introduction of the WWATC 2012 to govern wild animal circuses began in 2005, triggered by the passage of the Animal Welfare Bill. A public consultation carried out in 2009/2010 saw 94.5% of respondents support an outright ban on the use of wild animals in circuses.[4] In March 2012, a ban was promised by the government but was not implemented until January 2020, despite the deadline for implementation being set by government for the end of 2015. The WWATC 2012 were, therefore, implemented as a temporary measure while the ban was being processed through Parliament.

8.1 The Size and Shape of the Traveling Circus Industry

Over the years, campaigning for a ban continued and demonstrations and falling visitor numbers to shows with wild animals led to the lowest ever number of circuses using wild animals (4) and the lowest number of wild animals being used (~30–40) by around 2011, when the proposals for the WWATC 2012 were first mooted. Two of the circuses touring in 2012 with wild animals (Gifford's, which employed just one bird of prey in its 2012 season, and the Great British Circus, which toured with up to half of all the animals being used at any one time in English circuses) removed wild animals from their shows before its implementation. By the time the regulations were brought into force in January 2013, the number of circuses operating with wild animals had dropped to two circuses and 21 individual animals; however, later the same year, a new wild animal act was moved to England from Ireland, prompting suggestions that numbers of wild animals being used (and numbers of circuses using them) may, in fact, increase as a result of the perceived legitimately regulated status that circuses were now afforded.[5] In addition to the animals belonging to the circuses in question, other circuses could enter the United Kingdom from Europe or acts which are not affiliated with any particular circus might be hired in for any particular season. It has been the case in the past that circuses have hired in elephant acts, for example.[6] These animals would be brought to the United Kingdom by their trainers and travel with the circus for all or part of a season. In this way, the number of animals could fluctuate.

The English circus season usually begins in around March/April when the circus would leave their permanent base or "winter quarters" and travel the country. The season usually ends in around October of the same year when the circus and the animals would return to their winter quarters. The circuses usually visit one (or sometimes two) venues per week and perform twice a day (usually just once on the day of departure). Animals might be employed in the shows as "acts" where they perform tricks or stunts with the human performers. Big cats would go through routines whereby they sat on pedestals, rolled over, jumped through hoops, and so on. Elephants would sit or turn on pedestals, swing performers from their trunks, "dance" or make formations with other elephants in the show. Other animals might perform no obvious trick and simply be walked around the circus ring while people watch.[7] Some animals were used for photos (an elephant which traveled with Bobby Roberts circus until 2011, for example, did not perform for her last years with the circus) or to offer rides for children (e.g., the camel used by Circus Mondao was used for this purpose). Other animals simply travel as part of the menagerie. Some circuses would refer to the animal collection as a "zoo" and invite people to come and see the animals after the show for an extra charge.

Circus sites vary from town to town and may comprise a large field with amenities or a car park or other hard standing. The differences in location and type of site would have implications for the welfare of the animals involved.

8.2 The Introduction of the Welfare of Wild Animals in Travelling Circuses (England) Regulations 2012

Prior to the introduction of the Regulations, wild animals in circuses were protected, in theory, by the AWA 2006 which, broadly speaking, meant that circus owners should take measures to protect and promote the welfare of the animals under their care and also to ensure that the animals were not subjected to unnecessary suffering. If it were found that the owners were not providing the standard of care required to ensure that welfare needs were properly met to the extent required by good practice, then a prosecution could be mounted under the Act. The person responsible for the animal could be held liable for failure to comply with the provisions (s.9), as would they and any other person who inflicted unnecessary suffering on an animal (s.4).

Two arguments were leveled against the suggestion that animals in circuses were effectively protected by the AWA 2006 prior to the introduction of the regulations. The first was that, by its very nature, the traveling circus environment compromises the welfare of animals (and particularly wild animals) to the extent that their welfare needs could not be met in a traveling circus, regardless of standards imposed. This argument speaks to concerns already raised in Chap. 3 with regard to the demand that animal welfare needs are met only to the extent required by good practice and the idea that it is possible that the welfare needs of wild animal simply cannot be met when held "under the control of man", as discussed previously. The fundamental argument posed by those opposed to the regulations was that even the very best practice within the circus industry still imposed inevitable conditions upon animals which run contrary to their welfare need being met (predominantly the lack of appropriate living conditions, lack of natural social groupings, regular transport and training and performance to carry out unnatural behaviors—all of which are necessary parts of life for wild animals in circuses).[8]

The second argument to refute the suggestion that animals in circuses were adequately protected by the AWA 2006 was that it was near impossible to know whether the welfare needs of the animals were being met in traveling circuses due to the fact that the businesses operated as a "closed shop". While animals may be seen by the public during the daily performances for the short period of time that they appeared in the circus ring, the lives of the animals at all other times, and their treatment, was carried on predominantly behind closed doors and away from the public eye.

The "closed shop" argument was fueled by at least some evidence of animals being treated badly in circuses being released following undercover investigations into the industry. A number of investigations have been carried out by animal protection groups over the last few decades and have uncovered evidence of poor practice and some deliberate animal abuse in some circuses (in the United Kingdom and abroad). For example, undercover filming carried out in 2011 by one animal protection group in the United Kingdom showed that an elephant in a circus was shackled continuously by the ankles for up to three weeks and beaten on numerous occasions by a member of staff.[9] The cruel treatment was carried out at the circus' winter quarters and the treatment would not have come to light had it not been for the investigation. Charges were brought against the owner of the circus and he was convicted of three offences under s.4 of the AWA 2006 (causing unnecessary suffering).[10]

It should be noted that the arguments put forward by those who were advocating the ban were not based around the accusation that all circuses were cruelly beating their animals or inflicting suffering, as prohibited by s.4, on their animals. Instead, the argument was that the welfare needs of the animals set out in s.9 could not be met, regardless of the level of care that the animals were offered and even in the absence of overt, deliberately inflicted, cruelty.

In response to the case of the elephant and a number of years of concerted campaigning by other groups, the government announced, in March 2012, that they would introduce a ban on the use of wild animals in traveling circuses by the end of 2015 though, in practice, the ban was not introduced until 2020. In the meantime, they planned to develop an interim licensing regime which would "protect wild animals in circuses".[11]

The WWATC 2012 was introduced in January 2013 using powers granted to the Secretary of State under s.13 of the AWA 2006. Wild animals in traveling circuses in England were still protected by the provisions of the Act generally, and parts of the licensing regime introduced in early 2013 imposed additional obligations upon circus proprietors which, arguably, had the potential to improve welfare provision. For example, circus owners were required to develop and deliver care plans for each animal and group of animals and keep daily records; they had to provide tour itineraries to the authorities, formally identify which people look after the animals and devise detailed retirement plans for the animals in question. While failure to comply with these provisions would not, in itself, result in poor animal welfare, it seemed clear that introducing these aspects of planning, monitoring and increased scrutiny may help to better predict and manage potential shortcomings and thus help to prevent welfare offences occurring in the first instance.

The regulations came into force on 20 January 2013 with their stated purposes as follows:

> *[To] introduce a set of minimum welfare standards for all 'wild' animals (meaning an animal belonging to a species which is not normally domesticated in Great Britain) used by travelling circuses in England. These standards will be enforced by DEFRA through a licensing scheme.*[12]

It was confirmed in detailed correspondence between Freedom for Animals, Born Free, BVA, RSPCA and government officials that the intention of the legislation is to ensure the welfare of animals both on the road and in winter quarters.[13] This was formally confirmed again in September 2012, in a meeting with Freedom for Animals, Born Free and the BVA.[14] The importance of winter quarters being included is that this is where the animals were away from the public eye, and this is where the training was carried out. Some of the worst documented abuses of animals in circuses have been carried out in winter quarters and exposed by undercover investigation.[15]

The Secretary of State for the Environment at the time the regulations were introduced, Caroline Spelman, stated that the intention was a tough licensing regime which introduces additional safeguards to protect wild animals in circuses.[16]

8.3 Schedule of Conditions

A schedule of conditions followed the main body of the regulations, and lists ten criteria relating to the use of wild animals in circus which must be met if a license is to be granted, as per s.4(1)(a) of the regulations. These criteria range from record-keeping to the provision of veterinary care and welfare of animals during transport.

8.4 Guidance on the Welfare of Wild Animals in Travelling Circuses (Regulations) 2012

The conditions laid out in the schedule were relatively broad, arguably because they must apply to any and all species of wild animal kept by any traveling circus which ranged from reptiles such as snakes to mammals such as elephants. The guidance was intended to offer more information on the application of the regulations and "was intended to help the operator of a travelling circus that has wild animals, or any other interested party, understand the action that should be taken to comply with licensing conditions".[17]

The guidance also included specific guidance for certain animals deemed to have specific requirements when kept in circuses. Specific guidance was provided for big cats,[18] elephants,[19] reptiles,[20] sea lions[21] and ungulates.[22] Information was provided under the headings environment, diet, healthcare, display, training and performance, behavior, and transport. Not all criteria were covered for each type of animal. Specific instruction on display, training and performance, for example, was only provided for elephants.

This chapter has explored the development of regulation for circuses which use wild animals in England. In the next chapter, the way in which the regulations are enforced will be considered.

Notes

1. Captiveanimals.org. (n.d.). Our history. [online] Available at: http://www.captiveanimals.org/about-us/our-history [Accessed 24 Nov. 2017].
2. *Ibid.*
3. The Age. (1965). *Anti-Circus Bill Rejected.* London. Available at: http://news.google.com/newspapers?nid=1300&dat=19650218&id=GBwRAAAAIBAJ&sjid=SpUDAAAAIBAJ&pg=5043,3091196 [Accessed 1 Sep. 2014].
4. See House of Commons Library, (2016). Research Briefing Number CBP05992, House of Commons Library: London. Available at: http://researchbriefings.files.parliament.uk/documents/SN05992/SN05992.pdf [Accessed 1 Nov. 2017].
5. Captive Animals Protection Society. (2013). Breaking News: Big cats have joined English circus. [online] Available at: https://www.captive-animals.org/news/2013/08/4540 [Accessed 28 Dec. 2017].
6. For example, Courtney Brothers' circus hired Joy Gartner's elephant act in 2013, see http://www.irishcircuses.org/wp-content/uploads/2012/08/Ring-of-Cruelty-2-Summary-Report.pdf.
7. See http://www.irishcircuses.org/wp-content/uploads/2012/08/Ring-of-Cruelty-2-Summary-Report.pdf.
8. For example, see https://www.bva.co.uk/uploadedFiles/Content/News,_campaigns_and_policies/Policies/Ethics_and_welfare/circuses_joint_briefing_on_draft_Regs_Oct2012.pdf.
9. Wilkes, D. (2012). Owners of Britain's last circus elephant Anne accused of chaining her up for 24 hours a day and allowing staff to beat her with a pitchfork. [online] Mail Online. Available at: http://www.dailymail.co.uk/news/article-2235309/Owners-Britains-circus-elephant-Anne-accused-chaining-24-hours-day-allowing-staff-beat-pitchfork.html [Accessed 24 Nov. 2017].
10. BBC News. (2012). Elephant abuse circus boss guilty. [online] Available at: http://www.bbc.co.uk/news/uk-england-20464605 [Accessed 24 Nov. 2017].
11. HC Deb, 19 May 2011, c27WS.
12. Welfare of Wild Animals in Travelling Circuses (England) Regulations, Explanatory Memorandum.
13. Pers. Corr. between author and government officials in her then capacity as Director of CAPS.

14. A meeting attended by the author in her then capacity as Director of CAPS.
15. For example, the Anne the Elephant case mentioned previously.
16. HC Deb, 19 May 2011, c27WS.
17. DEFRA (2012). Guidance on the Welfare of Wild Animals in Travelling Circuses (England) Regulations 2012. London: DEFRA. p. 1.
18. Ibid., p. 47.
19. Ibid., p. 49.
20. Ibid., p. 52.
21. Ibid., p. 54.
22. Ibid., p. 46.

9

Enforcing the Welfare of Wild Animals in Travelling Circuses (England) Regulations 2012

The previous chapter considered the wider purpose and application of WWATC 2012, including the historical background to their introduction. The following section will consider the practical application of the regulations with a view to understand whether or not these regulations were effective in practice. This will, in turn, inform analysis of the Animal Welfare (Licensing of Activities Involving Animals) (England) Regulations 2018.

9.1 The Operation of the Welfare of Wild Animals in Travelling Circuses (England) Regulations 2012

Interpretations of terms were dealt with by s.2 of the regulations.

Section 3 identified the use of wild animals in traveling circus as an activity which was licensable under s.13(1) of the AWA 2006.

E. Tyson, *Licensing Laws and Animal Welfare*, The Palgrave Macmillan Animal Ethics Series, https://doi.org/10.1007/978-3-030-50042-9_9

Section 4 outlined the process for application and grant of a license. A traveling circus which intended to use wild animals in its shows must first apply to Secretary of State, providing all relevant information. The Secretary of State would grant or renew the license only if satisfied that all licensing conditions would be met and payment of fees had been received. No license could be granted before the circus had been inspected.

Any license could be granted for up to three years. The decision to refuse a license had to be given in writing and had to explain the reasons for refusal as well as grounds of appeal. In the guidance to the regulations, it stated that first licenses would be granted for one year. In practice, no license of more than one year was granted during the lifetime of the regulations.

Section 5 outlined a list of people who were not entitled to apply for a license by virtue of disqualification under different statutes. If a license was granted to a person disqualified under the relevant statutes, it automatically became invalid.

Section 6 dealt with temporary transfer of a license following the death of a license holder, allowing 3 months for the license to be formally transferred and 28 days for the Secretary of State to be notified of the death.

Section 7 stated that the Secretary of State could take such steps as considered necessary to ensure compliance with license conditions. What those steps might have been, other than suspension of license and eventual revocation in the case of ongoing non-compliance, were not made clear there or in the accompanying guidance to the regulations.

Section 8 outlined fees payable for the license and for the inspections, whose costs were borne by the circus.

Sections 9–12 dealt with license suspension and reinstatement, and s.13 dealt with full revocation of a license. Section 14 offered license holders the opportunity to appeal against refusal to renew a license or suspension or revocation of an existing license.

Section 15 stated that the regulations must be reviewed before the end of a five-year period.

9.2 The Ability to Enforce the Welfare of Wild Animals in Travelling Circuses (England) Regulations 2012

Given that, as mentioned above, one of the major concerns of animal protection advocates and vets lobbying for stricter controls over circuses (and in most cases an outright prohibition on the use of wild animals in circuses, which has now been implemented) was that any measures taken to regulate circuses must ensure that winter quarters were effectively captured, the way in which the WWATC 2012 were drafted appeared problematic. Concerns were raised during the passage of the draft regulations that the proposed method of suspension was unenforceable as there was no way in which a circus proprietor could comply with the suspension without finding him/herself in breach of the regulations. The issue with enforcement relating to process of license suspension can be outlined as follows (taken from government briefing document authored by me in September 2012):

> In the event that a license was suspended, the circus proprietor was not permitted to "operate a travelling circus" unless and until the suspension is lifted. The process for suspension was outlined in sections 9–15 of the regulations but it would appear that suspensions could not be practically enforced for the reasons outlined below.
>
> Considering the definition of "travelling circus" in the regulations (below), it is clear that the activity of operating a travelling circus includes *both* taking animals on tour and presenting them in shows and also simply keeping animals associated with the circus at any site, such as in winter quarters.

Interpretations of terms were dealt with by s.2 of the regulations with "travelling circus" defined as:

(a) *a circus—*

(i) *which travels from place to place for the purpose of giving performances, displays or exhibitions, and*

(ii) *as part of which wild animals are kept or introduced (whether for the purpose of performance, display or otherwise); and*

(b) *any place where a wild animal associated with such a circus is kept*

With this in mind, when a license was suspended, it is unclear what action a circus proprietor could have taken to ensure that they were compliant with the suspension. Common sense suggests that, if a license was suspended, there were a number of potential steps that could be taken to put the suspension into practice:

1. If the circus was on tour at the time, it stopped performances until the license was reinstated. The animals remained where they were.
2. If the circus was on tour at the time, it continued performances but did not use wild animals in the show.
3. If the circus was on tour at the time, the animals were returned to winter quarters.
4. If the circus was on tour at the time, the animals were moved somewhere else during the term of the suspension.
5. If the circus was not on tour, the animals were removed from winter quarters and held somewhere else during the suspension.

This creates a cyclical situation as options 1–3 all constituted "operating a travelling circus" for the purpose of the regulations and thus allowing any of these options to be fulfilled in the event of a suspension would have either put the circus proprietor immediately in breach of the suspension or rendered the suspension meaningless. Cognoscente of the fact that any place where an animal associated with a traveling circus was kept also required a license under the regulations, it would also appear that options 4 and 5 were equally unworkable as, while the license is suspended, the circus proprietor was effectively disallowed from keeping any animal associated with the traveling circus in any place without that activity being interpreted as operating a traveling circus and, thus, placing the proprietor in breach of the regulations (by virtue of "operating a travelling circus" during a suspension).

The only apparent option available to the circus proprietor in the event of a suspension would have been to move the animals to the site of another licensed circus. The Secretary of State was required to have 14 days' notice if a wild animal was introduced to any circus. This would have meant that moving animals from one circus to another would have required notice—particularly if the circus that was holding the animals temporarily did not, at that time, have provision for the specific species. Given that suspensions came into effect immediately, this was not a practical solution. In addition, and given that there were only two licensed traveling circuses in the United Kingdom at the time the regulations came into effect, the practical likelihood of one circus taking on the animals of another in the case of a suspension would likely have been fraught with complications and most probably unworkable.

In effect, this meant that during suspension, unless the circus removed the animals permanently from the business (so that they could no longer be considered to be "animals associated with the circus"), the circus could not put itself in a position whereby it was not "operating a travelling circus" and thus was likely to find itself in breach of the regulations and liable for prosecution under s.13(6) of the AWA 2006.

Revocation of license would not have had the same implications because, once the license was revoked, the circus was no longer a traveling circus with wild animals. However, revocation could only happen after suspension and so the problem outlined above remained.

When these concerns were raised with DEFRA by the author in a meeting during the drafting phase of the regulations, the government department could not provide an answer as to how the regulations would be enforced. Indeed, a senior official, in response to the question over how they intended to effectively implement suspensions, replied that "the circuses will just have to comply, so suspensions will not be necessary".

The concerns were then tested in early 2016, when information was released which confirmed one of the two circuses operating under a license in England had had its license suspended while in winter quarters in December 2015. This provided a case study to properly examine the weaknesses in the legislation in practice. This case study is discussed in Sect. 9.4 of this chapter.

9.3 The Inspection Process

In order to assess compliance, the standards outlined in the WWATC 2012 were underpinned by a system of inspection. Legally, only one inspection per license term was required under the regulations. This conferred a statutory obligation on the part of the relevant authority (in this case, DEFRA) to inspect the circus prior to the grant of a new license. As licenses could theoretically be granted for up to three years at a time, this meant that circuses might have been inspected just once every three years, prior to the issue of a new license. In practice, the Secretary of State outlined a more rigorous inspection regime in the guidance which accompanied the regulations, which was implemented until their repeal in January 2020. The regime as it was applied is summarized below.

Traveling circuses were inspected at least three times per year by a government-appointed inspector.[1] Two inspections were announced (i.e., the circus was given notice of the upcoming assessment) and one was unannounced (i.e., the circus was given no advance warning). At least one inspection had to be made of the circus' winter quarters and the unannounced inspection had to be carried out when the circus is on tour.

The government-appointed inspector could be accompanied by an animal health officer from the AHVLA. The inspection would be assisted by a member of staff from the circus—usually the license holder.

In order to assist inspectors in their assessment of a circus, a form (DEF-WATCIR[2]) was devised by DEFRA, which was to be filled in during an inspection. The form followed a similar format to those used under the ZLA 1981 inspection regime, but was comparatively simple and did not contain as many questions.

The form was split into two parts. The first dealt with seven specific topics relevant to license conditions[3] which all appeared to have a direct impact on animal welfare, health or safety. There were 26 questions relating to these seven topics. These included questions such as "Do all licensed animals appear to be in good health?" and "Do animals have sufficient access to exercise and enrichment?" For the most part, it seems that a "No" answer to questions in this section may have indicated poor animal welfare provision. The second part of the form contained a further ten topics (21 questions) which had a strong focus on record-keeping and logistics. They included questions surrounding the presence of the animals listed on the stock list, the keeping of daily records and evidence of accurate journey plans. As a general rule, a "No" answer to a question in this section may have demonstrated a breach of a license conditions but, in and of itself, was unlikely to be indicative of poor animal welfare provision. The exception to this was that assessment of provision of veterinary care and administration of medication was also carried out in this part of the form. Arguably, failure to provide appropriate vet care or treatment may have negatively impacted animal welfare. The section on veterinary care contained five questions in total. The form thus contained a total of 31 questions for which a "No" answer may have been indicative of poor animal welfare provision and 16 questions for which a "No" answer would not, in and of itself, have indicated poor animal welfare provision. It should be noted that, for the purposes of the regulations, no differentiation was made between conditions for which non-compliance may have had a direct and immediate negative impact on animal welfare and those which did not.

Unlike the form used to assess zoos for compliance with the ZLA 1981 which, for the most part, contains direct reference to the relevant clause of the legislation to which each question applies, the questions included in the circus inspection form did not make direct reference to the conditions to which they relate. The exception was the second part of the form which largely paraphrased or repeated the terms of the relevant conditions and therefore it was easy to identify which condition these questions related to. For the topics in the first part of the form, a matrix was produced by DEFRA as part of the guidance to show which topics related to which particular license conditions. The standards required of the circus with regard to each topic were then outlined in the guidance. Most topics contained questions which related to more than one license condition. This matrix (and the accompanying welfare standards in the guidance) allowed for both circus operators and circus inspectors to better understand what standards were required and for the latter to be able to assess compliance with the relevant conditions. The matrix has been reproduced for reference in Table 9.1.

The inspection forms were designed to offer a Red, Amber or Green (RAG) rating in relation to each topic (and its relevant questions). DEFRA explained the color code, on page 3 of the inspection form, as follows:

- Green = full compliance/minor breach (no action required);
- Amber = breach identified (remedial action recommended) and
- Red = significant breach (action required).

It is unclear how the inspectors differentiated between minor breaches which didn't require action, those breaches which simply required recommendations and those that required action. This information was not provided in the guidance which, arguably, introduced a margin of uncertainty for both inspectors and circus proprietors into the system. In addition to the RAG rating, the inspector provided notes next to each question under the relevant topic which served to explain the rating given and highlight any need for action. There was no mechanism to add new conditions to the license and so the circus would always be assessed against the existing ones. At the end of the inspection, the inspector made notes in relation to whether or not action was required, but these did not take the form of new conditions. Instead, they might have been listed as "items for attention".

In practice, the RAG rating was applied to the topic in the form, rather than each individual question. This meant that there were 17 ratings in relation to answers to 46 questions. This may have been problematic in that the questions grouped under topics may have related to compliance (or lack thereof) with a number of different conditions. The use of an R, A or G rating in relation to up to ten questions (e.g., in the case of the topic "Environment") may have been problematic as a means to identify specific breaches of conditions. It is argued that it would have been more beneficial to group questions in the inspection form into those which related specifically to conditions (similarly to the way in which the ZOO2

Table 9.1 Condition matrix for traveling circuses

License condition/ Topic	Topic 1: Circus staff	Topic 2: Healthcare	Topic 3: Environment	Topic 4: Diet	Topic 5: Display, performance and training	Topic 6: Breeding	Topic 7: Transport
Condition 3: Animal records		x					
Condition 4: Care plans		x	x	x	x	x	
Condition 5: Persons with access	x				x		
Condition 6: Veterinary surgeons		x				x	
Condition 7: Promote welfare	x	x	x	x	x	x	x
Condition 8: Display, training and performance		x			x	x	
Condition 9: Environment			x	x	x	x	
Condition 10: Transport		x				x	x

form, discussed previously, is arranged) so that it was clear whether or not a condition had been breached, and which one(s) it may have been.

After the form had been completed, a recommendation was made by the inspector as to whether the circus should continue to be licensed. Other options that the inspector could select were "Documentary evidence to demonstrate improvements to be provided", "Early visit recommended to confirm action has been taken" and "License refused/suspended". The inspector then provided the report to the Circus Licensing Panel, which took a decision based on the report and recommendations as to whether the circus should be licensed going forward. The options available to the panel were "license suspension" and the "circus being licensed in accordance with the regulations" (Figs. 9.1 and 9.2).

There was no legal requirement under the regulations for a report to be completed, only for the inspection to be carried out. In practice, for the lifetime of the regulations, a report was completed for each inspection and, indeed, it is unclear how the inspector would have communicated the relevant information required to the Circus Licensing Panel without completing a report.

Issues or concerns identified during an inspection could be noted by the inspector but there was no power to alter or amend the license. All licenses were subject to the same ten conditions and the Secretary of State had powers to "take such steps necessary to ensure compliance with the licensing conditions".[4] What these steps might have entailed was unclear other than the Secretary of State's ability to suspend a license if conditions have not been complied with. Problems with this process and questions over whether or not this was even possible in practice were outlined earlier in this chapter. If a license is suspended for 28 days, the Secretary of State *may have* to (but was not obliged to) revoke it.[5]

(1) Staff Is unsupervised access to licensed animals restricted to authorised persons?	NO. The reindeer are in unsupervised close contact during the day with the public at the rear of the garden centre , however, these animals appear very placid & are checked by staff every hour. At week-ends, the camels are brought into this area, but are out of reach of the public.	G
(2) Healthcare Do all licensed animals appear to be in good health?	Yes all the animals appear fit and healthy.	G
(3) Environment Are areas used by licensed animals operated in a way that provides good welfare?	YES	A
Are areas a suitable size?	See note re reindeer later	
Are areas in good condition and free from hazards?	YES	
Are areas sufficiently secure?	YES_apart from Camel paddock_see later	
Are areas suited to the social, behavioural and environmental needs of the animals?	YES	
Do animals have sufficient access to exercise and enrichment?	YES	
Are areas hygienic and clean?	YES	
Do areas have a suitable floor?	YES	
Are environmental factors managed, including shelter from the elements?	YES	
Is due regard had for species specific guidance?	YES	
(4) Diet Is food stored properly? Is food prepared properly?	Hay of good quality is fed ad lib . All other food was stored appropriately in one of the wagons in vermin & water proof containers	G
(5) Display, training and performance	No training or performance is undertaken during the winter rest period so this was not observed.	A
Are the precautions required by the assessment of welfare risks carried out?	YES	
Are animals fit for the activities expected of them?	YES	
Are only suitable areas used for display, training and performance?	YES	

Fig. 9.1 Column 1: Assessment criteria and sub questions; Column 2: Notes area; Column 3: RAG rating

Section 3: Inspectors Recommendation to Defra

Having inspected (name of circus) MONDAO

operated by (name of operator). CAROL MACMANUS

on: 10/11/2014

Summarise the potential impact of the issues found on the welfare of the wild animals in this travelling circus, noting the involvement of any other authority.

.All animals inspected were of excellent health and fitness. They have access to sufficient resources, exercise and behavioural enrichment to ensure a good welfare status. The only major concern arising from the inspection impacting on welfare, is the inadequate fencing in the camel paddock.

(This text will be transferred to the letter sent to the circus after the inspection)

Recommendation:

- Licence awarded / Continue to be licensed
- Documentary evidence to demonstrate improvements to be provided
- Early visit recommended to confirm that action taken
- Licence refused / suspended

(Please delete as necessary)

Signed: [redacted] Dated: 13/11/2014

Fig. 9.2 Recommendation made by inspector to DEFRA with relevant comments

9.4 Case Study: Attempts to Suspend a License—November 2015[6]

On 25 November 2015, Circus Mondao was subject to an unannounced inspection by DEFRA officials at its winter quarters in Spalding, Lincolnshire. What is perhaps unusual about Mondao's winter quarters was that they were a garden center which was open to the public. As such, the animals remained "on show" to some extent during the winter period, when the circus was not touring. The DEFRA report confirmed that reindeer and a baby camel were able to be accessed (and fed, unsupervised) by members of the public. Normally winter quarters are completely closed to the public and so there would be no element of display during the winter months. The relevance of this point in this case becomes clear when officials attempted to suspend the license.

During the inspection on 25 November, the following points were raised:

- Public access to the reindeer and camel were not adequately supervised (this had already been raised as an issue during inspections during previous inspections on 10/11/2014 and again on 18/12/2014 but remained unresolved by the circus the following year).
- The reindeer had insufficient space—their enclosure was smaller than licensing requirements demand.
- The reindeer were given insufficient exercise.
- Care plans did not include risk assessments for display, and individual records did not include any record of food being given by members of the public.

As a result of the above, there had been a clear breach of conditions 4, 5, 7 and 9 of the circus' license.[7] The DEFRA circus panel recommended immediate suspension of the license and the circus was informed of this in a letter dated 2 December. In that letter, DEFRA suggested that, in order for the terms of the suspension to be met, "wild animals must be off display and not perform at all times".[8] If the animals were species whose keeping was regulated by the Dangerous Wild Animals Act 1976,[9] DEFRA mandated that they must be licensed under that legislation. It should be noted at this stage that the issues with regard to the ability to effectively suspend a license, discussed in Sect. 4 (Chap. 8) of this book, now come into play. It appears that perhaps in order to make the suspension practically possible, DEFRA had dramatically narrowed the definition of a "travelling circus" from that which is included in the regulations. By suggesting that simply removing the animals from display and stopping performance for the duration of the suspension would constitute the suspension of "operating a travelling circus", it would appear that DEFRA did not classifies animals held off display and at winter quarters as forming part of the traveling circus, something which, as discussed in detail previously, was a major point of concern for animal welfare advocates and vets during the passage of the regulations. Indeed, this interpretation is in direct conflict with the definition of "travelling circus" utilized by the regulations which explicitly states that animals associated with a traveling circus remain part of that traveling circus anywhere they are kept. The activity of "operating a travelling circus" is an ongoing activity which continues perpetually while the business is traveling *and* while not traveling and while the animals are not on display.

On 12 December, the circus informed DEFRA that it would move the wild animals to the home of the owner of the circus—understood to be a farm near the garden center. This was confirmed as having been carried out on 14 December.[10] It is unclear whether or not the farm was henceforth considered to be part of the traveling circus or whether or not the farm was inspected. No documentation was made available with regard to inspections being carried out, and so it seems reasonable to assume that no inspection occurred and the farm was considered to sit outside of what was considered, by DEFRA, to constitute the "travelling circus".

9.5 Questions Over the Oversight of Winter Quarters

With just one case study available with regard to how the regulations might be enforced in the event of a breach, it is difficult to draw concrete conclusions. The Mondao case does, however, highlight a number of concerns which may come into play with regard to the ability of the regulations to achieve their purpose. The first issue is that DEFRA used a different working definition of "travelling circus" than is utilized in the regulations, a definition far narrower than intended by WWATC 2012. By limiting its interpretation of the activity "operating a travelling circus" to the period of time when animals are being displayed to the public and/or used in shows, it would appear that DEFRA have discounted the keeping of animals in winter quarters from the scope of the activity and, furthermore, are satisfied for the animals to be moved to a site not associated with the license in the event of a suspension.

Similarly, as was the case with Mondao, if a winter quarters themselves were inspected and the circus found to be in breach of standards outside of the touring season when the animals are not usually on display or involved in performances, DEFRA is again apparently satisfied that moving the animals to a site unrelated to the circus (and thus outside of the licensing regime's jurisdiction) would fulfill the demands of the suspension. There is no reason to suggest that any site unrelated to the licensed circus to which animals might be moved would necessarily be inadequate or that their welfare would be compromised simply by being kept somewhere which fell outside of the licensing regime's jurisdiction; however, it does raise two important points with regard to the regime itself, its extent and its efficacy:

1. First and foremost, the regulations made clear that the *anywhere* that an animal associated with a traveling circus was kept required a license so as to avoid breaching the regulations. As such, DEFRA's satisfaction at animals being moved to an unlicensed site during suspension may be a pragmatic way of enforcing poorly drafted regulations but is certainly not compliant with the letter of the law.
2. Perhaps more importantly, it would appear that the fears raised by animal welfare organizations and vets during the passage of the regulations that animals would not be adequately monitored and protected in winter quarters were founded. In the case of Mondao, when winter quarters were found to be lacking, the animals were simply sent elsewhere to a site which did not form part of the circus. It is perhaps lucky that the animals who were moved as part of the suspension were zebra and reindeer—animals who can be housed in similar accommodation as some domesticated animals, such as horses. Had the suspension been imposed in relation to wild animals with extremely specialized needs, such as lions, tigers or elephants, it seems unlikely that the circus would be able to provide, at short notice, a second site for the animals to be sent to. It therefore follows that, during the suspension, the animals would have to stay in the sub-standard winter quarters while the breaches were remedied or be removed to a different site, where inspectors have no right of entry other than the normal powers available under the AWA 2006 which would require a warrant and which may or may not provide an adequate standard of accommodation, husbandry and veterinary care.

Ultimately, the flawed suspension process as outlined in the regulations did not appear to have presented barriers to DEFRA taking action to suspend a license when breaches were found due to the pragmatic approach adopted by DEFRA officials in enforcing the suspension. That said, there are clearly flaws in the approach adopted, particularly if the suspension involves animals with highly specialized needs. While these regulations have now been repealed, analysis of the issues with them bears consideration in order to inform future regulation introduced using the same legal mechanism.

9.6 Conflating "Use" with "Ownership"

The WWATC regulations were put in place to regulate the activity of using wild animals in traveling circuses. Regulations introduced under s.13 of the AWA 2006 cannot imply power to deprive animal keepers of ownership of their animals. As such, to be enforceable, regulations must be able to differentiate between ownership of animals (which is an ongoing right to keep the animal) and an activity involving that animal. To avoid exceeding powers granted by s.13, it must be possible within the regulations to prevent/regulate the use of the animals in a particular activity without depriving the legal keeper of the animal of their right of ownership in the case that the regulations are breached. This is where, it is argued, the regulations in question failed.

In its definition of "circus", the regulations sought to capture every aspect of the animals' lives so that every activity the animal carries out (from sleeping to eating to exercising, whether while the circus was traveling and shows were being delivered or when it is not traveling and animals are housed in winter quarters) has been deemed to fall within the overarching activity of "being used in a travelling circus". As a license was required in order for a wild animal to be used in a traveling circus and the regulations defined "use" to include the simple keeping of an animal in a traveling circus or anywhere else while the animals is still considered "associated" with the circus, then the regulations were effectively regulating the ownership of wild animals by circuses or, by extension, circus employees. To suspend a license was to effectively demand that the wild animal was no longer able to be associated in any way with a circus. The only way in which to realize this demand was to remove the animals permanently from the site in the event of suspension, thus depriving the circus or individual of ownership. Proper enforcement would therefore clearly suggest that the regulations could be considered *ultra vires* in that they appeared to regulate ownership and not activity.

9.7 The Impression of Oversight Versus the Reality

An interesting and somewhat concerning point which became apparent from the correspondence in relation to the attempted license suspension of Circus Mondao relates to the breeding of animals. In the inspections reports studied as part of this research, carried out in August 2014 and November 2014 respectively, the inspector's answers to question 6 on the inspection form relating to health and welfare during the breeding process being met were as follows:

> August 2014: "The camels have been housed together for several years and no breeding behavior has been recorded. Both appear healthy and there does not appear to be any welfare problem or incompatibility".[11]
>
> November 2014: "No breeding has, or is likely to occur (the only entire animals are the camels, & these have been living together for many years & shown no breeding activity)" [*sic*].[12]

Camels have a gestation period of between 12 and 15 months and the female camel at Circus Mondao gave birth on 15 June 2015. As such, the camel was pregnant during both of the previous two inspections, but this went unnoticed by the vet. The female camel died just over a month later (21 July 2015) but post mortem records have not been made publicly available to understand the cause of death.

In the final inspection report made available publicly (6 August 2015), a note made by the inspector at the end of the report with regard to the camel's death reads:

> *The background to this event [the death of the female camel] is that the breeding of camels was not specifically planned. Mating behavior had been seen in previous seasons but had not resulted in pregnancy and it was thus assumed that breeding was unlikely.*[13]

This statement—that mating behavior had been witnessed by staff in the past—contradicts previous information provided to inspectors, whereby it appears that inspectors were told that there has never been any such behavior witnessed. This issue, and the failure to identify the pregnancy, raises questions with regard to the reliability of the inspection process as a means to gain a true indication of animal welfare provision. While it could be argued that with three visits per year and very few animals to be seen, it is perhaps more likely that animals used in circuses, due to their low numbers at this present time, would be subject to more thorough assessment and oversight than animals numbering in their thousands kept in zoos, but this was perhaps not the case in reality. Much of the licensing and inspection process necessarily relied on testimony from the staff, rather than direct observation by the inspector, which could be considered problematic if the information provided is not accurate. It is also clear that the inspector's visits did not necessarily identify situations which may demand further scrutiny or specific measures to be implemented in the interests of animal welfare. It is impossible to know, given the information available, whether or not the death of the camel was linked to the unplanned and unnoticed pregnancy; however, it is an issue worthy of further consideration when taking into account the licensing regime's ability to "secure the welfare of wild animals"[14] as stated by legislators to be its aim on implementation.

9.8 Conclusion

Having considered the development, implementation and enforcement of WWATC 2012, it appears that weaknesses can be found in the make-up of the regulations themselves, which led to DEFRA departing from the definition of "travelling circus" used in the regulations and, instead, adopting what appears to be a pragmatic approach to their enforcement.

Concerns were raised during its passage through Parliament that the highest standards of welfare possible in a traveling circus still fell below standards required to meet the welfare needs of the animals themselves in practice and, as such, welfare simply cannot be met in such an environment. Furthermore, the technical issues surrounding the ability to effectively sanction circuses in the case of non-compliance (highlighted in Sect. 4 of Chap. 8) which were raised during the passage of the Bill were found to be warranted in early 2016 in light of the attempted suspension of Circus Mondao's license.

It was made clear from the outset that regulations, to be effective, must protect animals both while on the road and in winter quarters. While this was explicitly recognized by policymakers and subsequently written into the legislation, the practical application of the legislation was far less expansive; with DEFRA taking a very narrow definition of what the activity of "operating a travelling circus" entails. In effect, DEFRA, in attempting to enforce the regulations, discounted keeping animals off-show in winter quarters as being encompassed in the overall activity of "operation a travelling circus". This created a two-pronged problem:

1. Proper enforcement of the legislation in the case of a suspension would have deprived the animal's keeper of ownership. This suggests that the regulations were *ultra vires* (exceed the scope of the powers granted by the enabling act).
2. Avoiding proper enforcement of the regulations and taking a pragmatic approach necessitated a far narrower interpretation of the activity of "using a wild animal in a travelling circus", in turn, creating the risk that animals kept in winter quarters or off display fell outside of the licensing regime in practice, if not strictly in law.

Finally, the case study relating to the unexpected birth of a camel and the subsequent death of his mother a little over a month later raised legitimate concerns that the oversight provided by the inspections, for reasons currently unknown, was not sufficient to properly assess, much less guarantee and protect, the welfare of individual animals.

The next chapter will go on to consider the new licensing legislation which was introduced using the same mechanism as the WWATC and explore whether lessons were learned from the circus legislation's shortcomings.

Notes

1. DEFRA (2012). Guidance on the Welfare of Wild Animals in Travelling Circuses (England) Regulations 2012. London: DEFRA. p. 4.
2. An example of the form can be found here: https://www.gov.uk/government/uploads/system/uploads/attachment_data/file/509834/rfi8126_cm_renewal_inspection_report.pdf.
3. Staff, Healthcare, Environment, Diet, Display Training and Performance, Breeding and Transport.
4. S.7 WWATC 2012.
5. S.13 WWATC 2012.
6. All paperwork relating to this case study has been published by DEFRA as part of Freedom of Information disclosure and can be found here: https://www.gov.uk/government/publications/licence-applications-and-inspections-for-travelling-circuses.
7. Condition 4: Care Plans; Condition 5: Persons with access to licensed animals; Condition 7: Responsibility of the operator to promote the welfare of licensed animals and Condition 9: Specific welfare requirements for environment.
8. Letter available as part of Freedom of Information disclosure. It can be found here: https://www.gov.uk/government/publications/licence-applications-and-inspections-for-travelling-circuses.
9. Circuses are explicitly exempt from Dangerous Wild Animal Licensing in s.5.
10. Letter available as part of Freedom of Information disclosure. It can be found here: https://www.gov.uk/government/publications/licence-applications-and-inspections-for-travelling-circuses.
11. Inspection report published as part of Freedom of Information disclosure is available here: https://www.gov.uk/government/publications/inspection-reports-for-2-named-circuses-since-october-2013.

12. Inspection report published as part of Freedom of Information disclosure is available here: https://www.gov.uk/government/publications/reports-on-2-circuses-between-26-june-2014-and-22-january-2015.
13. Inspection report released to author as part of Freedom of Information disclosure but not subsequently published by DEFRA in its disclosure log.
14. HC Deb, 1 March 2012, c41WS.

10

New Directions in Licensing: The Animal Welfare (Licensing of Activities Involving Animals) (England) Regulations 2018

10.1 New Regulations Under the AWA 2006

In October 2018, the Animal Welfare (Licensing of Activities Involving Animals (England) Regulations 2018 (AWR 2018) came into force. The introduction of these regulations fulfilled a commitment made by government at the introduction of the AWA 2006 to repeal outdated legislation and replace it with more modern and fit-for-purpose regulations. The regulations replaced the requirement in England to be registered under the Performing Animals (Regulation) Act 1925 or to obtain a license under the Pet Animals Act 1951, the Animal Boarding Establishments Act 1963, the Riding Establishments Act 1964 or the Breeding of Dogs Act 1973.

The licensing regulations cover the following activities:

- dog breeding
- pet selling
- hiring out horses
- boarding for dogs and cats
- home boarding for dogs

E. Tyson, *Licensing Laws and Animal Welfare*, The Palgrave Macmillan Animal Ethics Series, https://doi.org/10.1007/978-3-030-50042-9_10

- dog day care
- keeping or training animals for exhibition

Along with the regulations, guidance was published to inform both potential licensees and the local authorities charged with regulating them, on the operation of the regulations.

Generally speaking, licenses are granted for up to three years based on a risk assessment. New licenses are generally granted for one year as they are automatically considered "high risk". This creates a system whereby new licensees are afforded more scrutiny than long-standing license holders. Interestingly, in the case of the use of animals in exhibition and performance—an activity which has long been of concern to animal welfare organizations—licensees are automatically granted a three-year license due to the fact that the activity used to be governed by a system of registration. There is explicitly no risk assessment associated with the exhibition and performance license.

In practice, those businesses with lower risk rating will be granted longer licenses and, as such, which be subject to fewer inspections as inspections are carried out, generally speaking, on renewal. No license can be granted without prior inspection.

The risk assessment approach was not one that was employed for the WWATC 2012, which were subject to three inspections annually and, while licenses could be granted for three years, in practice, none of them were in practice and they were only ever granted for a one-year period.

There is relatively wide discretion for the local authority to decide who will be granted a license under the AWR 2018. Reasons for refusal are if the person is considered incapable of meeting license conditions, if there are concerns that the welfare needs of animals are not being met, if the operation appears inadequate in terms of management, staffing or accommodation, or if the person has been disqualified. Interestingly the guidance states that the local authority "can" refuse to grant a license to a person who has been disqualified, not that they "must". Applicants refused a license may appeal to the First Tier Tribunal.

There is also wide discretion to suspend, vary or revoke a license which is different to the WWATC 2012 regulations. Licenses can be suspended, varied or revoked as a result of license conditions not being complied with, in the case of a breach of the regulations, if information supplied by the license holder is false or misleading or if it necessary to do so in order to protect animal welfare.

Any decision to vary, suspend or revoke a license must be communicated to the license holder in writing and will take effect seven days after issue or with immediate effect if necessary to protect animal welfare. Interestingly, this provides a very wide discretion to the local authority as they can look outside of the regulations for reasons to vary, suspend or revoke—this is evidenced by the "necessary to protect the welfare of an animal". The local authority must provide information as to what action would be required to remedy the issue.

Following the notice, the licensee has seven working days to make written representation which the local authority must consider and then choose whether to continue with the planned action. The business must cease "trading" (this is the wording used in the guidance) once a suspension has come into effect and cannot do so until the decision is overturned by the First Tier Tribunal. Of course, if the animal activity is only an element of the business, the business cannot be stopped trading completely by a suspension, only that they cannot carry out the activity involving animals to which the license relates.

In the case of lengthy suspensions, the local authority must regularly check the animals to ensure welfare is maintained. It is unclear how this would play out if the suspension was put in place to protect welfare. Presumably, if the suspension is still in place, the issue which is affecting animal welfare remains an issue. In the case of boarding kennels, it could be that the business has no animals on premises during the suspension so animal welfare is not affected on an ongoing basis. If the suspension related to businesses which own and accommodate animals on a permanent basis, then it is possible that welfare concerns will be ongoing.

If the local authority fails to respond to a representation within seven working days of receipt, then their initial decision is overturned. The same applies to a suspension when no further action is taken on it within 28 days.

As there are no powers under the regulations to confiscate animals, any action to remedy serious animal welfare concerns would have to be carried out under separate legal proceedings using s.9 or s.4 of the AWA 2006.

Only horse-riding establishments have the requirement of an annual inspection, though it is unclear why these businesses, in particular, have been singled out for this higher level of scrutiny. Other inspections can be carried out for other activities or in the case of any activity in the instance of a complaint, but there is no obligation on the local authority to inspect (other than horse-riding establishments) other than on grant or renewal of a license. The "site" of the licensable activity must be inspected. For performance and exhibition, this is assumed to refer to the home base for the animals, which is interesting as, by default, this means that the activity itself will not be inspected, unless filming and exhibition occur on the day of inspection at the home base. Often, these businesses transport animals from the home base to the set of the film or to the place where the exhibition or performance will take place. It is unclear whether the inspection regime will ever therefore capture the activity itself.

In the case of the death of a license holder, the local authority must be informed within 28 days. The license will remain in place for up to three months (or less if the remaining time on the license is less) and the new licensee must apply for their own license. The local authority is allowed to extend the period by a further three months if it is required and deemed necessary and the time is needed to wind up the estate of the deceased.

Powers of entry are the same as those in the Parent Act—to enter a private dwelling, 24 hours' notice must be given. Parts of a premise which are not used as a dwelling can be entered if a license is in place or if a licensable activity is reasonably believed to be being carried out.

Breach of license condition is an offence, as is not complying with an inspector's request to take samples from an animal. Obstruction of an inspector is an offence. These offences could be met with an unlimited fine. Relevant post-conviction powers apply from s.34 of the AWA 2006.

Unexpired licenses under the Pet Animals Act 1951, Animal Boarding Establishments Act 1963, Riding Establishments Act 1964 and Riding Establishments Act 1970 would remain in force for the rest of their terms. Unexpired licenses under the Breeding of Dogs Act 1973, and associated legislation, would remain in force under the terms of those Acts until expiry.

Those registered under the Performing Animals (Regulation) Act 1925 has six months from the date the regulations came into force to register (1 April 2019).

The guidance provides a matrix as to how long a license should be issued for and the subsequent inspections required for those licenses based on risk. Interestingly, and despite long-term concerns regarding animal welfare in training and performance, and the explicit ban on the use of wild animals in traveling circuses, all licenses for training and performance are issued for three years. This means that these animals, by default, are only inspected mandatorily once every three years. This raises concerns over the value of the new regulations in relation to this activity and to what extent improvements have been made from the former system of registration which was deemed by the government itself as "not, however, intended to promote welfare and its provisions are widely regarded to be ineffective".[1] Of course, one inspection every three years is better than no inspection at all but it is unclear why, given the well-publicized concern over exhibition and training of animals for performance, this activity which is considered by many to be inherently problematic for animal welfare, has been given such a "light touch" in relation to other activities which, in and of themselves, appear to present fewer welfare issues (i.e., boarding kennels).

There are two levels of standards which establishments can meet—the minimum and the higher. Those meeting the higher standards will be inspected less frequently and those meeting just the lower standards will be inspected more frequently. Presumably, the idea was that this would act as an incentive for businesses to strive to meet the higher standards to avoid inspection. But this will depend on whether the cost of inspection is outweighed by the cost of meeting the higher standards.

UKAS[2] accreditation of the business can be used to give the business a higher rating and thus lower risk. This in turn reduces the need for inspection. This is an outsourcing of regulation which is of concern to some (many?) animal welfare organizations.

Schedule 2 of the Regulations outlines the general conditions which are to be attached to all licenses issued. They include demands relating to license display; record-keeping; use, number and type of animal; staffing; suitable environment; suitable diet; monitoring of behavior and training of animals; animal handling and interactions; protection from pain, suffering, injury and disease; and emergencies.

The schedules which follow provide specific additional conditions which are linked to the activities in question: selling animals as pets; providing boarding for cats and dogs; hiring out horses; breeding dogs; keeping or training animals for exhibition. Schedule 8 onward then covers people who may not apply for a license, repeals and consequential amendments, and revocations and consequential amendments.

10.2 Were Lessons Learned from the WWATC 2012?

These regulations are enforced at local authority level and adopt a risk-based approach with regard to inspection and length of license. Two arguably controversial activities—the use of animals in entertainment and the use of animals in "mobile zoos"—are captured under the "training and exhibition" activity but, despite concerns, this activity has been explicitly ruled out of the risk-based approach and is automatically licensed for three years at a time. When we consider that a static circus with wild animals could be established legally in England and immediately be granted a three-year license with no requirement for risk assessment at the same time that a traveling circus with wild animals is legally prohibited, the rationale behind this is unclear.

It is interesting that, despite repeatedly recognizing that the PAA 1925 was ineffective and did not, in any case, protect animal welfare, the fact that this activity was previously subject to registration appears to be the reason that these longer licenses are granted. The government has admitted that no assessment of the welfare impact of training and performance has ever been carried out and it was suggested that this would be done as part of the move to regulate or ban wild animals in circuses. While the use of wild animals in traveling circuses has now been banned, the same animals can be used in static circuses for largely the same purpose (albeit without the transport elements). It makes little sense that given the statement made by Lord Taylor at the time the proposal to ban was announced:

"There is no place in today's society for wild animals being used for our entertainment in travelling circuses. Wild animals deserve our respect",[3] that continuing to use wild animals in static circuses would demonstrate any more respect. It stands to reason, therefore, that the use of wild animals in circuses, whether traveling or otherwise, should have been banned when the legislative ban on wild animals in traveling circuses was introduced on 20 January 2020.

I would argue that it was also a mistake to include mobile zoos under these regulations rather than under the Zoo Licensing Act 1981. These businesses have been increasing in number in recent years with latest research suggested that there are at least 187 establishments, using over 3500 animals, operating in England alone.[4] Inspection once every three years at their home base will fail not only to capture meaningful information about the animals but, importantly, it will mean that the activity being regulated (taking animals away from the home base and exhibiting them) will never be witnessed by the inspectors.

When asked during a meeting during the consultation period why mobile zoos are being held to a lower standard than zoos, the government official responded that they were not considered to be "quite at the same level as zoos".[5] In the same conversation, it was acknowledged by the same official that mobile zoos used wild animals and often modeled themselves publicly as zoos. It was unclear how the decision was made that they were somehow something less than zoos and that this exempted them from the rigors of zoo licensing. Indeed, when asked to clarify how that decision had been come to, the official simply repeated that they did not intend to consider mobile zoos in line with the Zoo Licensing Act 1981. As outlined in Sect. 10.3 of Chap. 5, the operation of mobile zoos can be very easily, and in my opinion, should be, considered in line with the Zoo Licensing Act 1981. This is the approach that has been taken in Ireland and, to date, there have been no issues raised with regard to this approach from a legal perspective.

With regard to the suspension, revocation and so on of a license, elements of the issue found regarding circus winter quarters applies in that, if issues are found with the accommodation and the license is suspended or revoked, the animals remain where they are and this could prolong animal welfare concerns as one would assume that the income from the business is that which would fund any necessary improvements. What becomes important here is that the types of business regulated under this regime differ in that some own the animals which are being used in the activity and others do not. So, for example, if a dog-boarding kennels had its license revoked, it would not be allowed to accept boarders and thus any animal welfare concerns in relation to its operation would be negated by the fact there would be no animals associated with the business during the suspension or as a result of the revocation. A mobile zoo, or dog breeding establishment, however, owns the animals and so a license being suspended or revoked would leave the animals where they were. Of course, the argument would likely be that the business would need to amend the issues in order to continue and this would be motivation to make the necessary improvements and, in turn, this should remedy the issues in animal welfare. That said, it seems counterintuitive that the suspension of a license given to protect animal welfare could, in the short term, have the impact of reducing scrutiny over a failing business and thus potentially reduce animal welfare provision. The same issue applied with circuses. When a license was suspended, the animals stayed where they were and unless and until the license was reinstated, those animals were no longer subject to scrutiny. This would be a little like closing down a care home on welfare grounds but simply leaving the residents where they are.

It is therefore argued that a suspension or revocation should be accompanied with the appropriate action under the Animal Welfare Act 2006 in order to ensure that animal welfare is not compromised as a direct result.

Notes

1. Radford, M., (2007). The Report of the Chairman of the Circus Working Group (The Radford Report).
2. The United Kingdom Accreditation Service (UKAS) is the national accreditation body for the United Kingdom, appointed by government, to assess organizations that provide certification, testing, inspection and calibration services.

3. Gov.uk. (2012). Circuses to be banned from using performing wild animals—GOV.UK. [online] Available at: https://www.gov.uk/government/news/circuses-to-be-banned-from-using-performing-wild-animals [Accessed 24 Nov. 2017].
4. Mobilezoo.org.uk. 2014. [online] Available at: https://mobilezoo.org.uk/wp-content/uploads/2016/03/The-Growth-of-the-Mobile-Zoo-Industry-2016.pdf [Accessed 21 Mar. 2020].
5. Conversation with DEFRA officials during in-person meeting in November 2017 to discuss regulations.

11

Is Licensing an Effective Means to Regulate the Use of Animals?

The legislation under consideration is designed (and largely believed) to protect animal welfare. This narrative is strongly promoted within the rationale behind and wording of the legislation itself, in government statements with regard to the legislation[1] and among industry stakeholders.[2] This research has suggested that licensing *in and of itself* is unlikely to protect welfare, but it *can* be used as one tool within a wider regulatory framework to achieve a number of aims which certainly have potential to contribute to animal welfare. The specific benefits of a well-designed and implemented licensing regime is that practices which involve animals which might present specific welfare concerns can be monitored and given extra oversight and that standards can be set which allow those using the animals to understand what they need to do to comply. A good licensing regime will be underpinned by a range of enforcement tools, which can be deployed in the case of non-compliance. Whether or not these factors are met within the legislation under consideration will be considered shortly. First, and given the very strong assertions from various stakeholders that the very purpose of the legislation are to "ensure high welfare standards"[3] are met (WWATC 2012), to "ensure … that high standards of welfare are maintained"[4] (among other things) in the

E. Tyson, *Licensing Laws and Animal Welfare*, The Palgrave Macmillan Animal Ethics Series, https://doi.org/10.1007/978-3-030-50042-9_11

case of the ZLA 1981 and "to ensure that anyone who receives a licence for [the relevant activities] will need to meet … new minimum welfare standards. This should help to drive up animal welfare standards across all of these sectors".[5] It is clearly stated that the very purpose of the various statutes is to ensure high welfare standards. While it has been concluded this is not necessarily the practical impact of the legislation, it is important to attempt to explore why this is the case and, indeed, why under current legislative frameworks, the author believes that it could never be the case. In short, if the aim of the legislation is to ensure high welfare standards, then licensing is not the means by which to achieve this.

11.1 Why Licensing Can Never "Ensure High Standards of Welfare" for Regulated Animals

11.1.1 "Good Practice" Does Not Equal "Good Welfare"

As noted in Sect. 4.2 of Chap. 3, "good practice" in the context of the AWA 2006, does not lay down a universal minimum standard of welfare for any individual species or type of animal. Instead, as has been noted in the foregoing discussion on the development of WWATC 2012, the "good practice" caveat is necessarily interpreted based upon what is considered good practice within the industry itself. As such, existing good practice within the circus industry will act as the benchmark for welfare standards in circuses and existing good practice in pet shops, for example, will act as the benchmark for welfare in pet shops. The result of this is what O'Sullivan has referred to as "the internal inconsistency"[6] and practically means that an elephant, for example, can spend her entire life sleeping in a lorry trailer, being chained by the leg each night and in an unnatural social group in England and be deemed to have her welfare needs met under the law governing animal welfare in circuses. Likewise, an elephant can live in a concrete enclosure in a zoo, in a climate very different to that which she is adapted to and in a social group which is unnatural to her and be deemed to have her welfare needs met under the Animal Welfare Act (the extent to which needs might be better catered for under the Zoo Licensing Act itself will be considered shortly).

The result of this is that 100% compliance with the standards may result in animals of the same species and with (largely) the same needs, experiencing living experiences and welfare which are very different, depending on the situation in which they happen to be used. For this reason, it would appear that compliance with the law, without meaningful consideration of the content and demands that law makes, is not a good gauge of whether welfare needs are met in practice from the perspective of the animal themself. It may be an obvious statement to make but it would appear that the only way in which a licensing regime might be considered effective with regard to protecting animal welfare is if the standards which that licensing regime imposes on industry would result in good animal welfare if delivered. In the case of the WWATC 2012, it was widely believed that this was never and could never be the case.

To return to the example of shackling elephants explored earlier in Chap. 3, a circus which was regulated under the WWATC 2012 could be found to be compliant with welfare standards for circuses if it kept elephants shackled by their legs every night of the animals' lives. Conversely, a zoo would be found in breach of welfare standards for zoos if it were to do the same to the elephants under its care. This makes little sense if the two pieces of legislation have as their purpose the protection of the welfare of the (shackled or unshackled) elephants and highlights the clear weakness in relying on the "good practice" caveat to support the delivery of high welfare standards in practice.

11.1.2 The Limitations Created by the "Good Practice" Caveat Limits Potential Efficacy of Licensing

As noted, the ZLA 1981 is a piece of primary legislation, and WWATC 2012 and the AWR were introduced as secondary legislation under the AWA 2006. While the zoo industry is also governed by the AWA 2006, the standards laid out in the ZLA 1981 stand apart and can be considered in isolation. On the other hand, the standards previously in place for circuses and the current raft of licensing legislation under the AWR 2018 could not and cannot exceed welfare standards mandated by the parent Act due to the aforementioned caveat of "good practice" incumbent on the interpretation of any regulations introduced under the AWA 2006. In addition, while the ZLA 1981 must incorporate the demands of the EC Zoos Directive (Directive 1999/22 EC), member states are not precluded from implementing standards which exceed those of the Directive. As such, the EC Zoos Directive theoretically acts as a *minimum standard* which must be met but can be built upon. Having already considered that the AWA 2006 never makes a demand upon those responsible for animals to meet their welfare needs in full, the wording of the ZLA 1981 suggests the potential for more stringent controls. In place of the "to the extent required by good practice" caveat found in the AWA 2006 which, in turn informed the standards outlined in WWATC 2012 as well as the current AWR 2018, the ZLA 1981 demands that zoos must aim to "provide each animal with an environment well adapted to meet the physical, psychological and social needs of the species to which is belongs"[7] and "provide a high standard of animal husbandry with a developed program of preventative and curative veterinary care".[8] As such, there is potential for the very highest welfare standards to be delivered under the ZLA 1981 which are based upon the very specific physical, psychological and social needs of the species of animals held by the zoo. When we compare the demands of the ZLA 1981 with those of the licensing regimes introduced under s.13 of the AWA 2006, it becomes clear that the potential to meet animal welfare needs is constrained when interpreted in the context of the AWA 2006 in a way that they are not when the legislation in question seeks to further the aims of conservation of biodiversity, rather than animal welfare *per se*. It would appear from this that, somewhat ironically, if the true aim of the legislation was to introduce the highest welfare standards possible, policymakers might be better to introduce legislation outside of the constraints of the AWA 2006, and instead as primary legislation in its own right, such as under the banner or "conservation of biodiversity" which is the focus of the ZLA 1981. While this suggests that the ZLA 1981, properly interpreted and enforced, could therefore go a long way toward protecting animal welfare to a very high standard, what needs to be further understood is the real-life demands placed on licensees with regard to the extent to which they must meet those standards. High standards on paper are all well and good, but if no demands are placed on licensees that the standards outlined by the law have to be met, then this arguably reduces the legislation's ability to guarantee animal welfare needs are met in practice.

Further to considerations above, what also needs to be borne in mind is that none of the statutes under consideration explore the potential that the welfare of certain animals, and wild animals in particular, simply cannot be met in an environment where they are kept "under the control of man". It is argued that, as a starting point to any animal welfare legislation development, this question should first be asked and answered. If it is concluded that the welfare needs of the animal cannot be met in closely controlled human environments, then the correct course of action may be to ban the use or keeping of certain animals or to explicitly exclude those animals from being kept in certain circumstances.

11.1.3 Possession of a License Does Not Indicate Compliance with Standards

If the standards mandated as part of the licensing regime were adequate to ensure that compliance with them meant that animal welfare needs were met in practice, then this might go some way toward guaranteeing effective animal welfare protection. However, the next important point to note is that neither piece of legislation under consideration, if properly enforced, demands that license holders meet the standards required of them on a consistent basis. In fact, a zoo or a business regulated under AWR 2018 may theoretically hold a license yet be non-compliant with the standards outlined by law for long periods of time.

For example, the ZLA 1981 (properly enforced) makes the demand that zoos meet certain standards. If those standards are not met, then a condition must be attached to the license and a direction issued. If the condition relates to one of the demands made by s.1A of the Act, the zoo must comply within two years or it may face closure. This means that in theory (and as has been found in practice) zoos can retain a valid license while failing to meet fundamental legal standards for a period of up to two years (or more if the condition in question does not relate to demands made by s.1A). In practice, it has been seen that due to poor enforcement, zoos have retained licenses for far longer than two years while being non-compliant with at least some standards (see Chapter 6.10.3). In addition to this, zoos are only inspected by a government-appointed inspector once every three years. The two-year timeframe allowed for compliance only begins to run against the zoo once the issue has been noted upon inspection and a condition attached to the license (and a direction issued). Given that there may be a three-year gap between inspections, this further extends the time during which a zoo may be non-compliant with the law without being asked to take any remedial action. With the forgoing in mind, this means that zoos can hold a valid license while failing to meet at least some legal standards for up to five years if the law was correctly followed and enforced. This issue is further exacerbated by the systemic lack of enforcement action against non-compliant zoos.

In the case of circuses under the WWATC 2012, there appeared to be less potential for non-compliance to go unnoticed given that circuses were inspected three times a year under the regulations. Theoretically then, problems should only have gone undetected for a maximum of four months (on average). Notwithstanding the concerns that compliance with the standards did not equate to delivery of welfare needs in practice, the way in which non-compliance might have been dealt with in circuses was unclear from the legislation. Section 7 of the regulations made the, somewhat vague, suggestion that "The Secretary of State must take such steps as the Secretary of State considers necessary to ensure compliance with the licensing conditions". Chapter 9.4 explored how sanctions were delivered in practice and the process (and result) was found that the government department responsible for enforcement had to adopt a narrow (and from a strictly legal point of view, erroneous) definition of circus to allow them to carry out enforcement action. The long-term impact of applying this narrow definition suggests that the protection for animals held in circuses' winter quarters may have been limited (something which was a grave concern to campaigners during the passage of the regulations). Unlike for zoos, in the case of circuses, there is no minimum or maximum timescale by which compliance must be achieved before formal enforcement action is implemented and, instead, the timescale appears to be dependent on the will of the Secretary of State. As such, as with the ZLA 1981, circuses regulated under the WWATC 2012 were able to hold a license while practically being non-compliant with the standards outlined in the legislation.

Having used the WWATC as an example for analysis, it seems that the new AWR 2018 regulations create similar issues with less stringent and "risk based" approaches serving to limit oversight and suggests that breaches may go unnoticed as a result.

In effect, in all cases, businesses can be in operation over long periods of time, be non-compliant with standards outlined in the legislation, yet their license still be considered valid. The possession of a valid license is not, therefore, always an accurate indicator of welfare needs being met, but merely that welfare needs are being periodically assessed and, theoretically, the business is being encouraged (via the use of conditions, sanctions and other enforcement tools) to come into compliance.

11.1.4 Licensing Is Not Individualistic, Welfare Is

It is not just the specific make-up of the statutes under consideration which do not lend themselves to guaranteeing animal welfare needs are met, but the fundamental principles upon which licensing regimes are conceived that suggest that they are an unsuitable vehicle to guarantee the welfare of any individual animal, unless the practice in question is carried out on a very small-scale or large-scale investment in infrastructure allows for assessment of individuals within any one system subject to regulatory licensing. Welfare, by its very nature, is individualistic. Unlike licensing relating to driving, for example, whereby people are thoroughly assessed on the basis of individual competency, the licensing regimes under consideration are not, by their very nature, individualistic. Instead, the regimes largely consider processes and practices which impact upon the individual, rather than the individual themselves. For example, rather than providing a health check for all individual animals in a zoo, the vet inspector is, instead, asked to confirm whether the animals collectively "appear to be in good health" and to confirm that a veterinary care program is in place. Rather than accompany wild animals in circuses as they are moved from site to site, the inspector is required to confirm that an acceptable plan for movement of the animals is in place. This suggests, therefore, that licensing may be valid for considering "inputs" and processes within businesses by virtue of being able to examine systems, process and routines with regard to how the animals are cared for, but it does not, by its very nature, consider "outputs" in the sense of the way in which the various processes, routines and practices actually impact upon animals as individuals. It could be argued, therefore, that licensing of the type under consideration is simply not an appropriate tool to use to assess welfare, and yet it is used increasingly to do so.

Licensing regimes could, in practice, assess the individual in the same way as the aforementioned driving licensing regime. The issue with this is that assessing the welfare of each individual animal used as part of a licensed practice would be prohibitively expensive, unless the practice only involves a very small number of animals. The reason that aspiring drivers can be assessed individually is because it is the drivers themselves who pay the costs of their assessment. While the zoo industry does pay the costs of the inspection they are subject to, if those costs were to include sufficient funds for each and every animal to be individually assessed, the costs for zoos and other similar industries would likely be completely unviable. The practical implications of this point become clear on closer examination of the specific licensing regimes in question. For the circus licensing regime, there were only two businesses with only around 19 animals under during the time that the WWATC 2012 was in force. It is clear from the notes in the inspection reports that the inspectors see each and every animal on the list, verifying each one. When businesses are dealing with such a small number of animals, then it seems reasonable that personal, individual assessment can be carried out for each one as part of the inspection process. The assessments are carried out three times a year and a clear timeline of treatment of animals, on an individual basis, can be followed using the reports. It seems reasonable that the animals' welfare can be properly assessed, at least on the day of inspection, against the standards required. Small businesses such as horse-riding schools or boarding kennels under the new system could be similarly inspected, animal-by-animal, dependent on the size of the operation.

Contrary to this view, however, it became clear when analyzing the case study relating to Circus Mondao (Sect. 7 in Chap. 9) that the pregnancy of a camel who later died shortly after giving birth was completely missed by inspectors (and, apparently, by staff too).

In the case of zoos, which may house thousands of animals, the ability of inspectors to properly assess welfare becomes more difficult. The individual nature of welfare is lost when animals (often who might not be able to be identified individually by inspectors and, in some cases, staff) are kept in large groups and seen once every three years, often by a different inspector. Carried out over the course of one working day in most cases,[9] the inspectors may spend just a few seconds at best looking at each animal[10]—the reality is that many, or even most, animals in the zoo will not be seen at all by the inspectors. This leads to the, somewhat counter-intuitive, outcome that the larger the business and the more animals being used by that business, the lesser the ability for inspectors to assess individual welfare. To conclude, and notwithstanding the forgoing concerns with regard to standards and demands for compliance, the non-individualistic nature of the licensing regimes applied to zoos (and to a lesser extent, circuses) further challenges claims that the licensing regimes, in and of themselves, guarantee or ensure high standards of animal welfare. Indeed, any such claim made in relation to zoos must be qualified by the fact that it would be impossible for a proper assessment of individual animals to be made during a one working day visit to a collection of animals, often numbering in their thousands.

It is argued that the, necessarily, collective view of the licensing regimes in question is what leads to a tendency toward what Casamitjana referred to as the "yes, but"[11] problem in assessing standards in zoos, as well as a tendency toward considering compliance in a holistic sense, rather than on an individual basis. What this means is that when an inspector is assessing a zoo and the vast majority of animals that he or she sees that day are considered to be healthy and kept in an appropriate environment, the inspector will tend to answer questions as to whether or not the animals were in good health by responding "yes, but"—whereby it is noted that most animals are catered for well except for a few who are not. While these "yes, but" answers were not considered as part of the data analysis in this research, the principle remains worthy of discussion. As a general rule, industry representatives and government officials will point to the fact that most zoos are mostly compliant with the law, with the implication that "generally compliant" or "mainly compliant" is sufficient. This occurs both on an individual zoo basis (leading to the "yes, but" phenomena described above) and on a wider industry basis, where the failing of parts of an industry are dismissed on the basis that the majority of the industry is compliant. An example of this can be found in public statements issued following an investigation carried out by the Born Free Foundation which found that zoos were not meeting welfare standards. The public response from the British and Irish Association of Zoos and Aquariums (BIAZA) was "83 per cent of the 192 zoos were graded as meeting the standards for animal welfare assessments, which suggest[s] that the inspection system is working".[12] Of course, this means that 32 zoos, which may collectively house tens of thousands of animals, did not meet welfare standards. BIAZA's conclusion is clearly that "mostly compliant" or "mainly compliant" is sufficient to establish the system as successful.

If individual animals kept in zoos were considered under individualistic principle of the AWA 2006 then and the welfare of the individual animal was found to be unacceptable, there is no demand made on the person inspecting the animal to compare the living conditions of the animals living alongside the animal whose welfare is compromised in order to draw a conclusion. In the same way, an individual animal owner should not escape legal action if they keep five dogs but only neglects one of them. There would be no argument which would allow the cruel or poor treatment of one animal simply because other animals kept by the same person were treated well. This tendency toward accepting that compliance has been achieved when *most* standards are met further compounds the problem under consideration. Licensing therefore would appear to lend itself to interpretations that limit scrutiny on the individual and diffuse issues when instances of non-compliance are noted by pointing to the acceptable levels of compliance elsewhere in the business. To conclude, the collective, process-based assessment approach which the type of licensing regime under consideration lends itself to, as opposed to the individualistic approach required to carry out a meaningful assessment of any individual animal's welfare, suggests that licensing as an approach is not best suited to assessing, much less "guaranteeing" high standards of welfare for the individuals.

11.1.5 Conclusion: Licensing Is an Inappropriate Legal Mechanism for the Guarantee of High Animal Welfare Standards

In light of the above, it is argued that great care should be taken in interpreting the application of licensing regimes as a means, in and of themselves, to protect animal welfare, as well as noting that the possession of a license does not indicate that standards outlined in the relevant regulations are being met in practice. Indeed, while regimes of licensing and inspection may serve to add (sometimes extremely limited, sometimes extremely useful) scrutiny to practices involving animals which in turn may allow for the identification of welfare problems, the issues identified with regard to scope, enforcement and practical application raise concerns that these systems may provide a false impression that they are meeting animal welfare needs.

As noted previously, strong narratives surrounding the effectiveness of the zoo and circus licensing regimes have been promoted by government officials and industry representatives alike. For example, in response to welfare concerns raised by the RSPCA at Circus Mondao in early 2016, the circus responded in a public statement by saying, "We are licensed and inspected by the government and if anything was not up to standard we wouldn't have this license".[13] Not only does this statement refrain from any mention that the business had its license suspended due to animal welfare concerns just four months previously (see Sect. 4 in Chap. 9 for case study), but it also makes the clear suggestion that possession of a license is synonymous with welfare standards being met. The result of this is that industry representative and government officials may claim that animal welfare is well protected by the schemes but, in practice, the regimes may serve to legitimize—while largely failing to properly assess and scrutinize—activities which harm animals. It is often asserted that the legislation in place "guarantees" or "ensures" high standards of welfare. A more truthful description of a licensing regime which regulates animal use is that it provides an added level of monitoring and scrutiny which makes the identification of welfare concerns more probable than for those uses for which no such scheme is in place. It is clear from the above that the possession of a license neither confirms (nor does the law demand) that standards are met in full, something which is important to note as it runs contrary to the strong narrative promoted within the industry and from officials.

11.2 Licensing as a Mechanism to Enhance Monitoring and Scrutiny of Practices Which Impact Upon Animal Welfare

Having argued that licensing regimes do not *in and of themselves* guarantee that animal welfare standards are met, but that they can (and do) play a role in the monitoring and scrutiny of practices which may impact animal welfare, it is important to now consider how licensing can be put to best effect. Clearly, at present, it is unlikely that the zoo industry will be prohibited from operating; although circuses with wild animals have been banned, other animal-use activities have been brought under the umbrella of licensing. As such, it seems clear that the model of using licensing regimes to regulate animal use is here to stay. This is evident from the government's recent consultation on the issue of bringing other regulated industries under licensing regimes via secondary legislation introduced under the AWA 2006.[14] It is therefore worth exploring recommendations which might help to make existing (and future) licensing regimes as effective as possible. This research has highlighted a number of problems in relation to the two pieces of legislation under consideration which, in turn, can allow us to make a number of broad conclusions regarding what makes an effective licensing regime and what makes an ineffective regime. These findings will be explored in the following section.

11.2.1 Responsive Regulation

Before considering the specific problems identified as part of this research, it is worthwhile to consider whether or not the statutes in question meet the broad requirements of "good regulation". In the last three decades, and particularly under conservative, capitalist government rule, countries around the world have seen increasing conflict between a "command and control" approach to regulation where regulatory demands are placed on industry by the state and a desire to see a move toward deregulation, ostensibly to allow for industry competition and growth.[15] In the early 1990s, work carried out by Ayres and Braithwaite saw the development of the concept of "responsive regulation",[16] an approach which considered the pros and cons of traditional state-led, prescriptive legislation compared to a deregulation view and brought parts of each approach together to maximize efficacy in the development of regulation going forward. While the model created has been amended and expanded upon in recent years, it offers a logical means of assessing whether or not regulation has the potential to be effective, taking into consideration both social and legal elements.

The fundamental basis of responsive regulation can be demonstrated in the pyramid in Fig. 11.1.

The system works on a basis of increasing intervention in the case of non-compliance with regulation. Coined as the "benign big gun",[17] the principle is that it is neither helpful nor necessary to use harsh sanctions each time non-compliance is noted but that there needs to be the opportunity to escalate sanctions for persistent non-compliance. This is, in part, because regulatory resources are limited and therefore the cost of regulation would rise significantly if each instance of non-compliance was met with court sanctions or license revocation (and the subsequent actions that would have to be taken at that stage which may include redundancy, relocation of animals, etc.). In short, using harsh punishment in every instance of non-compliance is not possible—financially or practically. The principle of the "benign big gun" is that if industries are aware that the harsh sanctions can and will be used against them if they

Fig. 11.1 The responsive regulation pyramid

do not make efforts to comply at earlier stages, this acts as an effective deterrent, which will drive up standards in the longer term.

The system is not just driven by the need to limit the financial cost of regulation—although considering increasing cuts to local authorities and government departments across the United Kingdom,[18] in relation to the pieces of legislation in question, this is no small consideration. Instead, the system recognizes that the best way in which to encourage long-term and sustainable internalization of standards within industry is to work *with* industry to encourage them to improve, rather than sanction every instance of non-compliance. If industry is more concerned with avoiding punishment, this is thought to lead to either a focus on very specific practices or a narrow attempt to simply avoid punishment, rather than an interest and attempt to achieve good standards across the board.[19] Taking into account the social context of regulation and recognizing that people simply respond better to encouragement and feeling that they are trusted rather than punishment and feeling they are not trusted, is another key reason that the responsive regulation model is thought effective.[20]

For the purposes of this research, it is not necessary to explore the rationale behind responsive regulation further, but the reason for bringing it into the discussion is to consider whether or not the statutes in question are compatible with, or capable of facilitating, responsive regulation.

11.2.1.1 The Zoo Licensing Act 1981 as Responsive Regulation

The Zoo Licensing Act 1981 provides a set of standards which zoos are required to follow in order to avoid sanction. The enforcement tools available to the local authorities charged with implementing the Act are as follows:

1. Inspection of premises and identification of non-compliance.
2. When non-compliance is noted, a condition is added to the license and a Direction is issued in order to clarify the timescale by which the demands of the condition must be met.
3. If the condition relates to s.1A of the Act, the timescale for compliance with the condition cannot exceed two years.
4. If the demands of the condition are met within the timescale, the condition is removed from the license and no further action is taken.
5. If the demands of the condition are not met, then all or part of the zoo will be closed.
6. If conditions are not met, the local authority has discretion to bring criminal charges under s.19 of the Act.

The enforcement tools available appear to meet the criteria for responsive regulation well, with persuasion and long timescales being provided to zoo operators initially, along with conditions being removed from licenses once compliance was achieved. Only when non-compliance persists despite initial measures being implemented does the “benign big gun” come out. Zoos operate under the threat of closure if they do not comply with standards, but closure can never be imposed without first following the process of escalation. This allows for improvements to be made and allows for zoos to ensure that they avoid the “big gun” being used against them.

As such, in principle, the Zoo Licensing Act 1981 does appear to be structured in such a way as meets the criteria of responsive regulation and so issues with the structure of the Act do not seem to be the cause of the issues noted. If the Act was not structured in such a way, the complete absence of enforcement action might be explained. For example, if there was no escalation process for enforcement and local authorities were required to close a zoo on the first instance of non-compliance, it seems reasonable to assume that local authorities would seek to avoid this. Not just because this would seem somewhat unfair to the zoo operator, who is not given a chance to rectify the problems, but also as the local authority is ultimately responsible for the animals in the zoo in the event of closure. It is therefore understandable that local authorities would want to pursue zoo closure as an absolute last resort. However, the legislation makes no demand of local authorities to make immediate closure orders and, instead, offers a whole series of actions that can be taken before this becomes necessary. It seems reasonable to conclude therefore that the structure of the legislation is not to blame for the lack of enforcement action found as a result of this research.

11.2.1.2 The Welfare of Wild Animals in Travelling Circuses (England) Regulations 2012 as Responsive Regulations

The Welfare of Wild Animals in Travelling Circuses (England) Regulations provided a set of standards which traveling circuses with wild animals had to follow to avoid sanction. The enforcement tools available under the regulations were as follows:

1. Standard conditions were attached to every license upon its issue.
2. The Secretary of State was empowered to "take such steps as the Secretary of State considers necessary to ensure compliance with the licensing conditions". No clarification was provided as to what those steps might be.
3. The Secretary of State was able to suspend a license at any time if satisfied that the licensing conditions had not been complied with.
4. Upon suspension, the circus had to be informed of the grounds for suspension, what was needed in order for compliance to be reached and highlight the right of appeal to a magistrate's court (and the timescale within which an appeal must be brought).
5. The license had to be reinstated when the conditions had been (or the SoS is satisfied they will be) complied with.
6. At the time of reinstatement, the term of the license could be varied.
7. The license could be revoked if it had been suspended for more than 28 days (unless an outstanding appeal is awaiting hearing at a magistrate's court).

Unlike the escalating sanctions which form the enforcement tools available to the local authorities administering the Zoo Licensing Act, WWATC 2012 did not appear to fit the criteria of responsive regulation. The reference to the Secretary of State being able to take "such steps as necessary"[21] is ambiguous and gave circus operators no indication of what will happen to them and their business in the case of non-compliance. In addition, it is clear that a license can be suspended (and thus a business prevented from operating at all) at any time non-compliance is noted. This is far stricter than the zoo licensing regime which only prevents the operation of the business after various other steps, with potential for long timescales for compliance, have been carried out. After 28 days, the Secretary of State had powers to revoke the license completely, suggesting that a circus could be closed permanently after just 28 days of non-compliance, in comparison to two years (in the case of non-compliance relating to s.1A) or even longer in the case of non-compliance with the ZLA 1981.

Notwithstanding the concerns that the regulations cannot be properly enforced, it is clear that these regulations did not employ an escalating system of sanctions and, instead, had the potential to operate on a "one strike and you're out" approach.

11.2.1.3 The Animal Welfare (Licensing of Activities Involving Animals) (England) Regulations 2018 Responsive Regulations

The AWR 2018 is the newest animal welfare legislation to be introduced in England which implements a licensing regime. It bears some similarities in its structure to the earlier, now repealed, WWATC 2012 regulations, but has also introduced new mechanisms which would better lend the regulations to be considered "responsive regulation". This is not least because it employs a "risk-based" approach which limits scrutiny on businesses which are considered "low risk" and increases scrutiny on those considered "high risk". The specific enforcement process under these regulations can be outlined as follows:

1. All businesses must be inspected on application.
2. Standard conditions plus any specific conditions relating to that business are attached to the license.
3. The license can be granted for one, two or three years, based on the inspector's assessment and any accompanying guidance. In the case of exhibition of animals, licenses are granted for three years.
4. Inspections must be carried out on renewal of a license and, in the case of businesses which hire out horses, annually. Inspections can be carried out more frequently if required.
5. Licenses may be suspended by the local authority for breach of license condition, breach of the regulations, the provision of false information or if it is necessary to protect animal welfare.
6. Unless the suspension takes immediate effect with a view to protect animal welfare, the operator has seven days to make representations to appeal the decision, which the local authority must take into consideration.
7. If the suspension is subsequently implemented, it will last a maximum of 28 days, after which time the license must be reinstated or revoked.

If the local authority takes no steps to reinstate or revoke, then the license will be automatically reinstated after the 28-day period is over.
8. Revocation can be challenged by the operator in the First Tier Tribunal.

The AWR 2018 regulations lay out clear conditions for operators to meet and have the option for those operators who are considered lower risk to be issued with longer-term licenses. In the event of a breach, the local authority has discretion as to whether to suspend or vary a license. Presumably, this allows for local authorities to choose to pursue other avenues, such as discussion, training and encouragement before suspension comes into play. In the event that a breach is considered to impact animal welfare, licenses can be suspended with immediate effect. In instances where animal welfare is not deemed to be at risk, the operator is given a week to make representations against proposed suspension and the local authority is obliged to respond to these representations. If the local authority fails to take active steps to reinstate or revoke a license after a suspension has been in place for 28 days, this falls in favor of the operator, which will automatically have the license reinstated.

The regulations appear to be geared toward maintaining operation of businesses and ensuring that licenses remain in place unless specific action is taken to suspend or revoke them. There are steps that can be taken to prevent revocation and the steps required are made clear to operators and local authorities. With the foregoing in mind, these regulations appear to meet the requirements for responsive regulation well.

11.2.1.4 Is Responsive Regulation Good for Animal Welfare?

It can be recognized that responsive regulation may offer a longer term and sustainable means of industries improving and internalizing good standards, and may provide a more equitable outcome for operators who are keen to improve and do not perhaps deserve to have their business closed down (either temporarily or permanently) for one infraction. It also helps to ensure that regulators can direct resources and time to the "real offenders" by only using tough sanctions when all else have failed. However, this raises questions over how responsive regulation serves (or not, as the case may be) animal welfare. Certainly, the ZLA 1981 provides a fairer system for the zoo operators and long lead times for improvement whereas the circus regime operates with the potential to implement a "one strike and you're out" principle which could be deemed unfair from the point of view of the circuses, whose operators could find their license suspended immediately following an inspection and subsequently revoked entirely if the issues are not resolved within 28 days. But for the animals, the (potentially) swift-acting circus regime has the potential to tackle welfare problems almost immediately in that very real sanctions are placed on the business which forces the business to comply swiftly or simply not be able to continue. Animals in zoos, on the other hand, may have to wait up to five years in order to see changes made which may impact their welfare before any stricter measures are employed by the authorities.

On the one hand, responsive regulation appears to be a sensible approach with regard to ensuring that responsible businesses are supported, and long-term change effected, as well as reducing the burden on regulatory authorities. This suggests that, if properly applied over the long term, this might lead to industry-wide improvements. On the other hand, the disadvantage of using responsive regulation in place of more traditional "command and control" regulation is that the animals involved may be required to endure longer periods in which the business is non-compliant, and this could impact upon welfare in the short to medium term.

To conclude, and to come back to the conclusion that licensing should not be used as a means, in and of itself, to protect welfare and therefore should never be implemented in order to solve an identified animal welfare problem, then it would seem responsive regulation would be the best approach to achieve long-term change. This would require that licensing is only applied to practices which are "benign" in terms of animal welfare if carried out properly, but which might need additional oversight to ensure high standards are being met consistently. It is argued that the problem comes when the benchmark for animal welfare provision or "good practice" within the meaning of the AWA 2006 falls below the threshold required to meet basic animal welfare needs so that non-compliance with the legislation automatically implies the existence of an immediate animal welfare problem. For example, if a licensing condition whose purpose is to ensure that animals are not trained in such a way as to cause suffering is broken, the animal will already be suffering at the time that the condition is breached. A responsive regulation approach would favor giving the circus operator time to improve or change before sanctions were brought against the business, thus allowing for the suffering to be prolonged. Likewise, if a licensing condition such as "providing each animal with an environment well adapted to meet the physical, psychological and social needs of the species to which it belongs"[22] is breached in a zoo, this suggests that the physical, psychological and/or social well-being of the animal(s) are not being met. The application of a responsive regulation model allows for these needs to remain unmet for long periods of time while the use of the "big gun" is avoided and more benign persuasion techniques are employed in the first instance.

On the other hand, breach of conditions such as demand to keep stringent veterinary records in circuses and zoos do not necessarily equate to an animal welfare problem but suggests that, in the long term, this could cause problems if that condition continues not to be met. It can thus be concluded that a responsive regulation approach is appropriate and helpful for dealing with breaches which do not directly or immediately compromise welfare or cause suffering, whereas to use a responsive regulation approach to deal with breaches which either compromise welfare or cause suffering is likely to lead to those compromises or suffering being prolonged.

It should be noted that, within the AWA 2006, there are elements of responsive regulation. For example, on identifying an offense under s.9 of the Act, the inspector is empowered to serve an improvement notice upon the person responsible for the animal. There is significant flexibility in how these improvement notices can be applied, with the inspector being able to specify what steps must be taken to comply with the Act, as well as the timescale for compliance. In addition, the inspector also has powers to extend, or further extend, the compliance period. Where this differs from the ZLA 1981, while there is significant discretion to employ persuasion and more benign sanctions prior to using the "big gun" (prosecution or zoo closure), inspectors are not *required* to use the more benign options first. If the offense is serious enough, they can choose to forgo the improvement order and move straight to prosecution, with powers to confiscate animals prior to trial if required in the interests of stopping or preventing suffering from occurring. Section 18(5) and (6) of the Act allows for an inspector or constable to take an animal into possession if that animal is suffering or likely to suffer if circumstances do not change. Action can thus be taken to remove the animals before suffering occurs.

With the ZLA 1981, the relevant authorities are not empowered under the legislation to close a zoo before the various, more benign, sanctions have been employed. There is no legal means of overriding the process, nor powers to take animals into custody on welfare grounds using the ZLA 1981. Under the former circus regulations, while the Secretary of State can choose to suspend a license and then revoke a license if the suspension remains in place for 28 days, this still requires a 28-day delay before being able to revoke a license altogether. Not just that, but there were no specific powers granted under the WWATC 2012, nor under the new AWR 2018, to confiscate the animals. As such, if confiscation were to be required on welfare grounds, independent action would have to be taken under the AWA 2006, which does allow for confiscation of animals as part of post-conviction powers granted to the relevant authority in certain circumstances.[23]

As already noted, the AWA 2006 still applies to animals in zoos and circuses and therefore the relevant authority could choose to use powers under the AWA 2006 instead. It is argued that the licensing regimes create conflict and confusion in that they provide a raft of measures to deal with animal welfare problems which are different to those measures provided for dealing with the same or similar problems under the AWA 2006. It seems that the authorities are therefore in a position to choose which legislation to apply, allowing for the lesser sanctions of the licensing regimes to be implemented in place of the more flexible and immediate sanctions available under the AWA 2006. The case of South Lakes Safari Zoo demonstrates how administrative action may be instigated in place of court proceedings, even in cases where it appears clear that court proceedings would be appropriate. The outcome of the administrative proceedings against South Lakes also served to demonstrate that a zoo can simply assign a new license holder and continue operation. Even when the license holder was a senior member of the team for whom the previous license was denied.

In conclusion, a responsive regulation approach may be in the interests of animal welfare as long as it is used to support processes and practices which do not have the potential to cause immediate or direct suffering or compromised welfare if breached. However, for standards which, if breached, will impact directly on welfare or cause suffering, either a "control or command" approach should be used or the ability to bypass benign sanctions and move straight to the "big gun" should be employed. It is suggested that the best way of delivering this in practice is by removing conditions from licensing regimes which, if breached, have a direct impact upon animal welfare and ensuring that licensing deals only with those conditions which support good processes and practices.

11.2.2 Drafting of Legislation

As highlighted in detail earlier in this book, issues have arisen with regard to the drafting of legislation. In respect of the circus regulations, the enforceability of the regulations was questionable and, in the opinion of the author, exceeded the powers granted to the Secretary of State under s.13 of the AWA 2006. The key element to the enforcement problem is that the Secretary of State attempted to create regulations which apply to wild animals kept by circuses in every aspect of their life. This created a situation whereby, rather than licensing a defined activity involving the animals, the regulations had the, apparently unintended, consequence of licensing the keeping/ownership of the animals. This not only exceeds powers granted to the Secretary of State and renders the regulations, in the opinion of the author, *ultra vires*, but it is also the factor which creates the problems when it comes to enforcement.

With regard to the ZLA, and notwithstanding the concerns raised above about the available sanctions in relation to breach of conditions with regard to animal welfare, there do not appear to be any major flaws in the drafting of the legislation itself. No specific flaws with regard to drafting were identified in relation to the AWR 2018. Specifically, there is no element of the AWR 2018 which conflate the activity under scrutiny with the general keeping/ownership of the animal.

What is clear from this research is that when licensing of the use of animals, using secondary legislation introduced under the AWA 2006, it is vital that the activity which is being licensed is clearly defined and a clear line can be drawn between the activity and the normal ownership or keeping of the animal. If there is a wider welfare concern with the keeping of the animal and it is believed that the mere keeping of animals in a particular situation (such as a traveling circus) has the potential to seriously impact animal welfare negatively in a way which cannot be resolved, it is suggested that licensing is therefore not an appropriate solution and policymakers instead consider prohibition of keeping animals in specific settings or circumstances.

Notes

1. For example, HC Deb, 1 March 2012, c41WS.
2. For example, Penarth Times. (2016). Animal charity raises concerns over wild animals as circus comes to the Vale. [online] Available at: http://www.penarthtimes.co.uk/news/14424591.Animal_charity_raises_concerns_over_wild_animals_as_circus_comes_to_the_Vale/ [Accessed 17 June 2016].
3. Welfare of Wild Animals in Travelling Circuses (England) Regulations 2012, Explanatory Memorandum.
4. Defra.gov.uk. (n.d.). Biodiversity and ecosystems—GOV.UK. [online] Available at: http://www.DEFRA.gov.uk/wildlife-pets/zoos/ [Accessed 24 Nov. 2017].
5. HC Deb. Vol 790 c103GC.
6. O'Sullivan, S. (2011). Animals, equality and democracy. Houndmills, Basingstoke, Hampshire: Palgrave Macmillan, pp. 6–7.
7. S.1A(c)(i) Zoo Licensing Act 1981.
8. S.1A(c)(ii) Zoo Licensing Act 1981.
9. Draper, C. and Harris, S. (2012). The assessment of animal welfare in British zoos by Government-appointed inspectors. Animals 2012, 2, pp. 507–528.

10. Casamitjana, J. (2012). Inspecting Zoos: A study of the official zoo inspection system in England from 2005 to 2011. The Captive Animal's Protection Society, Manchester. p. 87.
11. Casamitjana, J. (2012). Inspecting Zoos: A study of the official zoo inspection system in England from 2005 to 2011. The Captive Animal's Protection Society, Manchester. p. 7.
12. Mail Online. (2012). British zoos 'failing' on animal welfare standards. [online] Available at: http://www.dailymail.co.uk/travel/article-2215044/British-zoos-failing-animal-welfare-says-new-Born-Free-report.html [Accessed 17 Jun. 2016].
13. Penarth Times. (2016). Animal charity raises concerns over wild animals as circus comes to the Vale. [online] Available at: http://www.penarthtimes.co.uk/news/14424591.Animal_charity_raises_concerns_over_wild_animals_as_circus_comes_to_the_Vale/ [Accessed 17 June 2016].
14. Consult.DEFRA.gov.uk. (2015). Consultation on the review of animal establishments licensing in England—DEFRA—Citizen Space. [online] Available at: https://consult.DEFRA.gov.uk/animal-health-and-welfare/consultation-on-the-review-of-animal-licensing [Accessed 4 Sep. 2016].
15. Lodge, M. and Wegrich, K. (2012). Managing regulation. Palgrave Macmillan, p. 8.
16. Ayres, I. and Braithwaite, J. (1992). Responsive regulation. New York: Oxford University Press.
17. Ayres, I. and Braithwaite, J. (1992). Responsive regulation. New York: Oxford University Press. pp. 19–53.
18. Local Government Association (LGA), (2014). Under Pressure: How Councils are Planning for Future Cuts. [online] LGA, p. 1. Available at: http://www.local.gov.uk/documents/10180/5854661/Under+pressure.pdf [Accessed 4 Sep. 2016].
19. Ayres, I. and Braithwaite, J. (1995). Responsive regulation. New York [etc.]: Oxford University Press, p. 21.
20. Ayres, I. and Braithwaite, J. (1995). Responsive regulation. New York [etc.]: Oxford University Press, p. 19.
21. S.7 WWATC 2012.
22. S.1A(c)(i) Zoo Licensing Act 1981.
23. S.33 AWA 2006 (Deprivation) and s.35 (Seizure in Relation to Disqualification).

12

Making Licensing Work for Animals: Recommendations for Change

In developing, implementing and enforcing animal welfare legislation, the lack of resources available to those who might be minded to bring challenges in relation to the pieces of legislation under consideration before a court (in most cases, small NGOs) means that failures in implementation or enforcement of these laws are unlikely to be met with formal legal challenge. With this in mind, it is vital that these laws are as well constructed as possible from the outset, with clear guidance for relevant authorities responsible for enforcement, if they are to achieve their aim. The debate and consensus around how, when, where and why the various elements of the legislation under question are implemented and enforced will not be carried out and resolved in a court room but via ongoing discussion, negotiation and lobbying between animal advocates, government bodies and industry representatives (and their relevant legal departments or individual counsels) in the policy development and lobbying process which has been in progress since the first piece of animal welfare legislation was passed. As such, the author of this book does not recommend that flaws identified as part of this research are remedied by bringing legal challenge, but by seeking improvement, amendment and clarity to the legislation itself.

E. Tyson, *Licensing Laws and Animal Welfare*, The Palgrave Macmillan Animal Ethics Series, https://doi.org/10.1007/978-3-030-50042-9_12

As the application of licensing regimes introduced as secondary legislation under the AWA 2006 and those introduced as primary legislation will necessarily differ in scope and structure, the recommendations which follow are split into those relating to secondary legislation (and particularly regulations introduced under s.13 of the AWA 2006, such as the WWATC 2012 and the AWR 2018) and those relating to primary legislation.

12.1 Effective Licensing as Secondary Legislation Under s.13 of the Animal Welfare Act 2006

The way in which effective licensing can be introduced as secondary legislation under s.13 of the Animal Welfare Act 2006 is considered in the form of a decision-making flow chart in Fig. 12.1. Further detail is then discussed and practical examples are provided.

12.1.1 Insurmountable Welfare Problems? Licensing Is Not the Answer

The case of the licensing of wild animals in circuses was hugely controversial due to the fact that all leading animal protection organizations and the leading veterinary association in the United Kingdom (The British Veterinary Association) maintained that the complex welfare needs of wild animals simply cannot be met in a traveling circus environment.[1] If this is the case, then no amount of monitoring of processes would serve to support the delivery of animal welfare objectives. As such, the first question that policymakers should address when considering the introduction of a licensing regime as secondary legislation under the AWA 2006 is whether or not the practice or use of animals in question is fundamentally or inherently damaging to animal welfare. This is particularly important to consider in the case of wild animals, whose welfare needs may be compromised by the simple act of being kept by humans. If it is concluded that it is inherently damaging, then prohibition of the use (or

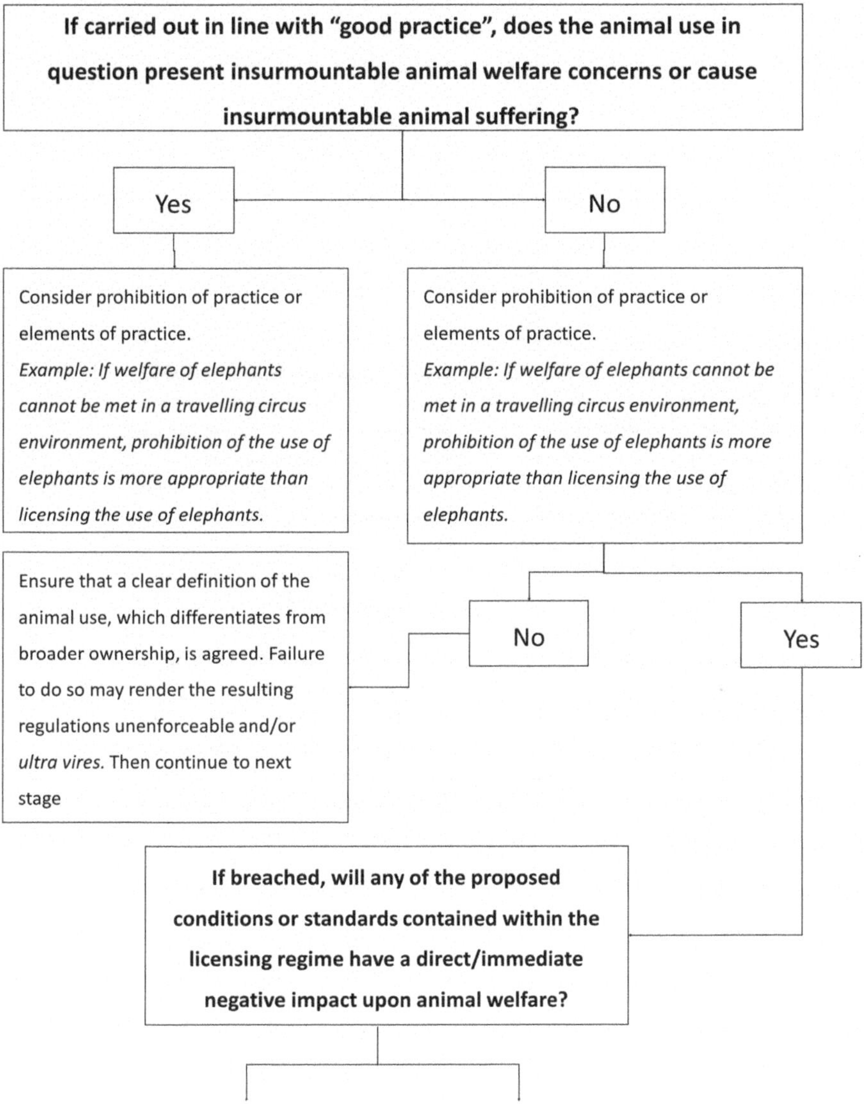

Continues on next page

Fig. 12.1 Decision-making model for licensing

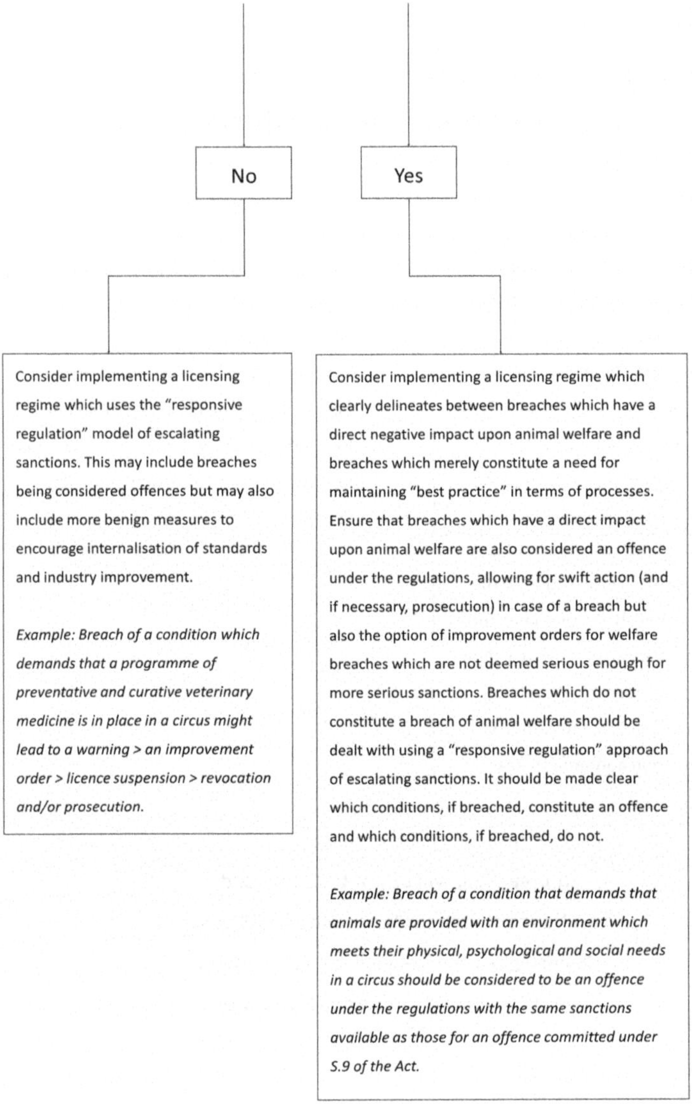

Fig. 12.1 (continued)

particular elements of the use) might be a more appropriate approach to take in place of licensing.

12.1.2 Ensuring that the Regulated Activity Is Clearly Differentiated from Ownership

As explored in the case of the WWATC 2012, the fact that the regulations failed to clearly differentiate the activity which was to be regulated (operating a traveling circus with wild animals) and the broader ownership of the animals created problems in interpretation when it came to attempts to suspend a license. In drafting new regulations, it should be possible to define the regulated activity in such a way as to ensure that suspension of a license does not necessitate deprivation of ownership, which would render the regulations ultra vires (as is believed to be the case with the circus regulations).

12.1.3 Standards and Conditions Relating to Processes to Be Implemented Using Response Regulation Model

Finally, if the licensing regime contains conditions which relate purely to processes and practices, sanctions available for breach of these conditions should follow the "responsive regulation" model of escalating sanctions. This may or may not include breach being considered an offense. For example, a licensing regime might provide for warning, followed by improvement order, followed by license suspension, followed by license revocation and/or prosecution. This will ensure that in relation to the processes that support the delivery of animal welfare objectives, but which do not impact directly upon animal welfare, inspectors have more flexibility and discretion and give operators a chance to internalize and improve standards in the long term.

12.1.4 Conclusion

In conclusion to this section, it is argued that if the model outlined in Fig. 12.1 is followed with regard to the implementation of licensing regimes as secondary legislation under the AWA 2006, future regulations have potential to be more effective than those introduced in respect of circuses in 2013. Using this approach in future will ensure that animal welfare concerns identified during inspection can be dealt with swiftly and easily, and breaches which impact animal welfare directly are given priority and harsher sanctions than those breaches which relate to procedure. The approach suggested combines a "responsive regulation" approach for issues which can be allowed more time to be resolved whereby inspectors can support businesses in improving standards across the board and a "control and command" approach which allows inspectors to act decisively to protect animals if needed. The incorporation of the improvement orders in the two proposed examples when breaches are considered offenses under the regulations also allows inspector discretion to use a more benign approach but also to choose harsher sanctions when it is in the best interests of the animals. The clear definition of the activity ensures that, in the case of suspension, this can be effectively enforced.

If this model were followed in future, it is argued that the regimes will have the best chance of supporting the delivery of animal welfare objectives.

12.2 Effective Licensing of Zoos

With regard to the piece of primary legislation under consideration, it has already been concluded that the ZLA 1981 is structured in such a way as could be considered to follow the "responsive regulation" model. There are a series of escalating sanctions available in the event of non-compliance as well as the potential for prosecution for breaches of condition. In terms of structure, then, it appears that there is a range of sanctions available. This research has found that those sanctions are not being used, and thus its failure is perhaps founded in lack of enforcement rather than any fundamental flaw within the legislation itself.

Notwithstanding the Act's, ostensibly, strong structure, there are a number of ways in which it is argued that the Act can be strengthened with regard to its ability to further animal welfare objectives. At present, any conviction can lead to a maximum fine of £2500 (the current level 4 on the standard scale). A fine of this size would certainly have an impact and thus potentially act as a deterrent to a small business, but many zoos are large, often multi-million pound, businesses and so a fine of this size is unlikely to present a significant deterrent in this case. In addition, there is no differentiation between offenses for breach of condition which impact upon animal welfare and those which are procedural. Following the arguments laid about above, it is maintained that it is important to provide swift and easy options to protect animal welfare in the short term and it is suggested that breaches which have a direct impact on animal welfare should be treated more harshly than those that do not.

It is therefore recommended that the following steps be taken to amend the ZLA 1981:

1. That an additional level of sanctions is added to the Offences and Penalties section to ensure that breaches impacting upon animal welfare are dealt with with the same severity as failing to meet animal welfare needs in any other circumstances. That is, to add sanctions which mirror those which stem from an offense under s.9 of the Act. This would allow for sanctions of imprisonment of no more than 51 weeks and a fine of no more than level 5 on the standard scale (which, as of March 2015, can be unlimited[2]) to be used against operators who fail to meet animal welfare needs. This clearly gives breaches of animal welfare conditions more weight than breaches of procedural conditions.

   It is suggested that any conditions relating to s.1A(c) "providing each animal with an environment well adapted to meet the physical, psychological and social needs of the species to which it belongs" are those which, if breached, will impact upon animal welfare and thus should be linked to the harsher sanctions.

2. Rather than include a section relating to improvement orders, as has been suggested by local authorities and members of the inspectorate,[3] it is suggested that the existing tools available under s.16 already provide in practice the same mechanism as improvement orders and so should be employed in conjunction with any action taken to tackle offenses under the Act.

As already highlighted, the issues found with regard to regulatory failures in relation to zoos were less to do with the structure of the Act itself, than with its enforcement and the sheer size of the industry (and individual businesses) that the Act is required to govern. With the minor changes above, coupled with effective, consistent enforcement, while the regime could never on its own ensure to maintain high standards of welfare, it may allow for improved delivery within the limitations of the industry.

12.2.1 Closing Loopholes

Section 10 in Chap. 5 considered the loophole relating to the exclusion of mobile zoos from regulation under the ZLA 1981. This can be easily remedied. Mobile Zoo businesses can simply be brought under the mantel of the ZLA 1981. This would not require any amendment to the legislation, simply interpreting the operation of mobile zoos as falling within the remit of the Act which, it is argued, is unproblematic. A detailed analysis of this was explored in Sect. 10.3 of Chap. 5.

12.2.2 Training

Considering the feedback from local authorities as part of the 2010 ADAS report, it would appear that there were gaps in understanding of the legislation and its application at that stage. The study by Casamitjana in 2012 and the present research suggest that understanding of enforcement obligations, at least, is still a problem. The fact that the explicit instruction from DEFRA to local authorities to use s.16 sanctions issued in 2012 resulted in no improvement in correct enforcement suggests that specific training or local authorities would be advisable in order to improve delivery.

Notes

1. Born Free Foundation, Captive Animals' Protection Society, RSPCA and British Veterinary Association (2013). The Welfare of Wild Animals in Travelling Circuses (England) Regulations 2012: unethical, ineffective and unenforceable.
2. Goucher, L. (2015). Unlimited fines in magistrates' courts | Insight | Nabarro. [online] Nabarro.com. Available at: http://www.nabarro.com/insight/briefings/2015/may/unlimited-fines-in-magistrates-courts/ [Accessed 4 Sep. 2016].
3. DEFRA/ADAS (2010). Review of local authorities' implementation of the Zoo Licensing Act 1981 in England and Wales. London: DEFRA, p. 27.

13

Conclusion: Toward Transparency and Universal Standards for Animal Welfare

This book has sought to consider how licensing regimes might be used to govern the use of animals, and particularly, in order to protect their welfare. A detailed, original analysis of the regulations of zoos in England detailed in Chaps. 5 and 6 showed that while the regulation of zoos was originally envisaged with a view to protect animal welfare, and despite the availability of a great deal of supplementary guidance provided to enforcement authorities to support their delivery of the Act, there is an almost complete absence of enforcement action taken against failing zoos. Arguably, despite the relative strength of the legislation itself on paper, its delivery in practice is significantly lacking.

Circuses were considered, in Chap. 8, as an example of how an industry might be regulated via licensing using relatively new powers granted to the Secretary of State under s.13 of the AWA 2006. While this particular licensing regime has now been repealed, reflections on its efficacy are valuable in order to inform newer regulations, such as AWR 2018 (explored in Chap. 9), introduced under the same section of the AWA 2006. Ensuring that any future regulations introduced under this mechanism are clearly drafted to ensure that their scope governs an "activity" involving animals, rather than the keeping or ownership of animals per se

E. Tyson, *Licensing Laws and Animal Welfare*, The Palgrave Macmillan Animal Ethics Series, https://doi.org/10.1007/978-3-030-50042-9_13

appears to be of fundamental importance. With this in mind, the fact that any regime implemented via s.13 of the AWA 2006 will always be subject to the "good practice" caveat found in s.9(1) of the same will always potentially limit the scope and impact of the regime.

With the foregoing in mind, this research has concluded that licensing, in and of itself, will never provide the "silver bullet" required to protect animal welfare, and members of the public should be wary of any claims that it is. Officials should be avoid making claims, such as those made by government department DEFRA, that that animal welfare needs are "ensured" simply by virtue of the fact that the business in question is in possession of a valid license.[1] In addition, statements made by representatives of the regulated industry which use the possession of a license to rebut welfare concerns should also be subject to further scrutiny.[2]

It is a reality that animal welfare, rightly or wrongly, will not be given priority as overworked and under-resourced authorities face cut after cut. Regimes which monitor animal protection, for the foreseeable future, cannot be expected to provide a thorough assessment, nor comprehensive oversight of the industries which they inspect—particularly when those industries may house hundreds of thousands of animals collectively. An inspection once every three years (e.g., for zoos) allows the most cursory inspection of processes, practices and perhaps some animals but, even when properly executed and enforced, the small team of inspectors visiting an establishment once every three years cannot be expected to categorically guarantee that standards are met all the time for all the animals. Even in the case of traveling circuses, which were inspected at least three times a year and had very few animals, it has been shown that important factors impacting on animal welfare (e.g., pregnancy) were missed during inspection. As explored previously, the legislation itself does not demand that businesses meet all animal welfare needs all of the time in order to possess a license. This raises the question: what can we reasonably expect, given the limitations, from licensing regimes which regulate animal use?

In has been argued that licensing on its own is not sufficient to ensure high welfare standards for animals; however, it certainly can be used to *support* the delivery of animal welfare objectives. To conclude this book, it is suggested that licensing regimes can be applied in the following ways for best effect:

1. as a monitoring tool which can facilitate the periodic assessment of animal welfare standards in its broadest sense and
2. as a means to enforce best practice within industries with regard to processes which, if properly maintained, can *support* the delivery of high welfare standards, such as ensuring that veterinary care programs are in place and maintained or ensuring that post mortems are carried out in the event of an animal's death.

It is firmly believed by the author that correctly applied and enforced licensing regimes to regulate animal use can be used as fundamental tools to support the delivery of high animal welfare standards, but only if implemented in conjunction with effective, responsive, and widely and properly enforced animal welfare legislation which implements minimum welfare standards based on the needs of the species to which the individual animal belongs, and regardless of where or how the individual animal is used. Vitally, research and genuine consideration must be given to the potential that some or all wild animals cannot be "kept" by people without their welfare being compromised and action to prohibit either certain practices or ownership itself for these species should be seriously considered. At present, the English legal system fails to recognize such minimum welfare needs and, thus, any licensing regime designed to facilitate the protection of animal welfare in England will be necessarily restricted by these limitations.

Notes

1. Gov.uk. (2011). Tough new licensing regime for wild animals in circuses—GOV.UK. [online] Available at: https://www.gov.uk/government/news/tough-new-licensing-regime-for-wild-animals-in-circuses [Accessed 20 Nov. 2017].
2. Derbyshiretimes.co.uk. (2017). Campaigners urge Derbyshire residents to shun wild animal circus. [online] Available at: https://www.derbyshiretimes.co.uk/news/campaigners-urge-derbyshire-residents-to-shun-wild-animal-circus-1-8751144 [Accessed 20 Nov. 2017].

Bibliography

Aaltola, E. (2012). *Animal Suffering: Philosophy and Culture*. Palgrave Macmillan.

ADAS. (2010). *Review of the implementation of the Zoo Licensing Act 1981 in local authorities in England and Wales*. [Online] London: DEFRA.

AHVLA. (2012). *AHVLA list of zoos operating in England* (November 2012). [Online] Bristol: DEFRA.

Ayres, I. and Braithwaite, J. (1992). *Responsive regulation*. New York: Oxford University Press.

Bekoff, M. (2007). *The Emotional Lives of Animals*. New World Library, Novato, CA.

Bentham, J. (1907). *An Introduction to the Principles of Morals and Legislation*.

Braithwaite, V. (2010). Do fish feel pain?. Oxford: Oxford University Press.

Brambell, F. W. R. (1965). *Report of the Technical Committee to Enquire into the Welfare of Animals Kept under Intensive Livestock Husbandry Systems*. London: Her Majesty's Stationery Office.

Broom, D. M. (1991). Animal welfare: Concepts and measurements. *J Animal Science*.

Casamitjana, J. (2012). *Inspecting Zoos: A study of the official zoo inspection system in England from 2005 to 2011*. The Captive Animal's Protection Society, Manchester.

Cobbett, W. (1806). *Cobbett's parliamentary history of England*. London: R. Bagshaw.

E. Tyson, *Licensing Laws and Animal Welfare*, The Palgrave Macmillan Animal Ethics Series, https://doi.org/10.1007/978-3-030-50042-9

Cochrane, A. (2012). *Animal rights without liberation.* New York: Columbia University Press.

De Waal, F. (1982). *Chimpanzee Politics: Power and Sex among Apes.* Johns Hopkins University Press.

Draper, C. & Harris, S. (2012). 'The Assessment of Animal Welfare in British Zoos by Government-Appointed Inspectors'. *Animals*, vol. 2.

Draper, C. and Glanville, G. (2013). *Application and enforcement of the Zoo Licensing Act 1981 by local authorities.* [Online] Horsham: The Born Free Foundation.

Heath, P. and J.B. Schneewind (Eds.). (1997). *Lectures on Ethics.* Cambridge: Cambridge University Press.

Francione, G. (1995). *Animals, property, and the law.* Philadelphia: Temple University Press.

Francione, G. (2012). *Sentience—Animal Rights: The Abolitionist Approach.*

Francione, G. and Garner, R. (2010). *The animal rights debate.* New York: Columbia University Press.

Francione, G. (2008). *Animals as Persons: Essays on the Abolition of Animal Exploitation*, Columbia University Press.

Frey, R. (1980). *Interests and rights: The Case Against Animals.* Oxford: Clarendon Press.

Gallup, G. (1970). Chimpanzees: Self-Recognition. *Science*, 167(3914).

Goodall, J. (1990) *Through a Window: 30 years observing the Gombe chimpanzees*, London: Weidenfeld & Nicolson.

Harrison, R. (1966). *Animal machines.* New York: Ballantine Books.

Honderich, Ted (ed.) (1995). "Animals: Peter Singer". *The Oxford Companion to Philosophy.* Oxford.

Hume, D. (1739). *A Treatise on Human Nature.*

Immanuel K. (1785), *Groundwork for the Metaphysics of Morals.*

Kemp Smith, N. (1952). *New Studies in the Philosophy of Descartes.* London: Macmillan.

Lodge, M. and Wegrich, K. (2012). *Managing regulation.* Palgrave Macmillan, p. 8.

Mason, G., Cooper, J. and Clarebrough, C. (2001). Frustrations of Fur-Farmed Mink. *Nature*, 410(6824).

O'Sullivan, S. (2011). *Animals, equality and democracy.* Houndmills, Basingstoke, Hampshire: Palgrave Macmillan.

Pepperberg, I. (2008). *Alex and me.* New York: HarperCollins Publishers, FAQs.

Pepperberg, I. (2000). *The Alex Studies: Cognitive and Communicative Abilities of Grey Parrots*. Harvard University Press.

Radford, M. (1999). "Unnecessary suffering": the cornerstone of animal protection legislation considered. *Criminal Law Review*.

Radford, M. (2007). *The Report of the Chairman of the Circus Working Group* (The Radford Report).

Radford, M. (2001). *Animal Welfare Law in Britain*. Oxford University Press.

Regan, T. (2010). *The case for animal rights*. 2nd ed. Berkeley: University of California Press.

Regan, T. (2001). *Defending Animal Rights*, University of Illinois Press.

Seligman, Martin E.P. (1975) *Helplessness: On depression, Development and Death*.

Singer, P. (1995). *Animal liberation*. 2nd ed. London: Pimlico.

The EU Zoo Inquiry. (2011). *An Evaluation of the Implementation and Enforcement of EC Directive 1999/22, Relating to the Keeping of Animals in Zoos*. Horsham: The Born Free Foundation.

Wise, S. (2013). *Drawing the line*. Cambridge, MA: Perseus Books.

Index[1]

[1] Note: Page numbers followed by 'n' refer to notes.

E. Tyson, *Licensing Laws and Animal Welfare*, The Palgrave Macmillan Animal Ethics Series, https://doi.org/10.1007/978-3-030-50042-9

The manufacturer's authorised representative in the EU is Springer Nature Customer Service Centre GmbH, Europaplatz 3, 69115 Heidelberg, Germany. If you have any concerns regarding our products, please contact ProductSafety@springernature.com

Printed and bound by CPI Group (UK) Ltd, Croydon, CR0 4YY
05/10/2026
02228121-0002